Chicken Soup for the Soul®

Here Comes the Bride

Chicken Soup for the Soul: Here Comes the Bride
101 Stories of Love, Laughter, and Family
Jack Canfield, Mark Victor Hansen, and Susan M. Heim

Published by Chicken Soup for the Soul Publishing, LLC   www.chickensoup.com
Copyright © 2012 by Chicken Soup for the Soul Publishing, LLC. All Rights Reserved.

The publisher gratefully acknowledges the many publishers and individuals who granted Chicken Soup for the Soul permission to reprint the cited material.

Front cover photo courtesy of iStockphoto.com/craftvision. Back cover photo courtesy of iStockphoto.com/rollover. Back cover photo and interior illustration courtesy of Photos.com

Cover and Interior Design & Layout by Pneuma Books, LLC
For more info on Pneuma Books, visit www.pneumabooks.com

Distributed to the booktrade by Simon & Schuster. SAN: 200-2442

Publisher's Cataloging-in-Publication Data
(Prepared by The Donohue Group)
Chicken soup for the soul : here comes the bride : 101 stories of love, laughter, and family / [compiled by] Jack Canfield, Mark Victor Hansen, [and] Susan M. Heim.

p. : ill. ; cm.

Summary: A collection of 101 true personal stories from brides, grooms, family, and friends, about proposals, engagements, wedding planning, weddings, and honeymoons. Includes brides of all ages and second marriages. Stories range from funny to heartwarming and cover the whole range of topics relating to becoming a bride and a newlywed.
ISBN: 978-1-935096-84-9

1. Brides--Literary collections. 2. Brides--Anecdotes. 3. Newlyweds--Literary collections. 4. Newlyweds--Anecdotes. 5. Marriage--Literary collections. 6. Marriage--Anecdotes. I. Canfield, Jack, 1944- II. Hansen, Mark Victor. III. Heim, Susan M. IV. Title: Here comes the bride

PN6071.B754 C45 2012
810.2/02/354/3   2012930594

PRINTED IN THE UNITED STATES OF AMERICA
on acid∞free paper
21 20 19 18 17 16 15 14 13 12   01 02 03 04 05 06 07 08 09 10

Chicken Soup for the Soul®

Here Comes the Bride

101 Stories of Love, Laughter, and Family

Jack Canfield
Mark Victor Hansen
Susan M. Heim

Chicken Soup for the Soul Publishing, LLC
Cos Cob, CT

Chicken Soup

www.chickensoup.com

for the Soul

Contents

❶
~The Proposal~

❷
~The Ring~

❸
~The Dress~

❹
~It's All in the Planning~

❺
~Meet the Parents~

❻
~The Wedding Party~

❼
~Marital Mishaps~

8

~Bucking Tradition~

9

~Never Too Late for Love~

⑩
~The Honeymoon~

Here Comes the Comes the Bride

Chapter 1

The Proposal

Come live with me and be my love,
And we will some new pleasures prove
Of golden sands and crystal brooks,
With silken lines and silver hooks.

~John Donne

The Perfect Proposal

You know you're in love when you don't want to fall asleep because reality is finally better than your dreams.

~Dr. Seuss

Growing up, I always wished my parents had a more romantic proposal story. Candles, roses, a serenade, an ocean sunset. My dad on bended knee with nervous, hopeful eyes; my mom gazing down at him, surprised and ecstatic, speechlessly nodding yes. But that is not their proposal story.

My parents met in college when my dad was a junior and my mom was a senior. After my mom graduated, she worked at a bookstore in town while my dad finished up school. When summer rolled around, they had a talk about what they would do next. And, as the story goes, my dad looked over at my mom and said, "We could get married."

And what was my mom's response? A gasp? Tears of joy? No, nothing like that. My mom burst out laughing. "I thought he was joking!" she would explain later when telling me the story. "You know your father. He's a kidder."

"And then what happened?" I would prod.

She would smile. "Then we got married and lived happier ever after."

It's true—my parents are amazingly happy, and they will have been married thirty years this September. They are a real-life love story, a guiding example for me of the comfort and joy that comes from building a life with the person you love. And yet, I also grew up on a steady diet of Disney songs and chick flicks. I'd ask my parents to tell the story again and again, hoping to bring out a new angle, discover a previously forgotten detail that might cast the whole thing in a new, more romantic light.

"You mean you didn't have it planned beforehand?" I would ask my dad.

"No, not specifically."

"Did you have a ring at least?"

"We picked it out together afterward."

"You didn't even get down on one knee?"

My dad would smile, his eyes far away, remembering. "Nope. I just asked her."

I would sigh, disappointed. How unromantic.

My grandparents were no better. "How did you propose to Grandma Auden?" I asked Gramps one Christmas as we spooned dinner leftovers into plastic containers. I was thinking of the romantic black-and-white movies we'd watched together over the years — *Casablanca*, *The Philadelphia Story*, *Meet Me in St. Louis*. Murmured voices, stolen kisses, three-piece suits and fancy dresses, and impassioned declarations of love.

"Oh, I don't really remember," Gramps said.

"What?" I paused my mashed-potato scooping and looked at him. "You don't remember?"

"Well, I didn't formally propose. We loved each other, and when she graduated college we decided to get married."

"You just decided?"

He met my eyes and smiled. "You know, I think it was kind of assumed between us from the very first time we met. There's an old saying, 'When you know, you know.' It was certainly true for me, and I think it was true for your grandma, too. When I met her, I just knew."

When you know, you know. I had to admit, it sounded pretty romantic. It could be a line from one of those black-and-white movies I loved. Still, I knew when it came to my own proposal one day in the hazy future that I wanted the works: an elaborate plan, a diamond ring in a small cushioned box, a man on one knee.

Throughout high school and college, I dated off and on, but never anyone serious. Never anyone I saw myself marrying. In some ways, that made it easier to daydream: I pictured a generic Prince Charming, who would soar into my life, sweep me off my feet, and take my breath away when he asked me to be his wife.

My friends only fueled the flames. We talked for hours about our dreams and hopes for the future. We shared extravagant proposal videos online: an artist painting a mural to pop the question, an amateur filmmaker creating a movie trailer to propose to his girlfriend, a flash mob surprising one woman at what she thought was a routine outing to the mall.

Then, one of my friends got engaged. It was the proposal of her dreams—a surprise in front of a gorgeous fountain in the park where they first met. But that didn't change the fact that they fought constantly, and she confessed to me at her bridal shower that she often got jealous because she "didn't really trust him." I saw that the "perfect" proposal didn't guarantee happiness or true love. In fact, my idea of "perfect" shifted completely. What makes a proposal truly perfect, I realized, is that it is genuine and filled with love, and built upon a strong foundation of a relationship that is similarly honest, open, and caring.

Flash forward two years to my first year of graduate school. At a luncheon for volunteers at the local senior center, I was seated across the table from Mike, a fellow graduate student in the English department whom I somehow had never met in the hallways at school. He was certainly handsome, with thick dark hair, glasses that framed his green eyes, and a contagious smile. But more than that, he seemed familiar to me in a way that no one had ever felt before. We spent the entire luncheon chatting over pizza and smiling at each other. And even though we were in a huge room with hundreds of other people, it seemed as if we were the only two people there.

We went out for coffee the next day, and dinner the day after that. Within a week, we were spending every waking moment together. I had discovered a new level of happiness, a deep contentment that came from finding the person who truly understands me, supports me, and loves me for exactly who I am—just as I love every part of him.

"I feel like I've known you my whole life," Mike told me. "I never used to believe in love at first sight, but I was in love with you from the moment we met." I felt the same way. When you know, you know. I finally understood what Gramps meant.

That summer, I went home for a month to visit my family, and Mike came with me. One evening, as we walked along the boardwalk beside the ocean, we stopped for a few minutes to watch the waves crashing onto the beach. Seagulls wheeled overhead. The clouds were tinged with pink, the sun just beginning to set. Mike's hand squeezed mine.

"Dallas," he said. I turned and looked into his warm green eyes. "Will you marry me?"

There was no bended knee, no rose petals or marching band or movie cameras. And yet, as tears sprang to my eyes, I no longer wanted any of that.

It was the perfect proposal, more romantic than anything I had envisioned in my years of daydreams. What made it perfect was the man standing there before me, looking at me with love filling his eyes.

"Yes," I said. And I kissed my future husband, the love of my life, happier and more excited than I ever dreamed possible.

~Dallas Nicole Woodburn

A Case of Cold Feet

We learn more by looking for the answer to a question and not finding it than we do from learning the answer itself.

~Lloyd Alexander

You've heard the old saying that if at first you don't succeed, try, try again. Well, that pretty much applied to how I proposed to the woman who would eventually become my wife. I tried and tried, and again and again she told me no. In fact, she told me no so many different times that any ordinary person would have gotten the idea she didn't want to marry me!

I had known Ann for two years. We'd met on the job, and had been first co-workers, then close friends, and finally, in a relationship. What began as shy glances at each other became spending every moment together at work and then finally dating.

Ann told me on that first date that she was not anxious to get married. She'd gone down that road, and the heartache and misery it had brought to her and her children was not something she was willing to risk again. I told her I wasn't interested in a serious relationship either, and, for a while, that was the truth.

But feelings deepen, and after growing closer to her and the kids, I knew I wanted to be part of such a wonderful family. I loved Ann, and I couldn't envision my life without her. But the shadow of her previous marriage was a long one, and every time I turned our conversation in the direction of marriage, she changed the subject or cut short our date. One day, I just came right out and asked her to marry me.

"I can't marry you," she said, tears in her eyes. "I'm too afraid of marriage. But I do love you. Please don't leave me."

I sighed and took her hand. "I'm here to stay."

That seemed to settle it for a while, but then one day I blurted out the question again. This time, she smiled and said, "I'm sorry, darling, but you know the answer is no."

So began a scene that was played out over the next days, weeks, and months. Time would pass, and then I'd be overcome with love for this woman and ask her to marry me, and she'd say no. She never said it angrily, but with the understanding that she loved me deeply and wanted me in her life. It made me want to marry her even more.

And so I kept asking her. I asked her while we danced, while we hiked, and while we shared a fine meal at a French restaurant. She told me, "No, no, and *non*." I proposed to her while we stood on the roof of an elegant hotel and counted down the seconds to the New Year, while we watched a close friend and his fiancée exchange vows at their wedding, and as we waved goodbye to her daughter and her boyfriend as she went out to enjoy her prom. Her answers were "Sorry, no, but Happy New Year!" and "No, now sshh, you'll spoil the wedding," and "Nuh-uh. Did her boyfriend say he was nineteen?"

Then one day when I was getting ready to ask her in the parking lot on our way to our cars, Ann turned and stopped me. I realized she had the saddest expression on her face. She took me by the hand and shook her head.

"I love you more than life itself. You know that. But I can't marry you. It isn't fair to keep giving you hope for something that will never happen. Maybe it's time we moved on with our lives." Then she took a deep breath and added, "Without each other."

I didn't know what to say. I wanted to argue the point, to make her see we could be great together, but the fear and sadness in her face were so great that I knew I'd be pushing her farther away. I released her hand, and the two of us walked away from each other.

A couple of months went by. Working together was heartbreaking, but I gave her the space she needed and pretended everything was all right. She seemed less stressed, a little happier. Life for me was an empty, yawning chasm that I couldn't fill. I went home each night numb from the pain. I told myself this was the price you sometimes paid for love. I would love Ann forever, but from a distance, far from her life.

Then one day I saw a note on my desk. It read, "Meet me at the café on the corner after work." There was no signature, and I figured it was one of the guys who wanted to grab dinner or just hang out at the end of a long day. I didn't feel like going, but I didn't want to go home to my empty apartment. So I went.

It was hard to be in that particular café. Ann and I had spent a lot of time there. As I went in, I wondered if this was a good idea. Then I looked at the table where the two of us usually sat. There was Ann, smiling and waving at me to join her. I nearly stumbled over a waiter getting to her.

"Ask me," she said softly as she reached out and took my hand.

"What?" was all I could manage. I took a drink of water. "Ask you what?"

Her eyes were big and bright and full of love. "All I needed was to know what it felt like to not have you in my life. It's not a feeling I ever want to feel again. Ask me."

I almost broke my kneecap dropping to the floor. "Will you marry me?"

She nodded, and then she started to cry. I pulled her into my arms.

"Of course, I will," she whispered, holding me tight. "What took you so long?"

~John P. Buentello

"With this ring, I thee beg."

The Bridge of Saint Mary's

*When the one man loves the one woman
and the one woman loves the one man,
the very angels desert heaven and come and sit in that house and sing for joy.*
~The Brahma Sutras

*I*t started with an acceptance letter from Saint Mary's College, Notre Dame, in the early spring of 2007. My sister and I were both happily admitted into the all-women's college and, upon receiving the good news in the mail, our family decided to make the forty-five-minute drive to visit our new college on a warm spring afternoon. I do not believe there is any college more beautiful in the springtime than Saint Mary's, and I will never forget our first stroll around the campus. We marveled at the secluded tranquility of the environment, the archaic charm of the 167-year-old architecture, and all around us, trees blossomed with little white flowers that filled the air with a delicately sweet aroma.

Its best feature of all was the small lake situated at the heart of the campus. Stretching over this small body of water was a narrow wooden bridge that connected to an even smaller island, with flowers and trees that grew thick all around. Benches were scattered here and there around the lake, and I remember seeing a young woman—a student, I supposed—seated on one of those wooden benches with a book in her lap. The girl caught sight of us and began to inquire

if we were new to campus. After exchanging a few friendly words with my parents, she asked, "Have you heard the legend about the Saint Mary's bridge yet?" Of course, we hadn't, so she proceeded to regale us with the legend of the bridge over the lake: The first gentleman with whom you cross the bridge, she said, is the man you will marry.

More than a year later, I was still making a solo trek across the bridge, all the while thinking about that silly legend and doubting that such a thing could ever happen to me. The island, however, became my quiet refuge for reading and writing. I would spend hours studying or writing short stories in this peaceful hideaway. Only the wild geese that inhabited the island would accompany me.

It wasn't until late July the following year that I suddenly received three new online messages from a gentleman I had never met, complimenting my web page and, in his third message, adding flattery to my profile picture by writing, "You have a cute smile." I succumbed to curiosity and responded to this stranger's comments. That simple response soon turned into frequent e-mail and phone conversations.

His name was Dinesh Rajan, a handsome, dark-haired, dark-eyed native of southern India. I learned that he was a recent graduate from the University of Notre Dame and worked as a software engineer in California. He later admitted to reading my online blogs for two weeks, in which he found himself intrigued by the girl behind the writings. After about a month of e-mail and instant messaging correspondence, we decided to meet. My father, however, proved more reluctant and wanted no part in my "meeting with a strange man from India we know nothing about."

Against my father's somewhat scornful protests, Dinesh purchased a plane ticket back to South Bend, Indiana, and we met for the first time at a bench by the Notre Dame basilica during fall break in 2008. I presented him with a batch of two-dozen homemade macadamia nut cookies, which I had carefully packed in a decorative box. We then exchanged a few nice-to-meet-yous before deciding to walk between the Notre Dame and Saint Mary's campuses.

Suddenly, I began thinking about the bridge. Would we cross it?

Did I want to cross it? Should I wait? What if there was truth to the legend? But it was too late. Side by side, we crossed the bridge. Did this mean I would marry Dinesh?

We sat on a bench on the island for an hour, talking about our respective childhoods, families, religions, and beliefs. I felt I had known Dinesh my whole life. I somehow felt natural with him. Safe. We planned to meet again two days later for our first official date and, later that week, he would take me to see *Manon* at the Lyric Opera of Chicago.

Our first kiss took place two months later at an oceanfront poolside in Florida, where we were vacationing with my family. I was twenty-two and had never even kissed a man up to that point! It was late evening, and we were counting shooting stars over the ocean while reclining in the lounge chairs. The air was cool and still, and the only sound came from the crashing of the waves. The kiss we shared was better than any romantic scene from a Hollywood motion picture, and when he flew back home later that week, I realized I was falling in love with him.

For two years, we endured a long-distance relationship; however, he would fly out once a month to visit. Sometimes, he'd even purchase a plane ticket for me, and we would spend a day sightseeing in various cities: wine tasting in Napa Valley, strolling the town of Sausalito, resting our feet in the refreshing tide pools of San Diego, crossing the Golden Gate Bridge in San Francisco, and even exploring Las Vegas. Each trip would last about eleven hours before I would fly back home that same night! It's true that some girls are treated like princesses, but Dinesh treated me like a queen.

In the spring of 2010, Dinesh made the decision to return to South Bend and finish his Ph.D. at Notre Dame, eliminating the thousands of miles that separated us. The talk of marriage became more frequent in our conversations. On October 1, 2010, he showed up on my doorstep with a bouquet of red roses. He said he wanted to walk each campus again for old times' sake. During our walk, he recounted all of the memories of our time together: our first date, the first time we held hands on the trails of a state park, our first kiss at the poolside, and the dreams we started building together.

When we finally reached the Saint Mary's campus, he said he wanted to cross the bridge just one more time. It was growing dark and chilly by then, but he took my hand anyway, and together we crossed the old wooden bridge just as we had done two years earlier. When we stepped onto the island, Dinesh dropped down on one knee. My heart leaped. From the pocket of his coat, he extracted a blue box. I felt dazed, like I was floating, when he proposed.

"Yes!" I said happily, fighting back the tears as we tightly embraced.

I guess there is magic in that old Saint Mary's bridge, after all.

~Sara R. Rajan

Hello, My Name Is Clueless

> *Some folks are wise and some are otherwise.*
> ~Tobias Smollett

Not many people can boast that complete strangers come up to them in the grocery store and say, "I was there when you got engaged." I can.

I'm getting ahead of myself. First, let me introduce myself. Hello. My name is Clueless.

On that gorgeous Sunday morning in August 1998, I had a wretched cold—and I was mad at my boyfriend. His family was in town, and although I thought the visit had passed very pleasantly, Christian had been short-tempered the whole weekend.

He picked me up for church that morning, his manner edgy and uptight as we zigged and zagged around campus to the Newman Center for choir warm-up. The air inside the church hummed with excitement. A fellow choir member was celebrating her fortieth wedding anniversary with a renewal of vows. Everyone anticipated a great morning with great music.

But my nose was running, my throat was sore, and I wasn't sure I'd be able to sing the two solos for which I was slated. Meanwhile, Christian's emotional state was deteriorating. Rapidly.

He pounded the piano keys with more than his usual energy, then leaped off the bench. "What is he doing?" asked a fellow alto, watching bemusedly as he dashed away from the piano hauling a clunky, hard plastic case.

I rolled my eyes. "Setting up a video camera," I said. "He promised he'd record the renewal of vows." His mood was rubbing off on me. This was turning into one of those days when I had to remind myself that love is a choice. My medicated brain felt fuzzy, and my throat hurt. And I had so wanted to sing well!

Christian darted moth-like around the church, worrying whether there was enough room on the videotape, whether his mom and his brother knew where they were going, and whether they would get to church before Mass started. He barely made it back to the piano in time for the opening song. "You okay?" he mouthed at me over the last chord. I gave him a look. Considering his mood, wasn't it kind of backward for him to be asking me that?

My obvious annoyance did little to settle his behavior. But church has a way of moderating bad feelings. By the time I had cantored the psalm without my voice cracking, both of us were feeling better. After the homily and the renewal of vows, the service progressed as usual. I was standing beside the piano, playing flute over Christian's shoulder as Communion wound down, when I glanced out over the congregation and saw my mother sitting in the back row. I was so surprised that I stopped playing. My mother lived forty-five minutes away.

"Christian," I hissed. "My mom's back there. What's she doing here?"

He shrugged and kept playing.

(In-laws in town. Video camera set up. Boyfriend freaking out. Like I said: Clueless.)

Communion ended, and I perched on the step beside the piano while Father read the announcements. Christian reached for my hand. His palms were ice cold and clammy.

"That's all I have," Father said, "but... I think Christian has an announcement?"

This was not on the agenda. Bewildered, I helped him disentangle a microphone from its stand. He stepped up onto the platform and promptly dissolved into a gibbering, incoherent mess.

All thought of being mad at him fled. It was agonizing to watch; he sounded so awkward, and he's usually so well spoken. I wanted desperately to get up and comfort him, because I knew that whenever he got to the point—whatever it was—he was going to be kicking himself for his blithering performance. Clearly, he needed moral support. But what was that he was saying?

"When I came to Newman," he said, "my life changed... because I met Kate."

Blame it on the cold medicine: My only thought was, Now what is he up to?

"Come up here, Kate," he said. I obeyed, and he rambled on while I stood beside him, holding his hand, offering mute encouragement while I tried to figure out where this whole monologue was headed, and what it had to do with me.

"And, um, Newman Center's been really special to us, because you all are kind of like a big family to us, so I kind of wanted to ask this in front of all of you...."

And that's when I figured it out.

Did I mention my name was Clueless?

He went down on one knee, and the whole community of people, 800 strong, rose up whooping amid a roar of applause.

I wish I could say that every moment since then has matched the romance and euphoria of that day at church. It hasn't. But any time a random stranger approaches me on the city bus, in the grocery store, or on the street and says, "I was there when you got engaged!" I realize all over again: I got a good one. And if I ever need proof, all I have to do is pull out the video.

~Kathleen M. Basi

Liftoff

Shoot for the moon. Even if you miss, you'll land among the stars.
~Les Brown

Ever since I was a little girl, I have dreamed about going into space.

I grew up in Houston, Texas, about a mile from NASA. On an elementary school field trip, we visited Mission Control and ate lunch in the enormous shadow of the Saturn V rocket lying on its side in a field of grass. A rocket like this one, our teacher told us, had taken Apollo 11 to the moon.

Since that day, I had wanted to be an astronaut. I would imagine myself sitting in a capsule at the top of that huge rocket pointed toward the heavens. The massive thrusters would fire on the launch pad in Cape Canaveral, and the countdown would begin in my head.

"10... 9... 8... "

I would flip some imaginary switches in front of me, legs up on the sofa in my living room, ready to head to the moon.

"3... 2... 1... Liftoff!"

Then my imagination would shift perspective, and I'd be looking out a window at all the people I loved. They would be cheering and waving, shrinking below me as I climbed higher and higher until the world became a swirl of clouds around a blue sphere, like in the pictures I'd seen taken from space.

Finally, I would be floating among the stars. That was the

favorite part of my daydreams, I would later tell my boyfriend, Drex. Of course, I didn't believe it would actually happen. Going into space had become a childhood fantasy.

Although on some deep level, I still wanted to be an astronaut, by the time I met Drex my freshman year of college, my career aspirations had become more down-to-earth. As an undergrad, I was pre-med, and he was a computer science major who lived in the dorm room right below mine. It wasn't love at first sight, but we got to know each other and then realized, to our mutual amazement about a year later, that we were actually soul mates.

We dated for five years. I started medical school, and he started graduate school. My second year, I got an opportunity to spend a month at a rural clinic in Honduras. Drex said that he would fly down after I was done with my work at the clinic so that we could have a long weekend together. Drex and I decided to go to the island of Roatan in the Caribbean Sea off the coast of Honduras. Since I was busy preparing for my clinic rotation and brushing up on medical Spanish phrases, Drex offered to make the arrangements for our getaway.

I felt comfortable leaving all the vacation preparations to him. On his apartment wall, Drex and I had a map studded with pins to mark all the places we'd been together. Through these trips and all the misadventures that came with them, we discovered that we had the same easygoing travel style, which involved minimal packing and planning. I knew we would have a good time no matter what.

We arrived at La Pura Vida Resort on the west end of Roatan. I took a shower and changed into my bathing suit, and then we headed out to enjoy an afternoon at the beach. Drex said that we only had one thing on our itinerary—he had planned it for after dinner that night. I tried to hold off plying him with questions because I have an intuitive knack for guessing his surprises.

After swimming in the turquoise water of Half Moon Bay, followed by lying on the sand doing absolutely nothing, we walked to a thatched-roof restaurant on the beachfront and had bowls of conch soup and plates of fried fish with spicy mayo. Then Drex steered us farther along the water to a wooden dock. On a post, it said: Roatan Institute of Deepsea Exploration.

Drex explained casually that he had chartered a submarine to take us into the Cayman Trench, a long and narrow depression in the floor of the Caribbean Sea. He had read about Karl Stanley, featured in *National Geographic Adventure* magazine, who had built his own submarine and now offered underwater adventures to a depth of about 2,000 feet below sea level off the coast of Honduras.

Needless to say, I was very excited when I saw the yellow submarine. It was round with a large Plexiglas viewing bubble in the front, like a giant fishbowl eye where we would sit. We climbed into the hatch on top of the submarine. Drex and I got strapped into our seats behind the Plexiglas bubble, and it briefly crossed my mind that the submarine was somewhat like a spaceship. We were going to be taken into another world. Karl would do the steering behind us.

As we started our descent, I noticed that Drex looked anxious. We were holding hands, and I could feel his racing pulse and sweaty palms. I asked him if he was nervous about the dive, but he shook his head.

Through our viewing bubble, in the bright submarine headlights, we saw unusual creatures like blood-red starfish and walking sea lilies. Karl started playing music—a CD of favorite songs Drex had made for our submarine adventure. Still, I didn't suspect anything. I was totally engrossed, like Jacques Cousteau, taking in this alien underwater world. It was vivid and surreal.

After about twenty minutes, we began our ascent to the surface. Karl turned off the submarine lights, and everything outside our bubble turned inky black. Then, all of a sudden, we were in a field of stars.

We were crossing a bioluminescent layer of tiny fish and squid that live in the Cayman Trench. They glow in response to the light from the submarine. Staring out from the capsule, I was in my girlhood dream, surrounded by a galaxy of creatures swimming around us. It actually felt like I was suspended and weightless in the darkness, an astronaut flying through space.

Overwhelmed, I barely heard the romantic speech Drex made, but when I saw the ring and heard him ask me to marry him, I said yes immediately. This incredible proposal made me realize that, no matter how ridiculous, unlikely, or out-of-reach they might seem, Drex would always, to the best of his abilities, help make my dreams come true.

~Mitali Ruths

A Month to Change Your Mind

There is no more lovely, friendly and charming relationship,
communion or company than a good marriage.
~Martin Luther

Walter and I had been seeing each other for about a year and a half when his father, Gus, became very ill. Gus was in his eighties, and although he was a tall, skinny drink of water like his son, he was also an insulin-dependent diabetic. The very first time Walter took me to meet Gus, he had a low blood sugar "incident," and I found myself calling 911 while Walter tried to revive him. So it was not really a shock when Walter got the call that his father had once again had an "incident" and was in the hospital. I requested some time off work, and we drove the hundred miles south from Boulder to Cañon City, Colorado, where Gus had moved when he retired. It was the last day of March 2002.

It turned out that this time the "incident" was very serious. Gus had been found on the floor of his house by a friend who'd stopped by. The doctors guessed that the night before, he'd accidentally taken a double dose of insulin. By the time he was found, he was in a coma. Although his numbers got better for a few days, by the end of the week he was slipping away from us.

Just after 6:00 A.M. on Saturday, we got the call from the hospital: Gus had died around 5:00. Walter and I had been staying in his father's house all week, looking after his dog and visiting the hospital daily. Walter's parents had separated when he was a child. His mother had died several years before, and his father had never remarried or even dated anyone, as far as we knew. He just lived with his dog, saw a few friends, and enjoyed fishing and hunting until the diabetes destroyed his eyesight.

We dressed quickly and went to the hospital. There, Walter spent a long time sitting beside his father's body. Finally, he said he was ready to go. Back at the house, he suggested that we change into hiking clothes. We took the dog, Molly, with us, and drove into the Rocky Mountains, up to Marshall Pass, one of the last places Walter had gone with his father.

There was still plenty of snow on the pass in early April, and I was glad I'd dressed warmly. We parked on the side of the road just before where the snow got deep, and I walked down the road a bit with Molly, exploring. When we returned, Walter said, "Let's climb up on this rock here so we can sit and talk."

This was unlike him, since he normally preferred hiking to talking. A Ph.D. engineer, Walter is typically stoic and no-nonsense. But it was a strange day, so I climbed up on the rock and prepared myself for a talk, perhaps about life and death and his relationship with his father.

Instead, Walter knelt down on the rock and said, "Margaret, will you marry me?" My heart sank.

I had been teasing him about the possibility of marriage for several months, but he had always rolled his eyes or changed the subject. Under any other circumstance, I would have been thrilled to finally hear those words. But not then. His father had just died. I was deeply afraid that Walter was asking me because he was in shock, not because he loved me. But on the other hand, how could I say no?

"Y-yes," I stammered. "But I don't think you should be asking me now. How about if we say you have a month to change your mind?"

"I'm not going to change my mind," he said, clearly offended.

"No, but you can, okay? Let's wait a month before we tell anyone, just in case," I went on.

"Don't you want to marry me?" he asked.

"Of course, I do," I said, feeling desperate. I so badly didn't want to hurt him on this sad day.

We drove back to Cañon City a little subdued. The next day, we returned to Boulder and our respective homes. I was very worried about what we'd gotten ourselves into. I didn't tell a soul about the proposal, not even my mother.

The next weekend found us back in Cañon City for the memorial service, and we were to go back many more times over the course of the next year as we cleaned out Gus's house. At the lunch we hosted for his family and friends, I wanted to mention our engagement, but I didn't because I was still waiting to see if Walter would change his mind.

The weekend after that, we stayed in Boulder. It was a quiet time for a change. We hung around his house, doing some cleaning and just relaxing. In the evening, as we snuggled up on the couch, I felt brave enough to bring up the subject again.

"Why did you ask me to marry you the day Gus died?" I said, trying to speak gently. "Why then?"

Walter sighed. "I just thought, I don't want my life to be like his," he said.

"In what way not like his?"

I thought Gus had had a rather pleasant life, with his dog and his friends and his hobbies. His house was full of books and music.

"Just living alone all those years, no family, no love. It's how I've lived my life up till now, but it's not how I want to live the rest of it. I don't want to die alone. I want to have a family. With you."

The month wasn't up. It was only April 21st. But I didn't need to wait any longer.

"How about next weekend we look for a ring?" I suggested.

I knew he wasn't going to change his mind.

~Margaret Luebs

Scrabble Surprise

Love is a game that two can play and both win.
~Eva Gabor

We met at a ball—I was in an indigo blue gown, he in a dazzling tuxedo. The moment we locked eyes, it was magical. We sipped champagne, giddy as we listened to David Benoit play "The Way You Look Tonight." The evening flew by as if we were in a dream, and by the end of the event, I felt hope for the first time in years.

Ours was a whirlwind romance. Everyone cautioned us to go slowly—we had both been through so much. And, despite my insistence that I really had no intention of anything serious, we quickly became inseparable. By the end of the summer, we had moved in together and achieved a peaceful harmony. Well, except in one department: marriage.

We had both been married before: he to his childhood sweetheart, who passed after twenty-one years of sweet union, and I to the father of my two children. Despite his desire to eventually marry again, he was in no hurry. I had professed for years that I would not remarry. Then, when faced with the idea of sharing my home, my life, and my children with another man, my traditional values pushed marriage to the surface of my mind once again.

I remember that first Valentine's Day: I was getting ready for work when my man walked into the master bath with a little velvet box. My heart leapt into my throat, I started to tear up, and suddenly

I just knew that life was about to be PERFECT! That is, until I opened the box. Staring back at me was a pair of the most beautiful diamond earrings. He looked at me with a grin from ear to ear, and I quickly tried to hide my disappointment. And, while I'm a fairly good actress, he quickly grasped the emotion I was trying to hide. "Hoping it was going to be a ring, huh?" he said. I nodded, putting the lovely gems in my ears. "It hasn't even been a year!" he laughed. I nodded again, and thanked him for the earrings as I darted into my closet to get dressed, desperate to hide my tears.

Two months later, we moved our home south when he joined a new firm. I had vowed I wouldn't move my children unless I was wearing a ring, but by then my heart was his. I just couldn't stomach the idea of ending the relationship just because he hadn't yet proposed. We created a new nest together and settled into our loft by the sea. We worked, played, and grew together as a couple and as a family.

As my thirty-eighth birthday approached, we began to talk more about further additions to our little family. I told him that I wouldn't even consider having children after my fortieth, and that marriage was an absolute requirement if we were going to have a child together.

Our second Valentine's Day arrived. That morning, I pulled on a beautiful red dress and heels as I prepared for the workday. I asked him if he needed me to come home early for any reason, and he just shook his head and told me he'd see me after work. Confused, and a little frustrated that he might not even have made dinner plans, I left for the office.

The day flew by, and I headed back home, eager to see what awaited me. I had always been a hopeless romantic, so I had gotten him a card and made him a beautiful scrapbook. I arrived home to find him in jeans and a T-shirt in the kitchen. I headed to our bedroom and asked him if I needed to change into anything special. He nonchalantly told me to throw on a pair of jeans and join him. I asked if we were going out to dinner, and he replied with a simple "no." As I pulled off my beautiful red dress and grabbed my jeans, my confusion and frustration turned to disappointment and resentment.

He walked into our bedroom, once again aware of the Valentine's Day Disappointment Look, and smiled. "Throw a few things in a bag. We're not going to dinner; we're going to Mexico!"

For the truly mentally healthy gal, this is the point at which she throws her arms around her lover's neck and screams, "Whoohoo!" and grabs her gear. And, while I like to think of myself as pretty together, his announcement was met by more of a glare. I packed my overnight bag, helped him grab a few things from the kitchen, and then climbed into the car. I sulked most of the way there, and didn't even bother to hide my disdainful disappointment in the "quaint" little home he'd rented for the weekend (one step up from a trailer, and not nearly as nice as the other places we'd visited in the past).

Despite my foul mood, his smile didn't leave his face. He offered me a glass of wine, threw dinner on the grill, and fed me Brie cheese from the cooler he'd packed. It may not have been what I was hoping for, but I softened with every kindness he showed me.

He suggested that we slip into more comfortable attire after dinner, and as I slipped on a red negligee (Hopeless Romantic again) in our bedroom, he prepared a beautiful fire and lounging area in the living room. He'd pulled a futon onto the ground, placed a *Scrabble* board in the middle of it, and poured us each a glass of champagne. To someone who didn't know us, this might have looked disastrous—*Scrabble* on Valentine's Day? But, to me, it looked like the perfect way to spend what could have been a nightmare of a day.

We shook the bag of letters and started the game as we had so many times in the past. Things started a bit slow, but soon gained speed. I was enjoying the competition, but also aware that the clock was heading toward midnight, and I was exhausted from the long day. I nearly emptied my deck and reached into the bag for more letters. I laughed to myself as I stared at the letters looking back at me. I spelled the word W-E-D, and he laughed as he took his turn. I pulled more tiles from the bag and laughed again, this time aloud. In the triple word space, I spelled the word V-O-W. Amazed, he pulled out tiles to complete a word of his own as I turned to grab my glass from the hearth. As I turned back around, I saw a little red leather box lying in the middle of the *Scrabble* board. I looked up at him, and he asked mischievously, "Where'd that come from?"

I gingerly picked up the box from the board and opened it to find the most extraordinary ring within. Tears ran down my face as my man offered the sweetest proposal a girl could receive. He kissed me tenderly, then as we separated, I glanced down at the tiles remaining in my deck: D-O-I-I. A warm smile crossed my face as I reorganized the letters and turned the deck to my fiancé. He laughed, eyes glistening, as he read them: I, I Do.

~Sage de Beixedon Breslin, Ph.D.

A Simple Proposition

What a distressing contrast there is between the radiant intelligence of the child and the feeble mentality of the average adult.
~Sigmund Freud

"I need to see you tonight." The urgency in the voice on the other end of the phone sent a cold chill curling up my spine. Why the man I was dating insisted on traveling thirty miles to see me on a weeknight, I wasn't sure. I'd worked all day, taught at a nearby university that evening, and my only plans had to do with peanut butter and jelly and a flannel nightgown. But something in his voice was compelling. So I pulled on an old pair of jeans and a sweater and agreed to see him.

Ernie arrived looking worried. Something was up. As we drove in silence to a nearby sports bar, my mind raced.

Perhaps, I speculated, he wanted to break off our relationship. After all, I had been less attentive lately, consumed by the demands of my new business and my son. Maybe he had met someone else and was a good enough guy to sit down one-on-one and tell me the news. Whatever it was, one thing was clear: This was the night I was going to hear about it.

As we slid into a booth, and ordered two beers and a platter of nachos, I found myself chattering to fill the silence.

"So, how about those Celtics?"

"Can you believe how windy it is?"

"Tom Hanks, you gotta love the guy."

Nothing I said seemed to warm him up.

Then, in a flash, he pulled a tiny box from his pocket. He placed it gingerly on the table in front of me without saying a word. For a moment, I hesitated. I looked around. The basketball game blared on the phalanx of television sets strategically placed throughout the smoky room. I glanced down at the salsa I had spilled on my faded jeans and smiled. Sometimes, life catches you when you least expect it.

Suddenly, I was the one who didn't know what to say. I picked up the box and opened the lid. This was it. The moment that could last a lifetime.

I knew he was hanging on my every word. And the only word he wanted to hear was "yes." But how could I say that? The commitment to marry someone isn't that simple. In fact, at that moment, nothing in my life seemed simple.

Refinancing my house, for instance. Same house. Same bank. Just a better rate. But after the application, credit checks and reappraisal, there was still a mountain of documents to sign. All for something that seemed so simple.

Even buying toothpaste, at times, seemed mind-boggling. Did I want to whiten or brighten? Should I add fluoride or remove plaque? Did I want the kind more dentists use or was Big Bird's endorsement good enough for me?

There I sat on the precipitous brink of what could be the rest of my life, face-to-face with the man who could be the one, if only I could say that little, three-letter word. So simple. Yet, so hard.

Disappointed by my silence, he drove me home. For the rest of that night, I dissected his proposal from every angle. Did I know him? I mean, did I *really* know him? What would it be like to live with him? Did his face turn red when he was angry? Did he snore? Where would we live? How could I trust in marriage again when it had failed me the first time? What would my family think? What would my friends say? Above all, what about my son?

For me, my little boy was the biggest question of all. In recent years, Geoff had grown accustomed to having me all to himself. What would he say? How would he feel?

From my purse, I pulled out the tiny box and showed him the ring. The look of doubt on my face must have been wildly evident even to a five-year-old.

"Mom, do you love him?"

"Yes."

"Then you should marry him."

In one quick exchange, my son had brought me back to the heart of the matter. Literally. With a child's clarity, he reminded me that some things really are quite simple. Not nearly as complicated as we grown-ups sometimes choose to believe.

"Do you love him?"

In my complex world, I had almost forgotten that there are some things in nature that are elemental. Primal, really. Love is like that. If you truly love someone, then all the rest will fall into place.

And as I write this on the occasion of our tenth wedding anniversary, I have to say it did. And it does.

~Rita Lussier

Mother Knew Best

One good mother is worth a hundred schoolmasters.
~George Herbert

When the phone rang, we were nestled under the covers. The double bed sat on a low wooden frame, and the sheets were dark and masculine with swirls of midnight black and forest green, a constant reminder that I had moved into his bachelor pad nine months earlier. Neither the pillowcases nor the duvet cover matched, but we didn't care. The smudges of dirt on the old graying walls didn't bother us either. As twenty-four-year-old new immigrants to Israel, Philippe and I were blissfully unconcerned with domestic details.

The shrill sound of the phone startled us out of our Sunday morning slumber. I fumbled for the receiver and said a groggy hello.

"Oh, good, you're up," my mom said. Even though it was late at night back in California, her voice was full of its usual vigor. "Quick, I need to know something." I was quiet, still wiping sleep out of my eyes. "I had an orthodontist appointment last week and was told I have to get braces — again. And I don't want them on for the pictures." I remained silent. "Can you please give me a date for the wedding so I can arrange to have them put on afterward?"

When my mom's words finally registered, I opened my mouth wide and rolled my eyes at Philippe. The queen of *chutzpah*, my mom had a ton of nerve and very blurred boundaries. Since there was only one phone and it didn't have a speaker, I asked her to hold.

"*C'est ma mère*," I whispered to Philippe, covering the receiver to tell him it was her. "*Elle veut savoir la date*—for the wedding. *Hahatonah shelanu.*" We spoke in a mish-mosh of languages—Hebrish, Fringlish—depending on our mood. I quickly told him about her orthodontic dilemma.

"*Attends*," Philippe said, turning his palm up and touching his fingertips together to indicate *savlanoot* or "wait a minute" in Hebrew. "I need *mon* agenda," he grinned.

Over the past few months, we had each landed jobs. I was working as an editor for a University of Haifa professor in the field of Arab-Jewish co-existence, and Philippe was a chemical engineer for the Israel Electric Corporation. Prior to this position, he had never owned an appointment book, planned ahead or written down dates. He reached across me to grab the book from his backpack on the floor.

Until this moment, we hadn't discussed the big "it"—getting married, spending our future together, starting a family—and I certainly had never mentioned anything about "it" to my mother. Not only had I arrived in the country with no more than a duffle to my name, never intending to make Israel my home, but I had also moved in with this man after an intense two-month courtship. My grandparents thought we were living in sin, but my perceptive parents had rented a car on their last visit to help me move in with him, transporting my worldly possessions from Jerusalem to Haifa.

Despite the intensity of our relationship, our union wasn't seamless. Philippe dreamed of growing old in the Promised Land, while I was en route to graduate school in the United States and had no desire to call Israel home. Upon moving to Israel, Philippe had decided to become more religious, observing the laws of the Sabbath and of keeping kosher; I had grown up in a God-less, pork-eating, do-what-you-want-on-Saturday Jewish household and had no interest in adopting an Orthodox lifestyle.

Still, in spite of our differing views, we were enraptured with each other's ability to speak several languages and our mutual yen for travel. We knew our relationship would evolve into marriage even though neither one of us had uttered the words. It was so like my mom to mention it first. She had always felt free to comment on my love life. She had been devastated two years earlier when I broke up with the man whom she thought I should marry, and she had stayed in contact with him long after he and I had parted company.

Flipping through his book, Philippe stopped at September. "How about ze nine?" I loved his non-perfect, heavily accented English. "It's good because nine-nine-ninety is easy to remember." I stared at him and smiled. In France, they say the day first and then the month and year. For this date, it wouldn't make a difference. In typical Philippe fashion, he was logical and unemotional; his voice didn't change its tone, and his facial expression didn't budge. Jittery and lightheaded, I uncovered the receiver and spoke.

"Mom, would September 9, 1990 work for your orthodontia? It gives us—you—nine months to plan." Somewhere in my subconscious, I realized it gave Philippe and me much-needed time to work on bridging our religious differences.

After we hung up the phone, I propped myself on one elbow and gazed at my unofficial fiancé. "*D'accord*, now you have to ask me," I announced, wanting more tradition. I was relieved that he didn't mind my mom's *chutzpahdik* intrusion, something I had accepted and probably inherited from her long ago. Staring into my eyes, Philippe proposed in French. I nodded my head yes.

"Now it's your turn," he said.

"*Quoi?* What do you mean?" I laughed.

"You ask me—to marry you," Philippe said with a semi-serious face. Clearly, nothing about our engagement was going to be done in a customary fashion.

I sat up in bed to face him. "Will you marry me? *S'il te plaît*," I asked with a smile, trusting that our unresolved issues—where to live and how much Judaism to live by—would be discussed and dealt with one by one, year after year. He laughed, and we kissed.

When I look back over the last two decades, I am amazed by our commitment, our deep desire to stay together despite our differing ambitions and plans. In an effort to achieve *shalom bayit* or peace in the house, we have each made tremendous compromises about country and religion, following an unconventional road, moving between Israel, France and America, with one, two and now three children in tow. We continue to talk, flirt, and fight in a mixture of three languages not found in any one dictionary. My mom has *chutzpah*, but she did know best.

~Jennifer Lang

A Gift of Faith

A horse is worth more than riches.
~Spanish Proverb

It had been a long weekend, but the results had been good. The hard work I had put in with Spenser had made us tough competition. The judge had loved my big horse, so we were nearly undefeatable. I smiled to myself. It had been years since I had been at the top of my game.

There was a rush of activity around me as everyone readied to go home. I had packed my stuff and stacked it outside Spenser's stall, but we were not going back home. It was the end of the last show of the summer, and Spenser was headed to a new home. The next week, I would start my senior year in college, and Spenser had a place waiting for him next to the campus.

I patted his neck as he neighed to the horses leaving around him. He was big and beautiful, a large gray horse with bright eyes and a long, silvery forelock. People would often approach me and ask if he was for sale or if they could at least pet him. He drew people to him and reveled in the attention they gave. His personality didn't change at all as people got to know him. He was a big boy with a big heart.

"I have my white horse. All I need for this to be perfect is my knight," I thought. But James was ten hours away at home. He had come and stayed almost a month for my birthday, but I couldn't expect him to stay all summer. I had been disappointed that our time together had ended so quickly, but we still talked as much as possible, and I would see him when we got to school.

James was pretty much as perfect as Spenser. He was smart and kind, and he didn't care that I didn't wear make-up or act girly. He let me be myself. We had met through James's older sister, Anna, at school two years ago. The following spring, I had come home with Anna to be in her wedding to Nate. We had only known each other for six months, but the connection was strong. At the wedding, I met James, and we danced and talked. All the while, Anna giggled and pointed out to Nate that there was a new couple forming right on the dance floor.

That spring, James and I talked almost every day and found we had a lot in common. I found a place for him in my heart and was smitten by the early summer. On my birthday that year, he came from ten hours away to ask me to be his girlfriend. I said yes, and we found ways to see each other despite the distance. It had been tough, but as the love grew within us, things fell into place.

Now, it was a year later. We were both in love, and neither of us could imagine life without the other. We fought, but it was nothing we couldn't solve. Our love was strong.

I sighed with thoughts of James. It had been a month since I had seen him in person, and I missed being able to hold him close to me, to look into his eyes and see the love shining back. I was hooked, no doubt.

Finally, the lot cleared momentarily. I motioned for Ronny, a trainer from Spenser's new barn, to pull the trailer around. I loaded everything into the truck's bed and led Spenser in. He was a saint, as usual, and went into the trailer without fuss.

"Wait," a familiar voice called as I began to lock Spenser in. "Another horse has to go in there!"

I looked up. Ronny hadn't said anything about taking another horse, and nobody had mentioned coming north with me. The horses here didn't normally travel that far.

My eyes locked on a familiar figure. My face broke into a smile, and I walked up to him.

"Hey there, beautiful," he whispered, kissing me gently.

"What are you doing here?"

He looked at me, and then looked to his right. I had been so wrapped up in seeing James that I hadn't even noticed the horse he was holding. And she was gorgeous. She was tall and lanky, and shone a deep golden chestnut, with a large, etched blaze and feet that looked like she had recently been knee-deep in white paint.

"Her name's Leap of Faith, or Faith, I guess," he said with a laugh. "She's yours."

I looked back and forth between the horse and my love. What had I done to deserve a wonderful man and this wonderful horse? I took the lead gently from his hands, my eyes thanking him while my voice failed to speak.

I looked back to the mare. She was about the same height as Spenser, but skinnier. She didn't seem hyped up by the show grounds, even though she appeared to be young. I reached up and scratched her neck. How had my boyfriend found and bought a great horse such as this? He knew very little about horses, only what I had taught him.

My eyes caught on the plate of the halter: "Will You Marry Me?"

My eyes widened, and I looked back at James. His hands were tucked sheepishly in his pockets, and he smiled carefully.

My mouth fell open, and I looked back and forth, my smile growing with every look. Ronny had caught on to what was going on and came to take Faith from me. I let go and ran the few steps to James's arms.

"Are you for real?" I asked, wrapping my arms around him.

"Well, we haven't known each other all that long. But I've been praying, and I've just got this feeling. I love you so much."

I smiled at him and wiggled in his embrace.

James laughed. "You never answered your horse."

I smiled up at him. "Well, we just met. I don't think I could marry her."

"How about me then?"

I bit my lip and smiled, my heart soaring. "Yes."

We kissed. By then, a small crowd had gathered and clapped for us. James slipped a ring on my finger and kissed me deeply.

"She's yours," he told me, "an early wedding gift. That way we can go riding together."

I smiled. I couldn't have found anyone better.

"Thank you, James. I love you."

"I love you, too."

The horses were loaded and taken north. We held hands for the entire eight-hour ride. When we arrived at the new barn, we unloaded the two gentle giants and took them out. The sun was setting over the small farm, and my ring caught in the fading light. I smiled to myself and then at my fiancé.

~Johanna Hardy

Mississippi Muddle

Time is too slow for those who wait, too swift for those who fear, too long for those who grieve, too short for those who rejoice, but for those who love, time is eternity.

~Henry Van Dyke

*L*onny and I grew up in a small town near the Illinois banks of the Mississippi River. We were high school sweethearts. I'm a romantic. A dreamer. Lonny was honest. Strong. Even at the tender age of sixteen, I was drawn to his dependable character and steadfast ways. Wild times? None needed. I was pleased to walk along the river and hold Lonny's gentle, warm hand.

"We're going to be married one day," Lonny said. We were flying kites along the dike. As our rainbow-striped nylon diamond dipped and curved in and out of a June-blue sky, I closed my eyes and hoped he was right. But we were young. Very young. Too young to be talking marriage. But we did, even though Lonny was about to head off for college and I still had two years of high school.

Two years blew by like a gentle wind. Then two more. Lonny and I continued to date, though we were now separated by miles. Lonny enrolled in an engineering work/study program. He earned some money, but it took longer to earn his degree. I worked in the admitting office of our local hospital. Lonny and I still talked of getting married, and I grew certain in my heart that one day we would.

"I've made some money," Lonny said when he was home for a visit. "Enough to buy a ring."

My heart began to flutter in my chest. "Is that so?" I asked.

"We could get married before I graduate," he said. "You've wanted to go to school. We could be students together."

It sounded like a plan. And my mind began to wander. When would he propose? How would he propose? All of my romantic hopes, dreams, and desires began to bloom like flowers in June. I just knew the proposal would be special. Lonny knew and loved my romantic dreamer's heart.

Lonny's job was with a printing company not far from where I lived. He came to visit most weekends. He'd pop into his parents' house, peck his mom on the cheek, and then drive over to see me. We loved to picnic. We'd pack my grandma's picnic hamper to the top and hit the road. Every time I loaded that basket with cold chicken or homemade pie and crisp, ripe apples, I'd wonder if this would be the time. Would he propose? What wonderful thing had he planned? Had he hidden the ring? Would he send me on a scavenger hunt? Was it buried deep in the petals of a dewy red rose?

But after each picnic, I was left to wonder. Oh, there had been opportunity. My own mind ran wild with possibilities. But nothing happened. Ever.

One evening, the two of us decided to go out for dinner. No place fancy. Then we stopped for ice cream. Lonny bought my favorite. Two scoops of butter pecan.

"Want to walk along the river?" he asked.

"Not so much. It's buggy. It's muggy-hot."

"Awww. Come on," he said. "The river's smooth as glass."

So we trudged along the river, the butter pecan making rivers of its own down my arms. We walked along quiet places where even the river seemed to make no sound. We walked along dark places where only the stars provided a far-off, hazy light.

Then we walked under the cranky old bridge that ran from Illinois to Iowa. The lights were bright. Shadflies batted harsh, annoying wings. Trucks roared overhead. I looked down at the path and picked up the pace.

That's when I noticed that Lonny wasn't beside me. He was a

few paces back. Under the bridge. Under the roar. Thick in the mix of river bugs.

And he was on one knee.

I tossed my ice cream and then pinched my forearm with sticky fingers. Was I dreaming? After all this time? All the missed opportunities? He was proposing under a river bridge?

But the look in his eyes had never been sweeter, and I'd never been more drawn to his solid, honest soul. Nothing pretentious. Nothing with frills. Just a solid "I love you, and I always will."

Of course, I couldn't hear a word. The trucks roared and the bridge banged, and I had to follow the movement of his mouth. I swooshed away the bugs and took his hands in mine. He stood and twirled me round and round, our laughter lost in the clatter overhead.

Romantic? Not so much. Not what I had hoped for. Not what I had planned. But I'm delighted to say that, twenty-two years later, my husband is the most romantic man I can imagine. We've grown into one another. I'm more practical. He's more romantic.

And I'll never, ever regret saying "I do" or accepting the promises made on that sultry summer night. He promised forever, and he meant it, too.

Even if the words were lost in Mississippi muddle.

~Shawnelle Eliasen

Here Comes the Comes the Bride

The Ring

With this ring I thee wed…

~Book of Common Prayer

Aunt Jane's Diamonds

Better a diamond with a flaw than a pebble without.
~Confucius, Analects

My son Andy wanted to ask Traci, his girlfriend of several years, to marry him. Problem was he couldn't afford a ring. Not one nice enough, in his mind, for Traci.

But I had a way to fix that: Aunt Jane's diamonds. Aunt Jane had passed away only a couple of years earlier, at the ripe old age of ninety-one. She was my favorite aunt, and I was her favorite niece. Because she had no daughter of her own, and she and Uncle Ed were quite well off, Aunt Jane had spoiled me rotten when I was a child. She bought me new clothes at the beginning of each school year. She took me out to eat at nice restaurants. She even helped me with the down payment on my first car.

But that's not why I was crazy about her. I loved Aunt Jane because she was smart and funny and interesting and kind. And because I knew she loved me.

Uncle Ed had always been a big kidder who loved to laugh and play practical jokes. After he died and their son moved out of state, Aunt Jane was terribly lonely. I made it a point to visit her as often as I could, even though she lived more than a hundred miles away. We'd sit together sipping iced tea and talking for hours on end. As is often the case when people grow older, Aunt Jane spent a great deal of time fretting over what would happen to "her things" when her time came.

She was certain that her son would not be interested in some of the treasures she held closest to her heart.

One afternoon while I was visiting, Aunt Jane insisted on showing me the contents of her jewelry drawer. She took out some beautiful pieces, many of which I'd seen her wear over the years. A pearl necklace. A sapphire ring. An elegant gold watch.

For every item of jewelry there was a story, often centering on when, where, and why Uncle Ed had given it to her.

The last thing she removed from the jewelry drawer was a small, velvet box. Face glowing, she handed it to me. "Open it, Julie," she said. Inside was a dazzling pair of diamond earrings. "Ed gave these to me on our fortieth wedding anniversary." She dabbed at her eyes. "I want you to have them."

"Oh, no, Aunt Jane," I stammered. "They're gorgeous. But I can't accept them. Why, I bet you still have occasion to wear these yourself."

"Nonsense! I don't need diamond earrings to watch silly game shows on TV. Nothing would make me happier than thinking about you wearing these diamonds to some of those fancy parties you go to!"

It was obvious that arguing would do no good. Telling Aunt Jane that I seldom went to fancy parties, or that wearing such huge diamonds would make me nervous about losing them, or that perhaps her daughter-in-law would like to have the earrings, clearly wasn't going to change her mind.

And so I drove home that afternoon, dressed in sneakers and blue jeans, with a dazzling pair of diamond studs adorning my ears.

On that drive home, I had an idea. A brilliant idea, if I do say so myself. My two grown sons had jobs they loved, but which didn't pay much. Both had serious girlfriends. I would lock Aunt Jane's earrings in my safety deposit box at the bank and give one to John and one to Andy if and when they needed a diamond for an engagement ring.

Not long after Aunt Jane died, Andy decided to propose to Traci. So I told him the story of the earrings and took him to the bank to get one. "Holy smokes!" he said when I opened the velvet box. "These things must weigh a carat apiece. Are you sure you want to do this, Mom?"

I nodded. "Nothing would make me — or Aunt Jane — happier."

So Andy took his diamond to a jeweler to have it set in an engagement ring. He discovered that he was right — the stone weighed in at .93 carats. But he found out something else, too. It was a fake. All those years ago, Uncle Ed had given Aunt Jane a pair of cubic zirconia earrings and passed them off as diamonds. And for all the years since, Aunt Jane had worn them with pride and then proudly handed them down to me.

I could only imagine Uncle Ed laughing uproariously from his grave at the great practical joke he had pulled on us all.

Andy didn't have the cubic zirconia set in an engagement ring. Figuring that one practical joke was enough, he bought a small but lovely genuine diamond for Traci. She was thrilled with the ring and even more thrilled about the marriage proposal. As for me, I moved Aunt Jane's earrings from the safety deposit box to my own jewelry drawer at home.

I wore them proudly to Andy and Traci's wedding where, I'm certain, Aunt Jane was smiling down on all of us.

~Julie Burns

Miracle of the Flying Diamond

Trouble and perplexity drive me to prayer
and prayer drives away perplexity and trouble.
~Philip Melanchthen

My daughter's beautiful new engagement ring was flying somewhere around the world underneath the floor of an aircraft. It had barely been on her finger a few days, and she hadn't even had a chance to show it to anyone.

Our daughter, Ardelle, had spent a good part of the winter in the Dominican Republic, working with a team from her church on a building project for a Christian school in a poor neighborhood, and then staying on to teach English to the children there. Now spring was coming to our home in central Alberta, and her job was nearly ended. Mark, a special guy she had been seriously dating, was inspired to fly out to meet her in the DR and sweep her off her feet with a marriage proposal on a beautiful white sandy beach. Then he would bring her home, and we would have an amazing celebration! The very idea was so romantic it nearly took my breath away, and I was only her mom!

The plan gave Mark little time to raise the money for everything. On short notice, airfare to the DR was going to be costly, and the ring he bought must be exquisite. The ladies who worked in the jewelry store in the mall near his workplace soon knew him by name as he visited their display case almost every lunch hour. Finally, in an act of sacrifice that impressed even a mother-in-law, he actually sold his car to complete the purchase! As parents, we thought he certainly deserved our blessing when he flew away, the secret jewel safe in his pocket.

Some days later, the scene at the beach on the Caribbean was as he had dreamed. To nobody's great surprise, Ardelle said yes to Mark's proposal. Thinking about how we would meet them at the airport in Calgary, Mark with his victorious grin, and Ardelle holding up her left hand, made the very days sing.

But what was this awful news I was now hearing on the telephone? It was the day of Mark and Ardelle's return, but Mark's mom was calling. Somewhere in the skies above the Gulf of Mexico, Ardelle had finished her lunch, brushed some crumbs off her skirt, and felt her ring go spinning off her finger. It had found its way to a broken space in the grating that covered an air vent running the length of the floor of the aircraft and disappeared! Of course, fellow passengers tried to help, and when the flight landed in Dallas, Texas, even the crew came out and rolled up the carpeting, but the ring was gone. When it was time for the connecting flight to Calgary, there was simply nothing to do but abandon the search and come home, leaving the aircraft that still held their special ring to continue on its flights elsewhere in the world.

Well, Mark and Ardelle's homecoming was happy but more subdued than we had planned. It's just harder to be ecstatic about your engagement when your ring gets lost. At church, the pastor announced their engagement and prayed for the couple, reminding people who wanted to congratulate them after the service not to ask to see their ring. It was hard not to cry.

But then folks started telling us amazing lost-and-found stories. We heard some tales so incredible that a small flame of hope seemed to light my heart, and I began to pray for a miracle. By Monday morning, I was praying and phoning. "Directory assistance for what place, ma'am?" I found myself talking with American Airlines personnel in the Dallas airport, in lost and found, in public relations, in management, in places that would transfer my call to other places. But finally I had someone's promise that in two or three days, when that particular aircraft would be down for routine maintenance, there would be a search for the lost ring. "Not to get your hopes up—this would be a needle in a haystack!" I was told.

A few mornings later, our phone rang early. Someone from American Airlines in Tampa, Florida, was speaking with an exotic southern accent. "I have something in my hand that I think y'all have been hoping to find," reported a man's voice. I had been praying for this moment, so why did it seem unbelievable? It had to be a miracle.

But most awesome was the part of the story we only discovered a little later, in a letter from our hero in Florida—an aircraft mechanic named Ted. Ted's assignment on night shift had been to complete his routine service duties, then search for an engagement ring lost by a passenger. He was working with a heavy heart, saddened by the death of his father-in-law. Ted admitted he did not believe he would ever find a ring, but he loosened between 200 and 300 screws to access the area where it might have fallen. This area was congested with electrical, hydraulic, air-conditioning and water lines, all covered with dust and insulation fibers. With his arms scratched and sore, Ted took a coffee break and looked up at the stars. Somewhere up there, his father-in-law was in heaven.

"Please," he prayed, "help me." Taking a small mirror in his hand, he stuck it into a crack and shone a light behind it. His letter continued, "I turned it left and saw nothing but dust, turned it right, and there it was! I started to tremble." Knowing that if he disturbed the ring it could fall farther out of reach, Ted paused to calm himself, then began the delicate task of getting a hold on it and finally extricating it from its dark hiding place. At last, it was in the palm of his hand.

Ted described what had happened as "a spiritual event for me." He knew that getting that mirror into the exact right spot was no coincidence. "Your prayers also helped this miracle happen for the both of us," his letter concluded. Mark and Ardelle have been married for almost sixteen years, and their diamond ring is as lovely as ever. So is the renewal of hope and faith I still feel when I remember this story.

~Sharon Pipke

A Tiny Ring

Our wedding was many years ago. The celebration continues to this day.
~Gene Perret

"I want to marry you, but there is just one thing," Bob said, as we were talking about our future and the possibility of marriage. "Mellissa."

Mellissa was my six-year-old daughter. I had married young, right out of high school. Mellissa, or Missy as we called her, was born the next year. She was diagnosed with medical problems, and my immature marriage couldn't handle the strain. I was divorced at twenty.

Bob and I had met when Missy was two. I was not looking for a relationship. I was a young mom working two jobs and trying just to make ends meet. Bob was like our weekend dad. He was fun-loving and full of joy. He would play Barbies with Missy and take us out for meals that included a toy. He won Missy's heart within a few months. It took a little longer for me to heal and trust. Four years later, Bob won my heart, and renewed my hope in marriage and the possibility of a family.

I couldn't understand what was so troubling to him now. "What is the problem, honey? She loves you," I said. "This will be so good for her, for us."

"This is so big," he kept saying. "Being Mellissa's father is so scary. I'm thinking about the importance of the role that I will play in her whole life. I mean, being a husband is huge, but being a dad?"

I wasn't sure what I should say or do. Was he changing his mind?

The next week, he came to me with a tiny ring and some handwritten vows. I could tell that he had been crying.

"I want to ask Missy to marry me," he said. "I want to give her a ring, and I have written vows to her, promises to be a good father." I was speechless.

"I want to commit to her in the same way that I will commit to you," he continued, "to be there for her for the rest of her life."

He paused. "If I marry you, I know—I have always known—I marry her, too."

Our wedding day came, and our friends and family gathered. When it came time for our vows and ring exchange, the ceremony went as planned. Bob and I read our vows to each other and placed the wedding rings on each other's hands. Then the pastor announced that Bob would like to give Missy a ring and share his vows to her.

I don't know why I thought that I would get through it just fine, but nothing could have prepared me for that moment. I watched my darling little daughter's face as Bob knelt down beside her, trembling and weeping, as he read his promises to her. He took her tiny hand in his big, strong hand while he slipped the little ring on her finger. It was then that I noticed the faces of my family. They were all crying—my dad, uncles, and brother were sobbing as they watched one of the most tender and loving moments ever witnessed.

Twenty-four years have passed, and each September we celebrate our anniversary—Bob, Mellissa, and me. It is hard to remember back to a time when I had lost my hope for marriage and a family. Sometimes, I take out my old jewelry box, open it up, and hold the tiny ring. I close my eyes and say a prayer of thanks for promises, second chances, and love.

~Lori Bryant

From Thin Air

It is not the mountain we conquer but ourselves.
~Edmund Hillary

*I*n December 2010, my then-boyfriend Dale and I flew to Ecuador for an eighteen-day backpacking trip. We were thrilled and terrified to be spending so many consecutive days together. Having a 2,200-mile, long-distance relationship did not allow us to spend much time together, and the short trips we had gone on so far had involved a few nights' stay in comfortable hotels in the U.S. and Canada. Thus, our developing-country backpacking compatibility was a scary unknown.

Our first three days revealed that we largely agreed upon the activities we wanted to do and the parts of the country we wanted to visit—hallelujah! So, on the fourth morning we set off to make reservations for a two-day mountain-biking trip and a three-day jungle adventure. Being the consummate consumer that he is, Dale insisted on doing due diligence before purchasing either trip. That involved an arduous three hours of talking to different tour companies and strategically discussing our options. Finally, at one o'clock, we walked out of The Biking Dutchman, our second and final reservation having been made.

Next, we bought sandwiches and flagged down a taxi driver to take us to a gondola that we would ride to the 13,000-foot trailhead of our 2,400-foot vertical climb for the day. The problem was, it was already two o'clock by the time we exited the gondola. The hike to the 15,400-foot peak was supposed to take three hours, and the sun would set at 6:12 P.M. Dale didn't seem concerned about our situation. I, on the other hand, realized we couldn't dilly-dally if we were going to reach our intended destination, which I fully intended to do. I had never been above 11,000 feet before, so this would be a momentous first for me.

Setting a quick pace, which likely wasn't the wisest thing to do at that altitude since we were breathing forty percent less oxygen, we managed to reach the top by about 4:50 P.M., ten minutes shy of the forecasted three hours—score! However, we weren't quite at the peak. Somewhere on a treacherous mound of rock there was allegedly a path that would lead us up the last one hundred feet to the peak. After diligently searching for the path for a few minutes, I suggested that we give up and start our descent. Unwilling to admit defeat, Dale insisted on continuing the quest.

"Okay," I said, "but we need to leave in ten minutes because a thick fog is rolling in, the temperature is dropping, the path is very hard to follow up here, and I don't trust them to keep the gondola open after sunset." Hastily agreeing to the somewhat prolonged search time, Dale continued to wander about until I finally had to tell him it was time to go.

My Girl Scout survival instincts kicking into high gear, I was ready to book it down the mountain. Dale, on the other hand, wanted to savor the moment. He pulled me against him so we could look at the foggy view together. Wondering why my affectionate boyfriend would choose this less-than-ideal moment to be close, I patiently humored him for about five seconds. Then, just as I was ready to explain, again, why it was important to head down the mountain, he said, "Being that this is the highest point in your life so far, I thought I would make it the highest point in another way."

My eyes grew to two times their normal size and my heart skipped a few beats as I realized what was about to happen. Although we had talked about marriage, I wasn't expecting him to propose in Ecuador. If he had been carrying an expensive engagement ring on our backpacking, hostelling adventure, he would have nervously monitored his belongings and likely would not have let me get close to his things. Since he had been doing neither of these things, I was convinced we would still be boyfriend-girlfriend when we returned to the States.

Turning me around, he managed to get down on one knee despite the uneven, rocky terrain and asked me to marry him. He slid a ring onto my finger as I kissed him and accepted his proposal. As we savored the moment, he explained that he had wanted to propose at the peak, which explained his persistent search for the apparently nonexistent path, but decided that one hundred feet shy of the top was just as good. We then took a few quick pictures to memorialize the beginning of our engagement and immediately began our descent.

As we hiked, I periodically glanced at the ring he had bestowed upon me. I should have been ecstatic that I had finally found the love of my life and had just been proposed to on top of a mountain in Ecuador. Instead, I was crestfallen because the ring was nothing like what I had wanted. The month before when Dale had prodded me with questions as to what type of ring I wanted, I responded by saying I wanted an ornate, antique band, and the size of the diamond didn't matter to me. I refused to say anything further because I wanted to be surprised. However, just to cover my bases, I e-mailed my younger sister, Holly, a website that had ring styles I liked. I figured that if Dale were to ask anyone what kind of ring I wanted, he would likely ask Holly during our Thanksgiving visit to my family in Iowa.

Contrary to my desires, the ring I wore had a thick, plain band and a massive solitary stone without any side diamonds. I tried to keep my tears in check. It's only a ring, I repeated to myself with every passing step. I would learn to love and appreciate it. His love and our life together were what mattered. By the time we reached the gondola, well after the sun had set, I had managed to convince myself that the ring was indeed a special item.

Settling into the gondola, Dale tentatively stated, "I should tell you how much I spent on your ring." Based on his tone, I slowly turned to face him, not wanting to know how far we would be set back by the mammoth stone I was sporting.

"I spent twelve."

"Dale," I responded in a state of shock, "$12,000 is a lot of money."

"Twelve dollars," he said with a goofy grin.

My clever sister had suggested that he get an imitation ring for proposing so he would not have to carry the real ring! For the remainder of the ride, we laughed as we recounted our separate stories about what we had each been thinking as we descended the mountain.

Upon returning to the hostel, Dale logged onto his e-mail account and showed me pictures he had sent to himself of the real ring. With tears running down my cheeks, I told him it was perfect—and I meant it.

~Heather Zuber-Harshman

Ringing In Our Wedding

I have always felt a gift diamond shines so much better than one you buy for yourself.
~Mae West

"Don't panic," my mom announced as I dressed for my wedding at our church, "but your wedding ring is missing." The guests were already arriving, so how could I not panic? My fiancé, Eldon, and I had agreed to follow tradition and not see each other before the ceremony. Maybe his groomsmen had set this up as some sort of bad joke. However, the look on my mom's face told me that it was serious. I tried not to raise my voice.

"My ring is missing? What happened?"

"Well…" she paused. "It may have actually been stolen."

"Stolen?" I felt the blood drain from my face and feared no amount of make-up would be able to turn me into a blushing bride.

She told me that Eldon's brother, Rolland, had been entrusted with the job of delivering my wedding ring. Neatly dressed for the ceremony, he'd placed the jewelry box containing the ring to his right on the car's bench seat before driving himself to the church. Moments later, he saw a hitchhiker and stopped, offering a ride to the straggly stranger. After dropping off the hitchhiker, Rolland arrived at the church. It was only then that he realized the jewelry box was missing.

The car had been searched, my mom said, but the box hadn't been found. The reality of the situation began to sink in. My wedding ring had disappeared right before the nuptials. It had vanished — poof — and its loss could put a big crimp in our ceremony.

I was a young bride — barely in college — and like most brides I'd dreamed of my wedding since childhood. My parents had offered to give us the same amount of money they'd spend for a wedding if we eloped. Without actually saying it, I realized that they probably thought that our youthful marriage wouldn't last, so why go through with the ceremony? But I believed in our love and wanted the wedding of my dreams. I turned down their offer before discussing it with Eldon. Nothing was going to get in the way of our big church wedding. Not even an absent ring.

Determined, I said, "So my ring's missing. Now what?"

"Eldon was really worried that you were going to get upset about this," my mom said. "But you seem to be taking it better than he thought. He's already found someone who will lend you her wedding ring for the ceremony." She opened the door and waved in a middle-aged, brunette woman I had never seen before.

"I'm Eileen," she introduced herself, "a friend of your soon-to-be in-laws. Eldon thought my wedding band might fit on your finger." She twisted off the ring. "Why don't you try it on?"

The thick gold band clashed with my engagement ring's delicate white-gold braid, but it slid onto my finger easily. I waved my hand, and it was neither too loose nor too tight. "It fits!"

"You may not believe this," Eileen said, "but you're the second bride I've lent this ring to for her ceremony. We've been married for a long time, and that couple's also been married for several years, so I think it brings good luck." Her smiling face reassured me that the wedding would turn out okay after all.

Not long after meeting Eileen, Eldon and I exchanged our vows at the altar, sealing our marriage with that borrowed ring.

Following the service, many people wanted to see "my" new wedding bands. At first, I was a bit embarrassed by the mismatched rings. But soon I was calmly repeating, "My wedding ring went missing this morning, so a lovely woman lent me her ring for the ceremony. It's my 'something borrowed.'" Some people seemed confused, but I smiled, and they smiled back.

When Eileen and her husband came through the line, she was positively beaming. "I enjoyed your wedding even more knowing you had my ring."

I gave her a big hug. "Well, I'm getting used to wearing it and might have some trouble giving it back."

Before the reception, Eldon and Rolland searched the car again for the jewelry box. Lo and behold, they found it, jammed in the corner of the seat right next to the passenger door.

Now, thirty-eight years of marriage have passed, and I'm sure of one thing: I don't remember all the little details that went right on our wedding day. But I'll always remember the episode of my missing wedding ring—and the borrowed wedding ring that still holds a huge place in my heart.

~Ronda Ross Taylor

I Love Lucy

One of the things I learned the hard way was that it doesn't pay to get discouraged.

~Lucille Ball

"Happy?" my brand-new fiancé asks. I smile and nod, pretty certain that I've never been happier.

Sitting mid-restaurant, puppy eyed and giddy, we share a bottle of champagne and appetizers. It's all very Disney's *Lady and the Tramp*, minus the shared meatball. He tinkers with the sparkling diamond, which has found its home on my left hand in just the past twenty-five minutes.

I think through the past four hours, trying to rejoin reality... I want to remember it all!

I recall a phone conversation with my father; he had uncharacteristically failed to ask about my plans for the evening, and then sounded funny when I told him about them anyway. My boyfriend and I had reservations at the nicest steakhouse in town. I'd chosen a dress he'd never seen.

"Wow, you look great!"

"Thanks! You, too." Dockers and a collared shirt, an extra effort, very handsome!

We went to church before dinner and arrived at five-fifteen for our six o'clock reservation. A typical Saturday night in one of the hottest spots—people crowded the corridor, the bar, and the tables inside the restaurant area...

The hostess giggled as she seated us early, making it clear that she had chosen a special spot, all the while looking cow-eyed and adoringly at John.

"Do you know her?" I'd asked.

"No."

"She acts like she knows you; why would she seat us so early?"

"She didn't," he'd said, though she'd done so, just as we'd gotten drinks from the bar. John had handed the bartender his entire wallet in payment. Both weird, but I'd had no reason for suspicion. He claims now that he'd been nervous but I hadn't noticed.

By the time we got our appetizers, it was clear this was no typical evening: the most beautiful engagement ring I'd ever seen was brought out under glass.

John got down on one knee...

"Will you marry me?" he'd asked.

"Absolutely!"

He'd reached for the ring box to put the ring on my finger, found it empty, momentarily panicked, then realized I was already wearing it!

"I guess that means you like it?"

"It's PERFECT!" Tears blurred my vision.

Since we were already center stage, he stood up and announced to the entire restaurant that we were engaged. Pulling me to my feet, he threw our arms up in the air as if we had just won Olympic medals. People everywhere clapped. By that point, simultaneous laughter and crying had overcome me.

We called both families from the patio of the restaurant on John's cell and planned trips to visit them the next day.

As we'd returned to our tables, he'd said, "You can see now why I wanted to get that out of the way before the steaks came... so I could eat my dinner!"

He confessed:

- He had gotten to the restaurant before picking me up and made arrangements with the manager, hostess, and wait staff.

- The previous night, he'd left work early, headed to my dad's barbershop, and waited his turn for a haircut that he never intended to receive.
- Dad had given "permission for my hand," a cliché that made me cry.

He had done everything correctly! It was all so romantic that it was hard to believe it was actually happening to me!

I heard myself babbling Lucille Ball-style... Nervous excitement had taken over. Relaxed, John ate his dinner as he'd hoped. Mine sat in a take-out box.

Now we're nibbling on fancy sweets. He's smiling like he's just won the lottery and playing with the diamond he's just put on my finger.

"You know," John says abruptly, snapping me out of the dream-night video playing in my head, "it's a little big; we need to get it sized as soon as possible."

"It's not that big!" I insist, waving my hand to prove that the diamond will remain on my finger.

As if on cue, it flies off and into a coin-size slot where the booth connects to the wall! Forgetting dress and heels, I wiggle to the floor and crawl around, searching like crazy. John meets me under the table and escorts me back to my seat.

"Oh, John, you scared me. Give it back to me."

"I don't have it, honey. It's not on the floor."

I look at him, through him, and try to laugh. "No kidding, give it to me!"

He's pointing to the tiny entryway. "Gina, we both saw that ring fly! It passed right by my face and slid into that slot! You couldn't make a shot like that twice! It's in the wall!"

The waitress comes over again to congratulate us and see if we need anything else.

"I LOST MY RING!" I hear the famous Lucy whine come from my side of the booth.

"You're not going to believe this," John says. "She waved her hand and the ring—it was a little big—flew off her finger and right here into the wall!"

"Are you sure?" She's as baffled as we are. She calls a busboy over, and he leaves and returns with a long stick of some sort. He is trying to swipe it toward the floor and out of the booth.

"You don't understand," John's voice quivers. "It's in the wall. I saw it. I'm sure it's in the wall."

Soon we are escorted to a different table where we watch busboys disassembling our booth.

People around us begin looking under their tables and passing the story amongst themselves. A woman in the crowd loudly accuses: "You'd think he'd get the right size!"

The manager comes over. "Are you sure you lost your ring? Could it be in your purse or in the bathroom or somewhere?"

John's voice is adamant. "It is in the wall!"

"Okay, then, when the dining room clears, we will take the booth apart from the wall. You are going to have to wait; we are already disturbing our customers enough."

We watch everyone slowly digesting meals. Time barely moves. We somberly swallow champagne and then dessert.

I ask: "Do you still want to marry me?"

"Yes."

(Whew!) "You know, my friends would say this was a typical 'Gina' thing to do. I can be a little *I Love Lucy*. You may be in for a lifetime of stuff like this."

He melts a bit. "Well, I guess I'm warned."

Eventually, only restaurant employees remain with us. The manager comes over holding a power drill. Two men pull out the booth.

Center wall, between plaster and paint, in the ridge that normally holds the booth's base, my diamond stares out at us.

The manager looks relieved. "And there it is!"

"Can I kiss you?" I ask, reaching for it, appreciating the man who has put all things right again with his hand drill.

"You should kiss *him*," he says, pointing to John.

John grabs the ring out of my hand and places it on my finger—and then we kiss.

~Gina Farella Howley

Planet Zirconia

There are many sham diamonds in this life which pass for real,
and vice versa.
~William Makepeace Thackeray

When we got married, Michael was a restaurant manager. I was a struggling student and a single mother, so our wedding was pieced together like a puzzle. A simple, on-sale gown for me, a rented tux for him, and a flower girl's dress for my daughter, Virginia, made by a family friend. The reception was at a neighborhood hall with cheesy linoleum and stained ceiling tiles. We tried not to look too closely at some of the details. The food was catered by us—the bride and groom—cooked up in our shag-carpeted apartment: roast beef slices rolled up *au jus*, tubs of mostaccioli, and chafing dishes full of green beans.

The rings we exchanged on that September afternoon were thin bands. Going shopping, we had settled on the cheapest ones. My band slipped on right next to my engagement ring, which Michael had picked out the year before. It was adorned with gems from "the planet Zirconia," as my husband would jest, and it became a running joke. There was no way we could afford diamonds, not even diamond dust.

Okay, so not all the pieces fit together to create a perfect picture. But at the end of the day, we were married, our friends and family had enjoyed themselves, we didn't run out of food, and my five-year-old daughter only lifted up her dress once during the ceremony.

And over the years, we stayed at nose-just-above-the-water level. After I finished with school, I became a third-grade teacher. Michael worked, too, but our goal was never to make loads of money. What money we did make went into Virginia and then Ian, our son. Soccer leagues. Music lessons. Braces. College loans. We started in a "starter home" and never left it. We began with simple gold bands and were still stuck with them, even though we tossed jokes back and forth for the next couple of decades.

"You know, one of these days I'm gonna get a rock on my finger to make up for all this aggravation!" I'd throw at him after he did something hardheaded.

"Well, actually, the stones from Zirconia are in higher demand than diamonds," Michael would claim. Since I was never really that enthralled with diamonds, it didn't matter. I liked my simple gold band. I didn't feel like I was missing out on anything.

When our 25th wedding anniversary rolled around, the two of us went out to dinner. It was a low-key celebration because my mom was in a rehabilitation center. Our son was away at college. It seemed silly to spend a bunch of money on a big party just to mark something we already knew: We had weathered lots of storms but were still together.

A few months later, we were at my in-laws' house, opening Christmas gifts. Earlier that morning, I had unwrapped some books and a sweater from Michael. Not expecting anything else from him, I was surprised when he handed me a plain, business-sized envelope. When I opened it, I read a lovely poem with such sweet sentiments about our twenty-five years together.

So blown away by the sentimental words, tears started flowing down my cheeks. I didn't even pay attention to the end of the poem, where it said that I should ask what was "hiding" in Michael's pocket. When he prompted me, "Ask me what's in my pocket," I blubbered the words. Out of his pocket emerged a small box—and in the small box was a diamond ring.

Even though I never wanted a diamond, after twenty-five

years, it mattered to him. In his mind, it was important to mark the anniversary with a grand gesture.

When I look at the ring—in a unique setting to mark our quirky relationship—I try not to think of what that money could have been spent on instead of an expensive piece of jewelry. I try not to think of how overrated diamonds are. When I look at the ring, what I see clearer than anything else is how we've arranged the puzzle pieces over the years. Sometimes, we've had to search for the right pieces, to the point of almost giving up. Sometimes, we've had to jam the pieces together, forcing them to fit. But in the end, we've made it work.

~Sioux Roslawski

Reprinted by permission of Off the Mark
and Mark Parisi ©1997

Humoring the Groom

Even the gods love jokes.
~Plato

My fingers fumbled with the cloth buttons on the jacket of my pink mother-of-the-groom suit. In a short time, I would welcome our first daughter-in-law into the family. I had no reservations. Lori had won my heart as quickly as she had won my son's. My anxiety was over something else — something that would happen during the ceremony.

Ron was and still is a weeper. He has been a sensitive child as long as I can remember. I feared it was going to be a boxful-of-tissues ceremony. As the wedding day approached, I wondered what we might do to help him keep his composure long enough to make it through his vows.

In addition to Ron's weeping, we had to contend with the best man's history of fainting during wedding ceremonies. His last had been his brother's, and he had buckled at the knees midway through. Certainly, we could find some way around both problems.

Drawing from something I had seen at a friend's daughter's wedding, I approached the groomsmen with my idea. Ron's two brothers were delighted to participate in my plan, as well as his friends who knew Ron's sense of humor would come through and save him from himself.

From my seat in the front row, I watched in awe as my child took the hands of his bride and began to recite his vows. Just as predicted, we could see the tears begin to flow. But then it came time to ask for the best man to produce the ring. The best man, Gary, was still standing, a slight twinkle in his eye. He had something else to think about other than keeping his knees from buckling.

When the pastor asked for the ring, Gary put a hand in his pocket. He then stuck his other hand in another pocket. When both came up empty, he checked the inside pockets of his tuxedo. Empty. He turned to the groomsman behind him who immediately began to check his pockets. And so it went all the way to the end where my youngest son finally fished the ring out of the last pocket he checked.

Chuckles broke out as the wedding guests realized what was happening. Lori's face softened as she saw the ring coming up the line of groomsmen. But the minister's face remained completely serious. Not a flicker of humor. My heart sank. I didn't want to create a problem. I had just wanted to break the tension for the guys. Now I may have gotten them into trouble.

The wedding reception over, we took the tape from the camera of a friend who had videotaped the whole day and went home to make copies. As we gathered around the television, my husband hooked up the video so we could relive our wonderful day. A shadow crossed my face as we watched the ring ceremony and the boys' antics. Just afterward, the pastor turned to face the back of the podium where our friend's camera was set up. As he did, his face broke into a wide grin! I relaxed. He had obviously enjoyed the prank as much as everyone else.

~Karen Robbins

Will You Marry Me... Again?

When dealing with people, remember you are not dealing with creatures of logic, but creatures of emotion.
~Dale Carnegie

My ring had gotten a little more "slippy" than I'd prefer for true peace of mind. Adam still wouldn't tell me what he paid, but even if he'd traded an old couch and a bag of cat food for it, losing it would break my heart. So, we decided to resize. This sounds so easy. All my engaged and married friends know all about it, went through it, and totally understand it. This doesn't make it any less scary. Kind of like going to the OB/GYN. Totally normal and yet completely terrifying.

Also, to add to the panic, the jewelry place that has been in the Shops at Mission Viejo for thirty-five years—the place that assured Adam that they weren't going anywhere, that they were as reliable as the sun itself—was closing. So we had to bite the bullet and resize the ring right away.

The guy at the jewelry place remembered Adam (he made multiple stops "just to visit" during the process of purchasing the ring) and called me the "lucky girl," which made me blush and Adam grin with pride. It all happened so fast. Before I knew it, the ring was off and signed for, a new size tried on, and a receipt was handed to us. We were told it would be two weeks, and before I knew it I was standing on the sidewalk outside the mall, eyes brimming with tears and my left hand feeling oh-so-naked. Adam was squeezing me, half sad that I was sad, but half over-the-moon about it since those tears meant that I REALLY LIKED HIS RING.

He tried to buy me a fake ring, you know, the kind you wear home from Spring Break junior year to freak out your mom, but I refused, absolutely sure that I could tough it out. We went to Chili's, but I didn't even make it out of the car before I started crying again. Side note: Getting engaged completely sets off your it's-okay-to-cry-about-everything meter.

We made it through dinner and the rest of the night, and I only teared up several times. The next night, Adam came over for dinner, and I was cooking in my tiny kitchen with my back to him.

"Hey," he said.

I turned around, and he was on one knee between the counter and couch, holding up a ring box and a very sparkly replacement ring, with his eyes shining, smiling up at me.

"Will you marry me... again?" he asked.

Guess what I said.

I wore the fake ring for two weeks, and I wear the real one every day now, two years after our wedding day. But any time I take it off or Adam holds it for any reason, I see that image in my mind — once on a snowdrift in Sequoia National Park, once in my tiny apartment kitchen — the love of my life asking for the privilege of being with me, forever. And even if he asks a million times, my answer will always be: yes.

~Dani Nichols

<... >

An Unconventional Proposal

The manner of giving is worth more than the gift.
~Pierre Corneille, Le Menteur

My husband Geoff and I met in college and dated for almost three years. I knew he was "the one" almost from the beginning of our relationship. I pestered him about marriage for several months, but he was reluctant to talk about it, so I dropped it. Even my grandfather, who was my guardian and best friend, knew my husband was the one for me. He offered Geoff a thousand dollars to marry me when he met him for the first time! Because I trusted my grandfather so much, I knew after hearing the story that I had made the right choice.

On my twenty-first birthday, Geoff had to work at a hunters' check station, so I decided to go home for the weekend to spend it with my girlfriends. When I returned, Geoff told me he still had one other birthday gift to buy me at the mall, and I begged him for hints. He told me it could cost anywhere from a few dollars to a few thousand, and that he would have to make it. I had no clue what he was talking about, so I was incredibly impatient! He let me accompany him to the mall where he purchased the items he needed, but I was banished to one part of the mall that was nowhere near the stores he was visiting.

When we returned home, he told me he had to go to the garage to make my gift, and I was forbidden from checking on him. My curiosity was overwhelming, but I left him alone. When he finally returned, I begged him to give it to me, but he said it was still "drying." Still, I harassed him non-stop until he finally gave in and went to the garage to retrieve it. He came to me where I was sitting on the couch and knelt in front of me. I stared at the item he was holding in confusion as he professed his love and asked me to marry him. I was so stunned that I actually laughed! His look of bewilderment only made me laugh harder, but I was able to say yes when I realized what he was holding.

Because he was a poor college student putting himself through school, he was not able to afford an engagement ring. Instead, he bought a crystal shaped like a diamond, gold spray paint, and some wire that he shaped it into a ring. The paint was still drying, so he brought the handmade ring in on a stick so he wouldn't touch it and smear the paint. And that was what he held out to me when he asked me to marry him. It was one of the most romantic and sweetest things he'd ever done. I couldn't have been happier with my ring, and I called all my friends and family to tell them the good news. My grandfather's words: "It's about time!"

Geoff spent the summer working in a different part of the state, so I did most of the wedding planning myself. We did not have much money and were paying for most of the wedding ourselves. My grandfather bought my dress for me, which made it even more special. And my parents paid for the venue, and made the food and the cake. We had no band or music, and there was no air conditioning on the hottest day of the year. The ceremony lasted about seven minutes, and the pictures and video that had been poorly taken by family members are almost not worth having. But it didn't matter. We were so happy to be married and call each other "husband" and "wife" that we laughed it off.

When we had been married for six years, my husband suggested we get married again and do it the way we would have wanted, so that's what we did. My grandfather had passed away the year after our wedding (after saying to me on my wedding day that he could leave me knowing I had someone wonderful to take care of me), so we honored him and our other relatives who had since passed by dedicating the ceremony and the day to them.

Almost twenty years later, we are still married and very much in love. I still have the engagement ring that Geoff fashioned for me so many years ago. It's hanging on a ribbon from the mirror of my car so I can look at it every day when I am in the car. People ask me what it is, and I tell them the story with pleasure as I remember Geoff coming toward me with it drying on a stick to ask me to share his life. It didn't matter that it wasn't a real engagement ring—only that he loved me enough to make it so he could ask me to be his wife. It's not the engagement ring or the wedding that matters anyway. It's the love that we share every day of this marriage and the happiness that we've given each other as partners for life.

~Kristi Cocchiarella FitzGerald

Here Comes the Bride

Chapter 3

The Dress

After all there is something about a wedding-gown
prettier than in any other gown in the world.

~Douglas William Jerrold

A Real Piece of Me

*Chains do not hold a marriage together. It is threads, hundreds of tiny
threads which sew people together through the years.*
~Simone Signoret

I dreamed of a small but whimsical wedding. I envisioned something low-pressure and fun, something everyone could enjoy
without being overly formal. I wanted the wedding to reflect my
personality: I didn't want anyone to be uncomfortable or worry about
etiquette or pay a fortune. I wanted to be relaxed. I was the exact
opposite of Bridezilla.

But my family made up for that.

Being the first to get married in my family and marrying an only
child, our families were perhaps more excited about our wedding
than we were! Mother, father, in-laws, sister… their eagerness about
planning our wedding quickly spiraled out of control.

My choice of wedding color was rejected by my fiancé, my choice
of location was rejected by my in-laws, and the food was chosen by
my parents. From party favors to invitations, everyone had an opinion and took advantage of my easygoing personality to make their
choices for the wedding—at the cost of my own. At first, it didn't
bother me, but when even my sister started listing characteristics she
"forbade" in my wedding dress, it was just too much.

It wasn't about control. It was about the fact that this was *my*
wedding—hopefully my only one—and I wanted it to reflect my
personality. Right now, it was just a mix of my family's demands. I had

to own just one element of my wedding. Something that reflected my personality. Something people would remember years after the wedding. Sitting on my couch and looking at pictures of the Halloween costumes I'd sewn for my fiancé and me, I knew just how to do it.

A memory of my first "surprise" date with my fiancé came to mind. Knowing it was my absolute favorite, he (then my boyfriend) had surprised me by securing opening-night tickets to the latest film installment of *Lord of the Rings*. As we sat in the darkened theater, an image filled the screen, and I squeezed his hand. It was an actress standing atop a cliff. The wind blew her hair up in long ribbons, and her medieval-inspired white dress billowed with it. The sleeves were long and open, the curves of the dress were simple, and the belt added a touch of elegance.

"That's the kind of dress I want to get married in!" I had whispered to my then-boyfriend. At the time, I was glad for the darkened theater: we had not yet discussed marriage, and I hadn't meant to bring up the subject. I blushed.

But sitting there on the couch, the memory rekindled itself in my heart. I knew just how to add my personal flair to the wedding.

"I'm sewing my own dress," I told my mother on the phone that evening. I sent her a dozen pictures I had found on the Internet. "It'll be a combination of all the ones I sent you. The sleeves from the first one, the trim from the next..."

My mother groaned. "That's a big undertaking," she told me once she regained the ability to speak. "You have so much else to focus on for the wedding. Perhaps you should leave it to the professionals."

I promised to make a prototype first, and if she really didn't approve, I'd consider a wedding shop. She hesitantly agreed.

I got to work. The sewing store had many patterns for medieval-style dresses, but nothing was exactly what I wanted. I ended up buying three different patterns and creating my own prototype. It was finished within two weeks—much to my mother's chagrin. But even she conceded that it would work.

Still, every once in a while she would e-mail me a picture of a professional wedding dress similar to the style I wanted. But the price tags, eight hundred dollars and up, were incentive enough to continue my project. I got to work finding the perfect elements for my dress.

At the fabric store, I spent hours scrutinizing fabric types. It was a summer wedding, but I wanted a fabric that would flow. It had to be the perfect weight. When I finally found the fabric, I needed almost two bolts.

"What on earth are you making?" the clerk asked me, eyeing the large pile of fabric.

I told her it was my wedding dress. I described the folds, the long train, the lace upper sleeves giving way to long, wide, flowing sleeves that gathered at the wrists with silver thread. Her eyes popped, and she treated the fabric with newfound respect. "To think," she said in awe, "that one day someone will be getting married in this fabric!"

I took the fabric home and slowly, carefully got to work. I measured four times before cutting. I double-checked the prototype to make the proper alterations. I vacuumed daily to make sure the floor and worktable were clear of any loose pins that might cause the dress to snag. And each time one of my family members got a little crazy about planning the wedding, I simply let it go and retreated to my work area.

The night before the wedding, I was still sewing on the last of the embellishments. My mother was sitting stiffly on the couch, adamant that neither of us move until the dress was finished. When I made the last stitch, she breathed a sigh of relief and finally admitted she was proud of me for completing such an ambitious undertaking.

The day of my wedding, family members were still arguing over details. My in-laws and parents couldn't agree on how to pass out the bubbles, my extended family argued over who got to sit at which table, and my sister and father argued over who they should ask to take candid video with their camcorder. But I put it all behind me. It was early July, but the weather worked out in my favor. The high that day, normally in the nineties, barely touched eighty. The dress's fabric was the perfect weight. The breeze was gentle enough not to mess up my hair, but it was just enough to kiss the fabric of my dress, billowing it almost like it did in *Lord of the Rings*.

I didn't tell many people I was making my dress. I hadn't done it for bragging rights or attention. I had done it for me. Still, the dress received many compliments, and people asked where I'd found such a unique dress. They couldn't believe I'd made it myself. Even the DJ made a special acknowledgment after learning I'd made the dress. It's been nearly six years since the wedding, and whenever the memory arises, one of the few details people recall is the beautiful and unique wedding dress that I had made. And here's why: It wasn't the fabric or the embellishments. It wasn't the sleeves or the lace. It was me. And that's all I ever wanted.

~Val Muller

23

The Peasant Dress

Just around the corner in every woman's mind—
is a lovely dress, a wonderful suit, or entire costume which will
make an enchanting new creature of her.
~Wilhela Cushman

*I*t's a little tight," I complained to the Macy's lingerie saleslady. "Sorry, hon. That top doesn't come in Extra Large."

When I had bought the cap-sleeve blouse to match my eyelet peasant skirt two months earlier, I had hoped to lose weight.

"But my wedding's ten days away!" I whined like a Bridezilla. Or, even worse—a wrinkled, overly tan sixty-two-year-old Bridezilla. I had been sure I could lose ten pounds and get down to my college weight. But I had only lost two pounds and I realized the fitted peasant blouse I wanted to be married in was made for the figure I had forty years ago. I'd be walking down the aisle popping pearl buttons like popcorn.

"Honey, you don't need to lose weight," the lady in lingerie reassured. "You need a waist cincher." That sounded painful.

She returned with a wrap-around corset as solidly boned as a standing rib roast. With Herculean yanking and stretching, I was finally able to secure its top hook. I was new to these lingerie innovations. During my previous thirty-year marriage, I had preferred loose, comfortable clothes. Then I did drop some pounds—actually cried them off in buckets when my husband left seven years before.

After securing countless waist-cincher hooks, the dressing-room mirror revealed a slimmer waist. But it was obvious where all the fat went. It was spilling out of my armpits and ballooning around my hips. The blouse now buttoned without pulling at the waist, but my back looked like the Michelin tire woman. Why didn't I listen to my future mother-in-law when she asked me if I was wearing a suit? A nice, respectable, age-appropriate suit.

"It's on the beach, a small casual wedding. The bridesmaids, our daughters, are wearing tropical color sheaths, and I'm wearing a hippie, calf-length sort of peasant dress."

"What color?" she asked, really meaning you never wear white for a second marriage.

"White," I answered.

"Well, I hope George isn't wearing a ponytail." I just smiled. My vote was for the ponytail and a baseball cap to keep the sun off his bald spot.

When I had married my ex, I wore a tiered muumuu that did little to hide my eighth month of pregnancy. I assumed our backyard wedding was forever, and any future wedding planning would be for our daughters. I never expected to be in a fitting room with a wedding dress, looking for undergarment alternatives to liposuction.

After my ex left, I dreamed about that wedding by the sea I never had. The white, hippie peasant dress. Gardenias in long, flowing hair. Hand in hand with a man who'd say he'd stay forever. A silly dream for a grandmother of five to have. But then I met George. With our grown children and former spouses gone (George was widowed and retired), we shared our Florida days swimming, snorkeling and cruising, top down, in my new convertible while singing John Denver songs. Sometimes, I needed to remind myself that I'm not twenty-two anymore. I just feel like twenty-two with George. And when George suggested a beach wedding, I knew it had to be by the South Florida turquoise sea, the one that lured me here from California and brought George here from Brooklyn. The sea that had brought us together.

After liberating my stomach from the cincher, I noticed the tape measure left on the dressing-room chair. I measured my waist.

How could my middle have grown by a whopping five inches? That couldn't be; I wasn't that much heavier than in college. I had heard that postmenopausal women thicken in the middle, but that wasn't supposed to happen to *me*—I swim, I do Zumba three times a week, and George and I just bought beach bikes.

The waist cincher did take off an inch, but what to do about the unwanted cleavage—on my back?

"Honey, you need a full-length body shaper, shoulder to thighs, a slip, and of course you'll want a padded bra." The saleslady peeked in, and then disappeared like a magician behind a curtain. She returned with several undergarments that resembled wetsuits. What was the point of wearing a light, cotton, flowing wedding dress if I had to wear a suit of armor underneath? I looked down at the red tape measure coiled ominously on the velveteen chair cushion.

My dream of a sleek peasant wedding dress blowing in the ocean breeze had been a delusion. Obviously, a sixty-two-year-old with long, blond hair in a hippie dress at an island themed wedding would look ridiculous to our guests. And the guest list was expanding every day, just like our budget and my waistline. George was inviting everyone. "Getting married to Barbara is the easiest thing I've ever done," he told our friends. Sure it was easy for him. He'd wear his white Hawaiian shirt, not even tucked in.

I folded up the cotton skirt I loved and the perfect blouse and put them both back in the Macy's bag with the receipt still in it. My perfect wedding dress wasn't perfect on me. The world's finest boned corset would not shape my body into the silhouette I wanted. I headed toward the escalator to find a dignified cream suit.

But before I could escape, the saleslady ran an interception, waving a long, stretchy camisole. "It tucks in the tummy and smoothes you out. All the girls are wearing Spanx." Spanx sounded like underwear you'd find in an adult porn shop. But I'd try it.

Our day arrived. George and I stood side by side at the edge of a turquoise sea with a makeshift altar between us—a small wood table just big enough to hold the candle we lit together and my mother's Bible. Our paparazzi guests overflowed the benches, snapping pictures under a canopy of pines. I loved the way the wind blew George's graying hair out of his ponytail—wisps that danced madly around his ears, making him look like a sweet Einstein in a Hawaiian shirt. And the whole time he was looking at me, not the dress.

My cap-sleeve blouse was snug but smooth and the peasant skirt blew in the breeze against the round curve of my stomach. Reading my vows, I could breathe easily, no extra—wires, bones, pads or wetsuits underneath—just one body-smoothing camisole. And when George read his vows to me, he had such love in his eyes that I thought he was going to cry. And when he did, my heart filled with such gratitude that every blouse button could have burst, but I wouldn't have cared. I felt beautiful that day—and, more than that, I felt loved.

Our wedding by the sea was beyond perfect, even if its casual, island, hippie-dippie theme was a bit hodgepodge. For weeks afterward, our friends and family kept telling us how much our wedding meant to them. I realized then that the true theme of our wedding wasn't a dress style or decor—but a simple message: It's never too late.

~Barbara Flores

The Perfect Dress

Why should we all dress after the same fashion?
The frost never paints my windows twice alike.
~Lydia Maria Child

When my husband and I were planning our wedding, we lived in a tiny cabin off the grid, with no running water or electricity, in the Vermont woods. He was a guitar builder, and I was a potter. We parked our truck at the road and hiked the half-mile through the woods and over the stream, carrying our groceries and laundry on our backs. We were young, and it was fun. We were poor. We were in love. We were happy.

Planning the wedding was fun, but also stressful because we didn't have much money. We decided to have a real Vermont wedding that would include a potluck buffet and an outdoor setting. The music would be performed by our friends. We had a couple of friends—professional photographers—who offered to take photos for free. One of my bridesmaids was a baker who decided to make the wedding cake as her gift. Another friend agreed to do my hair, and Andy and I would make all the gifts for everyone who helped with the wedding. We spent days in the pottery studio making candleholders with hearts carved on them and our names engraved on the bottoms. Inexpensive to make and a keepsake for all our loved ones.

We saved so much money! It was all going to be within our modest budget... except for one thing. The dress. This was the one area where there was to be no compromise. The dress mattered to me. A lot!

I took two of my bridesmaids with me to bridal shops and felt like a queen, a princess, a fairy and The Good Witch Glenda, all in one. We liked or didn't like the dresses we saw, and we figured out the perfect style for me. Once I knew what I wanted, I went to the best seamstress in town, and we designed the dress.

My mother-in-law came with me to pick out the fabric. We held every variation of white against my skin. Although white had never been my color, we were able to find one called Snowdrop White that would work. They ordered it and assured me it would be in the next week, just in time for the deadline my seamstress had given me. When we got the call that the order was in, my mother-in-law and I hurried to pick it up. I couldn't wait to see the yards and yards of Snowdrop White and imagine how it would look as my dress. My wedding dress!

I should have realized even before the saleslady opened the package that something was terribly wrong because right there, on the side of the box, was the word, "Banana." What did that mean? I didn't care; I just wanted to see my Snowdrop White wedding silk. The lady lifted the flap of the box and pulled out the fabric. My brain couldn't register what I was seeing. It just went blank. When I was finally able to focus, I looked at my mother-in-law in horror.

"What's this?" she asked the saleslady. "This isn't what she ordered."

The reason it said "Banana" on the box was because that was the color of the silk! It was not white. My head spun. How long would it take to order the right one? Would it come in time? How could it when my seamstress needed it right away?

The saleslady turned pale, and I felt like I might cry, but my mother-in-law was pulling out the banana silk and holding it up with a curious look.

"You know," she said, her voice soft as if she was discovering something, "it's actually quite beautiful."

Huh? What's she talking about, I wondered, and how am I going to get my Snowdrop White in time?

"Look at it," she said. Look at what? I was starting to feel annoyed.

"Honey, this silk is gorgeous. It's not banana; it's gold. It would be beautiful against your skin. It's a much better color for you."

And that was when I was finally able to shut off my mind and see what was before me. She was right; it was perfect. Gold, shimmery silk. Much better for me than white.

The wedding was a grand success. The photographs were great, and my hair curled and piled on my head as if a professional had done it. The food was fantastic, the music a blast, but most important was the moment Andy and I caught eyes as my parents walked me down the grassy aisle.

"Forever," his smile said to me.

"Forever," I smiled back, blinking away tears of pure joy.

When my parents hugged me and took their seats, Andy leaned in close and whispered, "Nice dress."

I was so happy with my low-budget wedding and have never regretted sticking with the not-at-all-low-budget dress.

"Wow, a gold dress. It's perfect," was the comment I heard most that day, maybe even more than "Best food I've ever had at a wedding" and "You two make such a great couple."

The dress has been in a box for fourteen years. My daughter says she wants to wear the golden dress at her own wedding some day.

"I'm so glad you didn't get white," she says, leafing through our wedding album. "Gold is a much better color for me."

~Lava Mueller

A Simple
Wedding Dress

Clothes make a statement. Costumes tell a story.
~Mason Cooley

My wedding wasn't exactly a typical wedding. My fiancé and I, young college students at the time, wanted a simple wedding. There was no rehearsal, no processional, no dinner, and no dance. We didn't go on a honeymoon. Instead of a warm Saturday afternoon in June, we set aside a Wednesday evening in November on what was sure to be a cold Wisconsin night.

We decided to get married in a Thanksgiving Eve church service. We'd stand at the altar and take our vows before the sermon, then enjoy the second half of the service as husband and wife with much to be thankful for.

With so few details to worry about, you'd think I would have had a goof-proof plan in place. But I haven't told you about The Dress yet.

Since this wasn't going to be a conventional wedding, I figured I could skip the traditional white gown and buy something nice that could be worn again.

And that was my first mistake.

I kept my eyes open wherever I went, looking for that perfect dress. One day, I was browsing through a sewing store and happened to see a dress pattern that I loved. The envelope showed a long, flowing dress with pretty, petite flowers printed on a pale pink material. It featured a fitted bodice and bell sleeves that flared gently from the elbows. I began to imagine myself walking down the aisle in this dress. I grabbed the pattern, bought it, and sang, "I found my dress! I found my dress!" all the way home.

That was my second mistake.

Now, who would sew this dress? I briefly thought of my sewing skills, but since a wedding dress is slightly more complicated than a throw pillow, I decided to ask my future mother-in-law. Not only was she excellent with a sewing machine, but it could be a nice way for us to bond over the coming wedding. Never mind that she lived 600 miles away, which would make fittings and alterations difficult.

That was my third mistake.

When it was time to purchase dress fabric, for some reason that understated pale pink flew out the window. In a fit of temporary insanity, I chose a smokey blue damask that would've been quite lovely as a set of curtains in our new home. But no. This was it. My dress material was promptly packaged and sent to my seamstress.

That was my fourth mistake.

It was October before I held the dress in my hands. Though not quite finished, it was close. Trembling with excitement, I took the dress into my bedroom and stepped into the blue folds for my first fitting. With my soon-to-be mother-in-law looking on with a tape measure and hopeful smile, I just couldn't say what I felt.

The dress was all wrong. Gaps of extra material at the waist coupled with seam-popping tightness in the arms. I looked like a cross between a large blue pear and a matronly lady-in-waiting. Something Maria von Trapp would have sewn had she married Robin Hood instead of the Captain.

Swallowing tears of disappointment, I asked if the arms could be let out at all as they were "a little snug." Pinching the waist on both sides, I suggested maybe "bringing this in a little." She promised to try, but didn't know if much could be done. "Whatever you can do," I said, hoping for a miracle.

That was my fifth mistake.

For the next month, I worried. How would I ever walk down the aisle in that dress? And what was I thinking with that blue material? The smallest drop of sweat would stain it dark and quickly spread. To say I was anxious would be putting it mildly, but what choice did I have? I couldn't turn back now, especially after all the hard work his mom had done.

The final weeks melted away, and soon it was the day before our wedding. My in-laws arrived in town, and so did The Dress.

The first thing my mother-in-law said to me was, "There's a problem with the dress."

A surge of hope raced through me. "What's wrong?"

"Well, I was doing some hand stitching, and I pricked my finger," she explained. "Some blood got on the dress." This sounds promising, I thought.

She continued, "I wanted to get the blood out, so I used some of Dad's orange goo cleaner." She held up my dress. In the middle of the blue bodice were two washed-out grayish smudges. "It took the color right out!"

My hand flew to my mouth. To hide a relieved smile. I wanted to jump up and down and celebrate at the top of my lungs. I didn't feel nearly guilty enough that she was obviously misunderstanding my reaction.

"It's okay." I hugged her. "We'll figure something out."

Later that evening, with less than twenty-four hours to go, I went out to buy a wedding dress. At the first bridal shop we came to, I pulled a beautiful white satin dress off the rack and tried it on. It fit like a glove, cost $100, and I loved it.

That was my lucky break.

As for the original wedding dress, for which I had a sentimental fondness, I passed it on to my sister. Not to be worn at her wedding, of course, but as an excellent costume for her annual trips to the Renaissance Fair.

~Debra Mayhew

Up in Flames

The Service you do for others is the rent you pay for your room here on Earth.
~Muhammad Ali

O
n April Fool's Day 2005, 7:10 A.M., the day before I was to be married, the telephone rang. It was our prankster friend, Brad.

"You're not going to believe this," he said, "but there are twenty-foot flames coming from Magic Moments Bridal Shop."

Neither my fiancé Aaron nor I believed a word he was saying. Brad insisted that it was not a joke. We tuned into the local radio station and heard the news ourselves. After months of looking for the "perfect dress," the one I found was now engulfed in flames along with three of the four bridesmaids' dresses. We were in total shock and did not know what this meant for our wedding. What were we going to do? Who should we call? Should we cancel the wedding?

The telephone rang again, and we were afraid to answer. It was The Bridal Boutique, the other bridal shop in town, asking how they could help; a dear friend had notified them of our dilemma. They offered to let the three bridesmaids and I come into their shop and pick out different dresses. Moments later, my mother and mother-in-law Shirley were at the door offering to help. A bridal shop in Eau Claire heard the news about the fire and called to see if they could help. One phone call after another, family and friends called to offer their services, wedding dresses, money, and sympathy. With all the offers to help, I began to believe that the wedding could actually go on.

In the midst of the commotion, I recalled that I had tried on the exact same wedding dress months earlier at Thelma's Bridal, an hour's drive from home. Maybe I would still be able to wear the "perfect dress." After an anxious hour waiting for the store to open, I called Thelma's Bridal. I blurted out, "I am supposed to get married tomorrow, and my wedding dress went up in flames this morning." Immediately, I had the salesperson's sympathy. She found the dress I described and agreed to sell it off the rack, something they don't typically do.

My mom and I drove two hours roundtrip and picked up the dress from Thelma's Bridal that by some miracle only needed hemming. We brought it to The Bridal Boutique where the Magic Moments alterations team, the owners of The Bridal Boutique, and my mother-in-law had gathered. They were cheerfully cutting apart and re-sewing the bridesmaids' dresses. It was an incredible and heartwarming sight to see everyone rallying to make our wedding day a reality. My cell phone rang at about 8:30 P.M. It was The Bridal Boutique calling to tell me they were locking up shop, and everything was ready to go for the next morning!

As I lay in bed that night, I reflected on the unbelievable day and the newspaper story that read, "No lives were lost. It was just bricks and mortar. Bricks and mortar can be replaced... and so can bridal gowns."

The big day arrived, and what a wonderful day it was! I had the "perfect dress" and the fairy-tale wedding I had envisioned. Yet, it was a richer and more memorable experience because of the many hands and hearts that helped to make it possible.

~Jennifer J. Heeg

Hand-Me-Down Bride

He who does not economize will have to agonize.
~Confucius

By the time I got married in 1995, there weren't many taboos left in Western dating and courtship. In the mainstream of society, the spirit of the times seemed to be that, as long as everyone was of legal age and happy, just about anything was permissible.

For instance, none of the saleswomen unlocking the glass cases of diamond rings for my future husband and me cared whether we were already having sex or not. But there was something about us that did make them raise their eyebrows. At ages twenty-one and twenty-two, we were fairly young to be getting married, and the four-month engagement we had planned was oddly short. Even so, it wasn't our sense of timing that made us stand out among most of the other couples shopping for wedding jewelry. It was our budget.

My future husband and I were both university students when we met and realized we were the same person. Our lives were simple and happy, but not prosperous. I was on track to finish my degree later in the year, but my husband was in a much longer program and wouldn't complete his training for another six years. His career path would turn out to be one of those inspirational stories about a gifted young man who rises above the poverty of the small-town, welfare-dependent family he was raised in to make a successful life for the family he fathered himself. But in 1995, dreams like those were still just goals and plans.

Financially, we had nothing but student loans the day we got engaged. Our parents were dealing with financial struggles much more serious than ours, and, despite their generous natures, they could offer us very little. I'd never wanted a lavish extravaganza wedding. Yet I was still surprised at how expensive a modest wedding could be.

Clearly, costs had to be cut—even slashed. It made sense to me to start economizing with myself first. In search of a three-figure price tag for my wedding dress, I went to a store that sold "gently used" prom and wedding dresses. Deep in the racks of rumpled white and white-ish gowns, I found nothing like the ultra-traditional dress I wanted for my mid-winter wedding in a cold climate. I wasn't particularly fussy, but I was sure I'd rather not end up looking like a bad wedding cake in a heap of outdated ruffles.

Then I noticed the corner of the store marked with a sign that read "Clearance." Here were the very cheapest-of-the-cheap wedding dresses. I held my nose and started sorting through the wire hangers. And there it was—a long, full skirt, a classic, fitted bodice, and long, elegant sleeves all in pure white. The dress wasn't perfect. It would need alterations and the tacky, sheer netting on the shoulders would have to go. But I had found my dress—and it was only going to cost me $300 instead of the $1,300 many of my fellow brides of the day were paying for their brand-new dresses.

Sometimes, when a shopper comes home with a fantastic deal, she'll brag about it to her friends—especially if those friends are in the market for the same kinds of items. My childhood best friend was shopping for her own wedding gear at the same time. But bragging to her about my clearance-rack find was the last thing I intended. She had already ordered her dress a year in advance. It was going to be custom-made out of ivory silk, fresh off the bolt, just for her.

I was a bit flustered the next time the topic of wedding dresses came up between us, and I was forced to admit what I'd done.

"What? You bought a used wedding dress?" My friend was livid.

"It's only been used once and for just one day," I defended myself.

"Yeah, but—it's a wedding dress."

"So?" I knew what she was suggesting, but I pretended I was so above caring that I didn't even understand her.

"So?" she repeated like an incredulous echo. "What would make someone sell off her wedding dress? I mean something must have gone terribly wrong. You don't even know. Those people might not even be married anymore."

She was probably right. I had nothing to say.

My friend went on, "You don't want to start your own marriage in a dress that comes with that kind of baggage. Do you?"

I'd known this girl almost all of my life. I didn't doubt that she loved me and wanted me to be happy. And I knew she was far more romantic than me—and maybe a little more superstitious than me, too. She really did see the cast-off wedding dress as a bad omen for my future. And that scared her. There was no way I could be angry with her for caring about me. To her, my cheap, secondhand wedding dress was taboo—an even bigger taboo than my teeny, tiny diamond solitaire engagement ring had been under the twinkly lights of the jewelry store.

But I wasn't just pretending I didn't care about where my dress came from. I answered my friend with an easy laugh as I told her not to worry. "Everything will be fine," I promised.

Our bargain-priced wedding went ahead as planned right after Christmas in the final days of the university's semester break. We didn't wait until my parents got their finances in order. We didn't keep dating for six years while my husband-to-be made his way through school. Instead, we pasted together a shabby little wedding and started our life together as a family. The romantics may have recoiled and the hipsters might have sneered, but we made the choice that was right for us.

I was still a young wife when a song was released called "Polyester Bride." I'm not sure exactly what the songwriter means when she asks, in every chorus, "Do you want to be a polyester bride?" It probably has something to do with a warning about settling for less. Whatever it means, I'm confident of my answer. Yes. Yes, I do want to be a clearance-rack, dry-cleaned, secondhand, and ridiculously happy polyester bride.

~Jennifer Quist

The dress was so expensive she could only afford half of it.

28

Two Women in Black

What the daughter does, the mother did.
~Jewish Proverb

"You're not wearing that to school!" I yelled at my daughter, Mary.

"Why not? It's clean," she replied.

"Because no daughter of mine is going out dressed all in black. That's all you wear lately. Every day. Black, black, black!"

"Oh, Mom, I like black. It's what all the kids are wearing."

Yes, with the right accessories and at the right time, a "little black dress" COULD be very cool. I smiled, remembering how I'd gotten married in one the night Mary's father and I ended up eloping instead of going to the theater.

I jumped at the slamming of the back door as Mary ran off to school. For a tiny freshman, she sure could slam a door.

My two older children were angels, but when it came to Mary we clashed on almost everything. My mother called her "Little Mary Sunshine," but when it came to her and me, it was mostly stormy weather.

Mary wasn't a bad egg, just very independent, willful, and outspoken. She had definite views on everything. Oh, and did I mention she was stubborn? I could coax my older two to do almost anything, but Mary always stood her ground. So, once again we were in our usual stance, at odds with one another.

Despite my begging and pleading, I couldn't get Mary to budge on her clothing choices. Then Mary's "Year of Darkness," as I nicknamed it, stopped abruptly when school ended for the year. I breathed a sigh of relief. After all, I had a lot to be thankful for; she hadn't gotten into drugs, alcohol or fallen in with a bad crowd.

As Mary got older, we seemed to become more in tune. I actually began to envy her independence. When she finished high school, she got her own apartment and began classes at the local community college at night, while working full-time during the day.

The years rolled by, and she acquired roommates who came and went along the way. Some were "bad boys" who wanted a meal ticket; others were girlfriends down on their luck. Mary was generous with whatever she could share, but one thing remained her own: Mary was true to herself.

Although Mary dated a lot, she was still single at thirty. It takes a special man to want a woman who will stand up for herself at any cost. Then she met Gary, or Bart as his friends call him and Mary began to change. Oh, she still kept her own counsel, but she softened around the edges. I actually found myself asking her opinion on matters. We met for dinner every couple of weeks, and I truly began to treasure her company.

One Saturday night when Mary had been dating Bart for about two years, we got a late-night phone call.

"Hi, Mom, you'll never guess what: I'm married! Bart and I eloped to Las Vegas. There, I said it. Are you hurt?"

"No… yes… I don't know. Dad and I really wanted to be at your wedding, you know."

"I know, but Bart and I have been planning on getting married for a long time. And then tonight, he said, 'Let's go to Vegas,' and here we are. I'm so happy!"

"Well, as long as you love each other," I replied.

"Oh, I do love him, and he loves me. I gotta go now, Mom. I just had to call and tell you the news. I love you, and give Dad a kiss for me." Her voice choked with emotion.

"Yes, of course I will," I said, gently replacing the phone in its cradle.

"Well, our daughter just eloped," I announced to my sleepy-eyed husband lying beside me.

"About time those two got hitched," he said and turned over.

The next night, we were just about to leave for Sunday dinner at a local restaurant when the phone rang.

It was Mary.

"You're home already?" I asked.

"Of course, Mom," came the reply. "We DO have to work tomorrow," our newly married daughter reminded me.

"How about going out for some dinner with us?" I urged.

Mary and Bart were at the door, arm in arm, before we knew it. There were hugs and congratulations all around.

The dinner moved along at a fast clip with Mary and Bart taking center stage. The happy couple relived their exciting weekend: the hurried plans to go to Vegas, renting a limo, calling their best friends to meet them there, going to the Graceland Wedding Chapel. Mary giggled as she confessed, "And I got married in black, Mom, just like you," and with that she whipped out photos taken with a minister who looked a lot like Elvis.

I stared at the pictures. There she was... radiant, glowing, and gorgeous — in a BLACK GOWN.

"Black? Who gets married in black?"

"Well, Mom, according to the stories I've heard, YOU did, and look how long you've been married. Getting married in black is a good-luck charm."

I will always remember what Mary said that night nine years ago, but this year our dual anniversary will be a different sharing time. It will be a bittersweet day. Paul passed away five months ago, and Mary and Bart are joining me for dinner. Mary and I will wear black to the restaurant — Mary glowing with happiness and faith in the years that lie ahead... mine for the forty-six years that are now becoming a memory, a memory of a wonderful marriage that began with eloping in a black dress, just like my daughter's.

~Sallie A. Rodman

29

The Second Dress

A successful marriage requires falling in love many times,
always with the same person.
~Mignon McLaughlin

M y friend, Pam, and her business partner, Kim, were wedding planner consultants. They had coordinated some of the most beautiful weddings I had ever seen. Quite often, Pam and I would talk about upcoming weddings, colors, and her special clients. All of them were unique. I can clearly recall back to 1996 when Pam asked me to go with her to a few bridal shops to look for a gown. For some reason, the bride — one of Pam's newest clients — was out of town and did not have time to shop for a wedding dress that particular weekend. Pam told me that I was the same size as the bride-to-be, so she wanted me to go with her to try on dresses. "How fun!" I thought.

So off we went to Cincinnati, Ohio, to look for wedding dresses. When we arrived, Pam and I began to look at some of the most beautiful gowns. After trying on several dresses, we concluded that the cream-colored, fully beaded dress with a sweetheart neckline was the prettiest gown of all. The fit and style seemed to be just right according to Pam. It did not take long — this would be the recommended gown. Pam asked the store assistant to put it on hold, and then we left the store.

While riding home, I asked, "Why would a lady not have time to shop for her own wedding dress?"

Pam laughed and said, "She is just one of those women who will pay for other people to take care of her personal matters. But, in my mind, that is just too personal to relinquish to someone else."

Fast forward a year later. My husband and I had planned a vacation get-a-way that I was really looking forward to. My girlfriend, Dawn, knew that we were leaving in a few days so she offered to give me a pedicure. I accepted her kind offer because she was really good. It wasn't something that I had planned—I was ready to go!

The weekend arrived, and it was time. Morton, my husband of almost ten years, told me that we needed to go by the church before we left. That was typical because we are very involved in church ministries. When we arrived at the church, I saw my cousin coming out the back door. I thought, "She's not a member. What is she doing here?" We spoke briefly, and then she rushed off. Then Marty, a family friend and Pam's husband, came out of the church door and said, "Tonya, I need for you to go downstairs and see someone."

I looked for Morton as I proceeded downstairs, but he wasn't around. Then I walked into the church choir room. All of a sudden, people came out from the shadows and shouted, "Surprise!" I was stunned! Some of them were family members and friends. Then I spotted my cousin from Dallas, Texas, and I started to cry. "What is going on?"

Marty brought Morton into the room, and everyone was crying and laughing. And then Morton looked deeply into my eyes and said, "It's been ten years, Tonya. Would you marry me—again?"

Then Pam walked out with a wedding gown in her hand and hung it up for display. I cried, "YES! And that's the dress!" I glanced over at my mom and saw her looking at me with so much love and pride. She appeared speechless. More people walked into the room, and I realized it had turned into a bridal shower! Cameras were flashing, gifts were appearing, and people were hugging.

Pam said, "Okay, we have forty-five minutes for the shower, and then everyone must get dressed. Your wedding is in an hour!"

Later, Pam told me that it had all begun the previous summer when we were at Kings Island Amusement Park. While Marty and I were riding a roller coaster, Morton told Pam that he wanted to do something different for our tenth wedding anniversary. Since Pam was a wedding consultant, she agreed to help him. Many people became involved, and it seemed that everyone knew about this wedding except for me.

The shower was finally over. Out came the shoes, my veil, garter, hosiery, undergarments, jewelry, bouquets—everything! I was amazed. Within a few minutes, I was a bride again. I walked out the door, and my uncle Spunky greeted me. He was ready to walk me down the aisle and give me away—again! All of my bridesmaids and even a few new ones were all lined up and looking lovely. The colors were cream, gold, and black. Just dazzling!

The doors to the sanctuary opened to reveal a church filled with guests. Music was playing. My eyes were so full of tears that I could barely recognize the guests. As I made it down the aisle and stood with Morton, I looked out into the pews and zoomed in on my aunt from Dallas, Texas. There went the tears again… I didn't know that she was in town. Our friends from Virginia were in town as well. I think more men were amazed that Morton had pulled this off.

After the wedding, there was a wonderful reception with the most beautiful cake and décor. Ms. Shirley—a great friend and a wonderful cook—was the caterer. We ate and danced the night away. A day later, we drove to Suffolk, Virginia, with our friends. It was a beautiful time that I'll never forget. We now celebrate two anniversaries, and I have two wedding gowns.

~LaTonya Branham

30

Something Borrowed: A Wedding Gown Encore

There are two lasting bequests we can give our children. One is roots.
The other is wings.
~Hodding Carter, Jr.

The color was blush—a trifle paler than pink and rosier than white. It was gossamer light, as if woven by elves. Even on the hanger, it seemed to float.

On Jill's shoulders, it repeated that performance, drifting down to her ankles in gentle folds and gathers.

Our daughter's wedding dress, kissed with lace and decidedly in the Victorian spirit, was worn nearly two decades ago, and is now on loan. Another bride will be wearing it on another wedding day that hopefully will be rich in joy.

I could never have guessed that Jill, a feisty feminist, would have chosen that particular dress. "Dress, not gown," she had stressed, because Jill wanted no part of hems dragging in the grass at her home wedding.

I remember the day we chose it better than I can remember the name of the book I read last month, or the movie I saw a few days ago.

There I was, sitting on a pink velvet sofa unofficially reserved for anxious mothers of the bride, suddenly in the grip of this singular experience with our firstborn daughter.

The sight of Jill, standing incongruously in sneakers—and that swirl of lace and ribbon—literally took my breath away. I think I actually gasped.

But in this archetypal suburban bridal salon, there was still the sense of a little girl playing one last game of dress-up in a stranger's closet.

As Jill and the sales consultant went on to discuss veils, I was still lost in memories of a little girl with unruly blond curls stepping up to the microphone in the second-grade play to blurt out her line: "I'm cold—please take me home."

And then, after some other detours into sentiment, the real insight flashed. Once again, Jill and I were playing out my own might-have-beens-that-never-were. In the endless game of dreaming, hoping, yearning that the children you love beyond all reason will somehow live out your own failed expectations, Jill was doing just that.

Until that moment, I had never fully realized what I had actually missed when I had pulled a friend's borrowed wedding gown over my head, content to be practical, if not sentimental.

It had been a perfectly lovely bridal gown with tiny seed pearls and lace, and it all seemed so sensible back then when my bride-groom and I were struggling to make the down payment on a little Cape Cod house so that he could begin to practice law while I went off to teach eighth-graders who didn't share my reverence for grammar or lyric poetry. Why blow money on a wedding gown? Why not celebrate the good luck that the gown I borrowed from a generous friend fit perfectly, and was quite lovely enough to sail through the occasion?

Everyone applauded how sensible I was being.

But from some long-buried place, the ghosts were back to haunt a mother of the bride who was suddenly almost reeling with regret.

I had missed out on this experience that Jill was having. Maybe I shouldn't have. Maybe I really should have had that gown of my own, and practicality be damned.

My daughter would not miss out.

Despite her absolute certainty that she was, of course, going to keep her own name, not take her husband's, this feisty bride was still going to splurge big-time on this one beautiful dress she would wear for several hours.

And my thought, then and now, was "How wonderful!"

Who knew then that the very same dress, in pristine condition, is now considered "vintage"—practically antique—and that a friend's daughter will be thrilled to wear it. Her circumstances are challenging, and much as she may want to throw caution to the winds of indulgence, she can't. So Jill's gown will walk down another aisle.

And to my own bridal gown regrets? Gone and almost forgotten.

My borrowed gown brought me decades of the kind of happiness that sounds sloppily sentimental, but there it is: I'll take the marriage over the gown any time. So the blush dress is having a second run. Another day with a dress trimmed in lace—and dreams.

Not such a bad thing after all.

~Sally Friedman

It's All in the Planning

Life is what happens to us while we are making other plans.

~Allen Saunders

Just a Few Little Changes

In matters of principle, stand like a rock;
in matters of taste, swim with the current.
~Thomas Jefferson

Our wedding? It would be a small affair, my fiancé Bill and I quickly decided. No fanfare for us plain folks—just an afternoon with a few select friends and family members as we took our vows—me in a white dress and he in his favorite suit.

In the weeks that followed, I happily spread the news of our upcoming nuptials. Yet, when I got to the point in the conversation where I outlined our wedding-day plans, the enthusiasm balloon deflated, and I was generally met with the same glazed stare a listener gives when she notices a piece of spinach stuck on the speaker's tooth, but is too embarrassed to point out the problem. One evening as I sat at dinner with my parents, I voiced my confusion.

"I don't get it," I said. "No one seems excited about my wedding."

My mother looked up from her plate. "Of course, we're all excited, dear. It's just that…"

My father interjected. "Excited about what? I mean, your wedding doesn't sound like much."

Now, weddings in our neck of the woods are big business. Caterers and bridal shops can be found on almost every main road, it seems, and every hair salon within a fifty-mile radius of my home advertises "wedding party specials." Most receptions in our community are large affairs, and those in our extended Italian-American family were no exception. I thought back to all the weddings I had attended—and enjoyed. The buffets, the live band, the floral arrangements, the Viennese hour… I was starting to see Dad's point. True enough, what Bill and I were proposing was nothing more than an afternoon party. Surely there would be nothing wrong with a little compromise, I surmised. With a bit of tweaking, Bill and I could still have a scaled-down affair that fit our more modest style and at the same time would not disappoint common expectations.

Later that evening, Bill and I reviewed our plans. It was decided that I would wear a tea-length gown, with an understated spray of flowers in my hair; he would spring for a new suit. Our bridal party would consist of two of our closest friends, no more. The afternoon luncheon would become a sit-down dinner, and for those who enjoyed dancing, the services of a DJ would be retained. Bill and I shook on the deal. No matter what well-meaning advice we received, we agreed, we would not budge from our parameters. And so, with all good intentions, it began.

The next week, I went to a bridal shop in search of my tea-length gown. The salesperson looked around. "Hmm," she breathed thoughtfully, "I have something else in mind for you." She turned toward a rack, and then fluttered back with a full-length satin number covered in lace, crystals, and beads. "This would be just perfect," she said as she hurriedly ushered me toward the fitting room.

My first impression: It was big and flashy and not anything like the dress that Bill and I had agreed upon only a few days earlier. But it was beautiful. I tried it on and fell immediately and totally in love. And I had to have that dress, complete with four-foot train. It was just a little more material, I convinced myself as I wrote the check for the deposit. As long as I kept to the small spray of flowers in my hair and didn't wear a veil, what difference would a few feet of satin and lace make anyhow? Of course, now this development would require

Bill to be fitted with a tuxedo. Just a small difference from a new suit, really; it was no big deal at all.

My mother-in-law soon caught wind of these developments. "Well, then, you'll need gowns and tuxedoes for the entire wedding party," she advised.

Bill and I reminded her that our wedding party consisted solely of two witnesses, and the decisions on what they would wear would be left to them. I watched as the color drained from her face.

"Only two?" she gasped before she rattled off a list of friends and family who would "simply never forgive us" if they were not included in the procession. The result of this discussion: a full bridal party, including a flower girl and a ring bearer dressed, of course, in matching gowns and tuxedoes.

From there, my parents accompanied us to the reception hall where dinner plans were to be finalized. "Just a dinner," I said to the caterer as I planted my fist firmly on his desk to emphasize my resolve.

He cocked his head. "For only a few dollars more per person, we can add a full cocktail hour. It's a special package. The wedding cake even comes out on a flaming cart."

I hesitated, trying to imagine flames shooting from between layers of vanilla sponge cake and lemon frosting.

"If you take it," he bargained, "I'll even throw in the invitations for free."

My mother leaned in closer to me. "Free invitations," she whispered.

I held my breath and looked at Bill. "Might as well take it," he answered.

"Now, what about entertainment?" the caterer inquired. "I have a very good band that I can recommend."

I felt my father's hand on my back. "I don't know about this DJ thing you were thinking about. I'd take the band."

I sighed as the runaway train that had become my wedding took another unexpected turn. "We'll take the band, too," I conceded.

Next, my mother and I went to the florist to order bouquets.

Nosegays of pink carnations and baby's breath were quickly selected for my three girls. Feeling confident, I proposed a full bouquet of lively red, orange, and yellow roses for me. The florist lifted her hand to write the order.

"Not so fast," my mother said. She turned to me. "I think if you're wearing white, you should carry white flowers."

"But that's so dull," I argued. "I'd like some color."

"Red, orange, and yellow," my mother harrumphed. "That's just a little too bright. Really."

Needless to say, I left the flower shop that afternoon with an order for three pink nosegays for my girls and one bouquet of white roses for me.

My big day neared, and our final step before the wedding arrived: the church ceremony rehearsal. Carefully, Pastor Roy walked us through the choreography that we would recreate the following Sunday afternoon.

"First," he said, "the bridal party marches down the aisle. Then wait a few beats before the bride and father follow. When you arrive at the altar, Father lifts the veil and kisses Daughter before taking his place next to Mother."

I raised my hand meekly. "Um, Pastor, I'm not wearing a veil."

Pastor Roy's eyes opened wide. "No veil?" he said. "That's highly unusual in a church wedding."

Like a chorus, I heard my bridesmaids whisper "amen" from the sidelines, and my face flushed as I made a mental note to buy a veil first thing in the morning.

When the afternoon of Sunday, September 23rd arrived, it was as beautiful a day as any bride could have hoped for. The sun shone brightly in the sky as leaves of red and gold tumbled across the ground in the warm autumn breeze. I made my way into church precisely on time and stood patiently in my full-length, bridal-consultant-approved gown behind my large mother-in-law-approved bridal party. I walked down the aisle, and when I reached the altar, I handed my mother-approved white bouquet to my maid-of-honor. My father lifted my pastor-approved veil and kissed me on the cheek.

I turned and looked at my husband-to-be. What had happened to our modest affair? I wondered as I gazed at him. It seemed as though my choice of groom was the only facet of our wedding I had not been convinced to change.

As we said "I do" I realized I was marrying the man of my dreams. In the grand scheme of things, the other details didn't truly matter. Well, except for one detail, I mused—keeping a safe distance from that flaming wedding cake later. That would probably be important, too.

~Monica A. Andermann

My Husband
the Wedding Planner

If you surrender to the wind, you can ride it.
~Toni Morrison

My husband and I are married not because I said, "I do," but because he said, "I'll do it." When Jay got on one knee in Battery Park in Manhattan and proposed, I accepted and realized I was filled with joy—at the prospect of spending the rest of my life with him—then panic, associated with the idea of becoming a bride.

We were eight years into our monogamous relationship, so I wasn't a commitment-phobe, but the thought of donning a big white dress and playing the lead role in a family-filled wedding drama inspired a tsunami of anxiety I couldn't quell.

So after saying yes, I said, "Let's elope!" trying to make it sound bright, shiny and enticing. To my frustration, his response was, "No way!"

I threw my hands in the air and issued my challenge: "Fine. You're planning this thing."

Part of my PR job revolved around arranging events, but a press conference is not a wedding. I'd seen friends plan elaborate affairs with hundreds of guests, and I knew it required diplomacy and stellar organizational skills—as well as passion for the project. I possessed none of these prerequisites. Would I flunk the nuptials test?

Jay, a Jets-worshipping, Adidas-flip-flop-wearing NYC fire-fighter, wasn't the most obvious candidate for the role of wedding planner either, but mind-blowingly he replied, "No problem," without hesitating.

I wanted to grill him on his folly, but I recognized what was at play. His father was from Pakistan, a culture that celebrated marriages with multi-day affairs involving everyone the couple and their families have ever met—from the neighbors up the street, to the corner vendor, to a fifth cousin twice removed. Though my future father-in-law had been in the U.S. for forty years, he'd tried to bring a live elephant, a symbol of good luck, into one of his daughters' weddings at an exclusive Manhattan club. My parents, on the other hand, had gotten hitched in Rome, my mom in a yellow mini-dress, with one witness looking on. We'd come from distinctly different matrimonial traditions.

As the only child born to two only children, I'm a member of a neat, little family tree with few branches. Jay, on the other hand, is one of five. His tree is massive and has a huge root system.

I feared our families would meet and spontaneously combust. In eight years, we hadn't introduced them, imagining that our mothers—two strong-willed alpha females—would battle for supremacy. My mother, a Fox News fanatic, was a convention-flouting ex-Rockette. His, a Democrat, was a committed Catholic with an entrepreneurial streak. My mom was opposed to a wedding, calling it "a silly indulgence," while his felt the planet would stop spinning if I didn't get the perfect Vera Wang gown.

When Jay said he'd spearhead our marital march, I was relieved. Then I wasn't.

The night he grabbed the wedding reins, I dreamed I was walking the aisle in a flesh-colored pantsuit from the Gap. I was halfway to the altar before I realized it wasn't a pantsuit, but my birthday suit. The epiphany made me panic because my vows were in my pocket, but I had no pocket. I had nothing to say when I arrived in front of Jay and the officiant except "Hi."

I just wanted to slip quietly into married life. The thought of a gargantuan party intimidated me. Plus, after living together for years, I didn't feel the need to register for pots, pans and plates, nor did I relish fielding comments like, "What took you so long?" I felt like I was missing a critical bridal gene. Jay was, however, incredibly stubborn. As a teenager, he'd ripped his braces off with pliers—twice. I realized there was no hope of fulfilling my fantasy, but like a reverse Bridezilla, I fought doggedly anyway.

First, I lobbied to get the fest off-shored to winnow the invite list. I suggested Italy. Jay was on board initially, but soon realized our dollars weren't worth much versus the Euro, so he torpedoed the idea.

Next, I deviously handpicked a couple I knew who had a particularly tough time managing the family feuds and invited them to join us for dinner. At a Turkish restaurant in Tribeca, I leaned over the baba ghanoush and said to the pair, "If you had to do it again, would you do anything differently?" They glanced nervously at each other, and then in unison replied, "We'd elope."

My friends, who'd opted for the big white wedding, launched into their fairy tale gone wrong. At the horror story's conclusion, I turned to Jay, hoping he'd be aghast. Instead, he was completely composed.

Finally, I trotted out the last weapon in my arsenal—my ability to pitch a fit. One morning, after I'd awoken drenched in a nudie nightmare-induced sweat, I checked my e-mail and found a missive from one of Jay's sisters chastising me for falling down on the bridesmaids' dress-hunting job. I called Jay at work sobbing.

"I can't do this. Please, please don't make me," I pleaded.

"I'll handle it. Tell her to talk to me," he said. "We'll be fine."

My bridesmaids' dress freak-out marked a turning point in our engagement. I can't say that the path was problem-free from that point on, but that morning, once I stopped hyperventilating, I decided to lay down my arms and stop sabotaging my fiancé.

Once I started to relax, Jay morphed from adversary into protector. He shielded me from everything, just as he'd promised he would. Since he no longer had to battle me, he was able to focus his attention on fending off relatives, managing vendors, and making his vision come to life.

When my mother referred to the lake we were getting married on as a "puddle," he accompanied her on a visit to the site and reassured her. When the florist called claiming she'd been verbally abused by a member of our family, he spent two hours consoling her. When our parents overrode our music selection, insisting on golden oldies, he accommodated them.

Finally, I saw the authentic beauty of Jay's gesture. He wasn't giving me what I'd been asking for, but he was giving us what he thought we needed—something symbolic and grand to honor our union.

In October, on a stunningly sunny day, I met Jay in a spot between two trees. In front of our fourteen-person bridal party and more than 200 friends and family members, we read the vows we'd written to each other. As I made my pledge, I felt the weight of everyone's expectations—including my own—fall away. It was the most romantic, most hopeful day of my life.

~Victoria Grantham

A Mother's
Wedding Dreams

Because that's what kindness is.
It's not doing something for someone else because they can't,
but because you can.
~Andrew Iskander

"Mom, I want to get married this weekend."

"Oh... yeah..." I stammered, struggling to sound positive. They'd been engaged four years. Why the sudden hurry? I was afraid to ask.

"Sunday is Valentine's Day. Mom, don't you think that would be the best day for a wedding?"

"Yes, but it's only three days away. Where would you go? Reno?"

"I suppose. It just hit me this morning as a great idea."

"Why don't we give it some thought and get together this evening for a family meeting?"

That night, we flushed out the real reason for the sudden elopement and long engagement. Jessica dreaded having a big ceremony. She'd seen her sister agonize over every detail of planning the perfect wedding. Even the thought of doing the same stressed her out.

Her sister, Danielle, is a professional meeting and event planner, so she wanted a big, fancy wedding. That's her thing. She worked a year and a half carefully selecting everything from invitations and dresses for their large bridal party to DJ and candle-lit decorations. It was a fairy-tale wedding in a charming French restaurant, complete with gourmet food, champagne, and designer cake. We all had a great time.

Now, with the bar set so high, no wonder Jessica balked. As we talked and listened, we discovered Jessica's idea of the perfect wedding was a simple ceremony and fabulous honeymoon. But to avoid the stress of planning, she would settle for a justice of the peace if they could then escape to a tropical paradise.

I was devastated at the thought of skipping my daughter's wedding. I wanted to watch with joy and tears as my white-veiled princess floated down the aisle. I wanted to witness their sacred vows exchanged in the presence of God. I wanted to toast and celebrate and throw rice. But this wasn't about me, was it?

"I know," Danielle's face lit up. "We could rent a cabin at Lake Tahoe just big enough for immediate family and a couple of friends. Don't worry about the planning—I can do it all. It'll be easy. What do you think?"

All eyes turned to Jessica.

"That sounds great if I don't have to plan it."

I breathed a sigh of relief—the essence of my dream revived.

True to her word, Danielle searched the Internet and found a suitable cabin overlooking the lake, available in April. Each week, she e-mailed Jessica two or three choices of items to pick from. Invitations, bouquet, food. Jessica selected each one with a simple click.

I asked Danielle to cc me on the e-mails so I would feel included. I wanted to at least see what they were doing. But on one matter I held my ground: Selecting the dress is a mother-daughter affair. I insisted on going with them to the bridal shop.

I knew from the e-mails that Jessica had decided to wear a bridesmaid's dress because of the casual cabin atmosphere and the cost. When she stepped out from behind the curtain, we all agreed the first dress looked hideous. I'm convinced they make bridesmaid's dresses look frumpy to guarantee no one outshines the bride.

I tried hard to muster an enthusiastic response when the second one looked just okay, then made a quick exit to search the racks for another choice. Glancing over at the next aisle, I saw a white gown encased in dry cleaner's plastic, and I got an idea. "I'll take this in and have Jessica try it on just for fun." This was my one opportunity to see my daughter in a wedding gown. At least I'd be able to enjoy the vision for a couple of minutes.

On closer inspection, the dress I carried looked exceptionally gaudy, like a poufy wedding cake. Jessica is not a foo-foo kind of girl. She's very down to earth. I chuckled as I imagined her in such an outlandish style. Back in the dressing room, I convinced her to try it on—just for me. Reluctantly, she agreed.

As the dress slipped into place, the gathers and pooches disappeared as the gown molded perfectly to her form. All chatter stopped, and our faces dropped. I stared in awe at my daughter adorned in regal splendor.

"Wow. You look beautiful. In a rustic setting, it's okay for the bride to stand out. Imagine Jon's face when he sees you in this."

"You have to get it, Jessica," Danielle said as she straightened the train folds.

Jessica had to agree. The choice was clear.

And so all the preparations came together. When we arrived at Tahoe the night before the event, crisp pine air filled my lungs and ribbons of smoke from neighboring chimneys hung all around. I was relieved to see the cabin looked as cute as the Internet photos. However, as I stepped into the main living room, my chest tightened.

"This room is smaller than I thought it would be. Danielle, do you think there's room for everyone in here?"

"Let's see. We can move the sofa over there, slide the table next to the wall and use it for the food. There won't be much legroom, but we should be able to squeeze in all thirty rental chairs. Don't worry, Mom, it'll be fine."

The morning brought a blur of hustle and bustle. But all details faded into the background when I caught that first glimpse of my radiant daughter strolling down the aisle. My little girl, all grown up. Years of triumphs and trials welled up in my soul as the past gave way to the future.

She stopped beside her beaming groom—so close I could have reached out and touched her. A spectacular panoramic view of Lake Tahoe framed the pair, with the pastor backed against the window.

In the cozy cabin, Pastor Dan's sermonette sounded more like a chat among friends. "A successful marriage needs the support of family and friends. Do you agree to help Jon and Jessica's relationship grow and flourish?"

"We do."

When the couple finally turned to face each other, I had a perfect view of Jon's face over Jessica's shoulder. Too perfect. The passion in his eyes felt too intimate for me to view at such close proximity. But look I did as they exchanged their heartfelt vows.

Then they ducked and dashed amid confetti poppers and cheers. Joy filled the room.

Today, two wedding albums adorn my coffee table, each filled with wonderful memories. Both of my daughters had beautiful weddings, special in their own ways. We all have different dreams, and dreams don't always come true. But Jessica and Jon got to enjoy a great off-season honeymoon package in Cancun, and this proud mother saw her dreams for her daughters' weddings fulfilled.

~Kris Lindsey

Turn Around

Who, being loved, is poor?
~Oscar Wilde

"Stand there underneath that gazebo and look out over the park," my boyfriend ordered one sunny Sunday with an old-fashioned 35mm camera in hand. "No, turn around! I want a picture of you gazing out over the landscape. Look pensive."

I dutifully did as I was told, patiently turning my back and entertaining myself by watching a young family playing on the hill in front of me as he artistically snapped the picture he'd already framed hundreds of times.

"Okay, you can turn around now."

I spun, trivial statement playing on my lips... to see the camera abandoned on the ground in front of his knee, the antique diamond ring winking at me, his hands shaking and words jumbling as he tried to find the right words to ask me to be his wife.

In that instant, that one turn, I'd twirled from a girl to a woman, a college sweetheart to a fiancée, a "me" to an "us." We were ready to dance off into the sunset, plan our fairy-tale wedding, buy our first little home, and live happily after ever.

And then the floor dropped out from underneath us.

You see, that momentous walk in the park was in 2009. While I was tearfully saying yes to my future, banks were crashing. As we were salivating over bacon-wrapped scallops and bruschetta and debating the merits of filet mignon versus prime rib, the unemployment line was growing exponentially, and the rations at food banks were flying off the shelves.

One day, curled up in my apartment after a long (successful!) day of wedding dress shopping, perusing bridal magazines flaunting elaborate centerpieces and exotic honeymoon locales, my mom sheepishly informed me that four of the nine support staff positions at her small elementary school would be cut. She wasn't sure if she'd be returning from her weekend trip to a job, to a steady paycheck.

A little voice in my head piped up, nudging me back to a reality the rest of the world was already dealing with. Flowers and four-tier cakes and favors... those trappings were merely the icing on the cake. Who needs pounds of sugar-filled frosting on the already-sweet-enough cake of true love?

So wedding planning took another turn.

A scrapbook-savvy aunt spent hours deciding between mellow yellow and canary sunshine cardstock, imprinting tulip stamp after tulip stamp onto my save-the-date cards—as a wedding gift to us, and a fun craft project to keep her busy when her husband's job was transferred across the country.

My soon-to-be mother-in-law continued my tulip theme, purchasing a flower-shaped chocolate mold so she could make our favors. She toiled in the kitchen at midnight, flecked with pink sugar glitter and chocolate, mixing yellow food dye into white chocolate to prove she could come up with just the right shade to match my flowers. She spent hours tying white ribbon onto the green stems of the tulip lollipops.

A former co-worker of my mother made me a garter belt after she happened across an antique blue tulip pin that made her think of me.

Her aspiring baker daughter volunteered to break out her icing tips and baking pans for me, not even flinching at the mention of the food allergy that would've made ordering a professionally made cake a major financial investment. (I've never met this girl.)

My grandmother offered up a beautiful pearl clutch that perfectly matched my ivory lace dress without even being asked.

I put my crafty self to work, too, creating table numbers, invitations, place cards, thank-you notes, and more, presenting each piece of art to the steering committee composed of my top-notch wedding coordinators: my mother, sister, and husband-to-be.

On April 24, 2010, I walked down the aisle toward the man of my dreams and a new life as "the wife."

Was it the wedding I've always dreamed of?

No.

It was better.

My wedding was a perfect balance of convention and professionals and pure, unadulterated talents, favors, and love. In the midst of stock market crashes, layoffs, and a deluge of negative headlines, the sun shone on an unseasonably warm spring day, and 110 people forgot their own troubles and laughed, cheered, cried, ate, and danced right along with me.

Did I mention the groom was perfect, too?

I married a man who loves cooking at home and saves fancy restaurants for "special occasions." Who knows a Sunday afternoon matinee is the perfect way to watch a movie, and that a glass of wine and a paper cup full of dark chocolate M&Ms beats a dozen red roses every time. Who couldn't wait to rip down wallpaper and paint in our new home — all by ourselves.

Every time we kneel down in the pews where our friends and family witnessed our vows, we both know we have so much to be thankful for. While a recession may not have been the ideal time to start a life and embark on such a busy, crazy, expensive roller coaster of a journey, it taught us that we can treasure the best of times — and survive the worst of times.

Together.

~Caitlin Q. Bailey O'Neill

35

It Had to Be Perfect

When you look at your life, the greatest happinesses are family happinesses.
~Dr. Joyce Brothers

rom the right flowers, which just happened to be light blue and violet hydrangeas, to tackling the headache-inducing seating charts, I spent months planning every detail of my traditional wedding, and it had to be perfect!

The venue that I fell in love with was a private country club in Connecticut that neither I nor my family could ever afford to join. The reality was that I was cursed with champagne taste on a beer budget. What would my wedding be without the perfect venue, though? My "perfect wedding" obsession forced me to make some serious compromises (I now regret my lack of passed hors d'oeuvres), but I knew I had to have the venue. And after weeks of haggling and negotiating, it was mine.

As time went by, I started to get lost in the details as if they were the only things that mattered. I bought four different pairs of wedding shoes because I couldn't decide which shade of ivory matched my dress just right. After that splurge, I actually started doubting my dress as I delved back into bridal magazines searching for one that could have possibly been better. I admit that if my wedding planning had gone on another few weeks, I would have morphed into a full-blown "Bridezilla."

Although I didn't realize it at the time, I was actually one of the lucky brides-to-be. By that I mean that I got a reality check. It came in the form of a life-changing event that reminded me what really mattered… and it wasn't the frosting on the cake or the length of the bridesmaids' dresses.

I received a phone call two weeks before my big day. I had just returned from my "hair and make-up dry run." My dad was on the other line telling me that he thought he was having a heart attack and was on his way to the hospital. I grabbed my bag and jumped in the car with my fiancé. The ten-minute car ride to the emergency room seemed like an eternity as I relived a phone call I had received eight years earlier. I was in college at the time, three hours away from home, when my aunt called to inform me that my stepfather had died of a heart attack that morning. I couldn't bear the thought of losing my dad, too. As tears started streaming down, I kept telling myself that he was going to be okay.

Thankfully, he was okay. He had indeed suffered a heart attack but was lucky enough to get medical attention immediately. He underwent surgery to open his clogged arteries and stayed in the hospital for a few nights for further testing and observation. My sister and I visited him in his hospital room every day to keep him company. It was the first week since my engagement that I didn't think about wedding details. There was no stress, no fighting, no meaningless energy wasted. It was the first time that I realized how silly I had been to get so caught up in the small stuff.

When I woke up on my wedding day, September 5, 2009, I knew my wedding was going to be perfect. It had nothing to do with all of my hard work, planning or even money. It was going to be perfect because my dad was going to be there to walk me down the aisle. I realized that not a single wedding detail would have mattered without my dad being there that day.

~Kate Sugg

36

The Paws in Our Plans

What greater gift than the love of a cat?
~Charles Dickens

After five years of dating, including four years of sharing a flat and the affections of a little cat called Figuero, it was time for us to make it official!

Neal's proposal came over an ice cream cone, simple and sweet. Smiling so wide I could only nod my acceptance, I became his fiancée and was soon wearing the engagement ring of my dreams—gemstones and diamonds.

Together, we threw ourselves into wedding plans, sharing each decision regarding the ceremony, the guest list, the menu. Like every couple, we wanted our wedding to reflect who we were as a couple. The cake would be vegan. The reception at an historic hotel. The bouquet and boutonnieres would contain not only orchids and roses, but also the joyful greenery of carrot tops, dill weed, and parsley.

But one of the most lasting decisions—our wedding date—we left up to our cat. The beautiful, long-haired tabby was the light of our young lives, an integral part of every day since his unexpected arrival one cold winter night. From his frostbitten ears to his elegant sweep of tail, he exuded personality and immediately warmed our hearts.

He woke us up each morning, taking quite seriously his role of Alarm Cat. He greeted us each evening, waiting none too patiently to share dinnertime. He cuddled between our knees at night, ensuring sweet dreams all around.

If he couldn't be at the wedding, we decided, he could at least have a part in the plans.

We looked at the calendar and chose three dates in the autumn. Then came Figuero's turn.

Neal wrote each date on a separate scrap of paper while I held Figuero in my arms. Crumpling each scrap into a ball, Neal tossed them randomly onto the kitchen floor one at a time. Loving nothing more than a crumpled bit of paper, Figuero watched with great interest, as if sensing the extra importance of this particular game.

The first piece he walked over to, we had decided, would be the date of our wedding.

As soon as I set Figuero down, he trotted over to the paper ball that had landed in front of the stove. With his big paw, he gave it a little swat of approval.

I scooped him up again, squeezing him with excitement. Neal smoothed the paper out and, with our heads together, the three of us read the date that would be special for the rest of our lives: October sixth.

Neal and I have been married nearly twenty-five years now, sharing fifteen of those years with our little man, who lived to the ripe old age of twenty-one. On every anniversary, I remember the way Figuero helped make our wedding special. I think about the joy he added, not only to that day, but to every single one we knew as a family.

A gift that goes beyond the years, his legacy is our lifetime of love.

~Kate Fellowes

"The nerve. This wedding invitation clearly excludes you."

The List

Details create the big picture.
~Sanford I. Weill

As a single parent for more than thirteen years, I didn't think I would ever wed again. That changed in October 1999 when the man I had been dating for nearly a year popped the question. We chose a date in February 2000, coincidentally exactly a year from our first date.

Things were on a whirlwind pace to get a wedding planned in four months amid the Christmas and New Year holidays, but I took the planning in stride. You see, I was a fundraiser at the time, and special events are a staple in the fundraising world. I had planned successful garden parties, silent auctions, golf tournaments, and black-tie galas. All of that took planning and attention to detail. So, what was a wedding? Just another special event!

I decided I would plan our wedding accordingly. First, I drew up a budget. A second marriage for each, we both had financial obligations. We believed we could have a meaningful ceremony and a wonderful reception if we were really savvy about how we used our money. Second, I developed a very detailed "to-do list," complete with deadlines and the person responsible for completing the tasks. My soon-to-be husband, Terry, laughed at me.

"What is all this?" he inquired one afternoon, looking through several pieces of paper.

"It's how we're going to get the wedding done and make it come in on time and at or under budget," I replied.

"With all these lists?"

"Sure. Hey, I do this all the time at work. It's my mantra for success... Plan your work and then work your plan."

Terry picked up my to-do list, seeing his name in several places on the sheet of paper. "I can already see how our marriage is going to be," he said with a smirk on his face.

And my plan was working beautifully! My matron-of-honor and I spent an entire Saturday afternoon choosing beautiful silk flowers and then fashioning bouquets, corsages, and boutonnieres. I found Victorian-inspired stationery with matching envelopes and response cards, and printed our invitations on my home computer. Terry and I decided that our groomsmen and ushers would be outfitted in what it seemed every man possessed: a navy blazer, gray slacks, and a white shirt. We would buy matching ties to coordinate with my attendants' dresses, which, of course, I found on clearance.

But the real bargain was my dress! Shopping for what my daughter would wear, I stumbled across a gorgeous white tea-length dress, with a sparkly beaded bodice and sleeves, and a chiffon skirt. Not only was it my size, but it was on sale for only thirty-five dollars! Right then and there, I decided I would decorate a wide-brimmed hat to wear instead of the traditional veil.

As our special day neared, Terry and I really kicked into high gear, packing boxes with some of our own things to use at the reception to continue to keep the expense under budget. A friend asked Terry how things were going.

"Betty has all these lists to check before she packs the boxes! But as soon as I suggest that I'd like to take a box to church to put in the storeroom, she has to check the box again—just to make sure it's all in there. It's starting to drive me nuts!"

Didn't Terry understand that paying attention to detail was how a special event was planned and implemented? Didn't he want our day to be perfection? I was sure that when it was all said and done, he would appreciate my strict adherence to both our budget and time constraints. What a good wife I would be!

However, the day of our blessed event, I was starting to have a few doubts of my own. We had stayed up late the night before making cream-cheese mints and preparing raw vegetables for the reception. The next morning, we arrived at church right after the men's group breakfast so we could decorate the room. After that was my trip to the hairdresser. When I arrived back home, Terry informed me that he had received a call that our pianist for the reception was on the way to the hospital with severe flu-like symptoms. Both of us frantically searched our CD collections to find suitable music. Things were not going according to plan!

The time was nearing that we were scheduled to arrive at the church. With my ever-present list, my soon-to-be husband, two children, and I started loading the car.

"Rings?"

"Check."

"Guest book?"

"Check."

"Flowers?"

"Check."

"CDs?"

"Check."

"It looks like we have everything, Mom," my son said.

"I want to check the house one last time."

I could hear all of them groaning as I walked through every room in the house looking for any boxes or other items that were left behind. I was confident that everything we needed was in the car. I got behind the wheel for the ten-minute trip to the church.

I pulled up in the circle drive in front of the church, and four car doors opened simultaneously. Boxes and other items were unloaded and placed on the concrete sidewalk.

There was a sick feeling in the pit of my stomach. My wedding dress was missing!

I checked the lists I had in my hand. Nowhere did I have a check mark for my wedding dress. In fact, the entry for the dress hadn't even made the list!

"I've got to go back home," I told the family.

Three sets of eyes looked at me questioningly.

"I seem to have forgotten my dress. It must still be hanging on the back of the bedroom door," I said sheepishly.

We all looked at each other and started laughing. "The list" had failed me! I drove home and fetched the gown, laughing hysterically at the irony.

A few days later, after returning from a short honeymoon, I found my wedding to-do list among what was brought back from the wedding. As I ran my finger down the check-marked entries, I realized that "the list" had served a lot of purposes. Sure, it had kept us focused and on-task during a crazy time. But it also reminded me that, no matter how hard we try, not everything turns out the way we want. And, sometimes, it's better that way.

~Betty Ost-Everley

Nothing Can Change This Love

If music be the food of love, play on.
~William Shakespeare

After people ask about the proposal, the ring, the date, and the dress, they have either completely lost interest in your wedding ("Well, it's got twenty-two layers of French tulle followed by sixteen layers of Austrian lace going down the back...") or they come to their next question: the song. You know, the one that will play when you awkwardly dance in front of your family and friends for the first time as husband and wife.

Oh, to be the shamed couple that doesn't have a song! My fiancé Peter and I were such a couple a few months ago.

To be fair, though, we're not living in the dancehall days of the 1940s when the average couple was likely to have a song they called their own. Now, hardly any young couples have a song. I know because during our early engagement, I polled every couple we knew, hoping to shed some light on this important business.

Realizing we were not alone didn't make the song-picking struggle any easier. For one, Peter and I have vastly different musical tastes, which until that moment hadn't presented much of a problem—other than the fact that Peter could probably do for one less round of Tony Bennett's "Duets" collection on the dinner music rotation.

It is difficult—way more difficult than I initially imagined—to find a song two people will love equally. Add to that the pressure of (at least mildly) impressing your family and friends with the cool and impressive quality of your song and its clear representation of your relationship. Darn near impossible.

We pulled our coffee to the side night after night and practiced dancing to the Beach Boys, David Byrne, and Michael Bublé. It took a few months, and I'm embarrassed to admit that a few tense discussions took place along the way. ("You want to dance to that?") But in the process, I learned that Peter had excellent dance skills and could effortlessly orchestrate dips, turns, and spins. We laughed a lot. And when we finally heard it — the song that would become ours — I was filled with joyful excitement. It was a classic — Sam Cooke's "Nothing Can Change This Love" — but not overplayed — sweet, but not saccharine. It felt comforting and fun and just, well, perfect: very similar to how I felt about marrying Peter.

~Julie Turner

39

Groomzilla

We find comfort among those who agree with us—
growth among those who don't.
~Frank A. Clark

I've heard that some brides get annoyed when their husbands-to-be don't participate enough in the wedding planning process. But when I was planning my wedding, such a situation didn't sound like a problem at all. In fact, it sounded dreamy. I fantasized every day about having a less involved fiancé.

My future husband, Tobias, was full of ideas for our wedding. Big, horrible ideas. For instance, at one point he was struck with the idea of renting a big yellow school bus to transport our guests from the church to the reception site.

"It'll be great!" he'd exclaimed, his eyes glowing. "The guests will love it!"

Would they? I remember trying to imagine my mother, dressed in her finest, bridesmaids in their silky gowns, elderly aunts and uncles, all clambering up the stairs of a grimy yellow behemoth that still smelled of dirty sneakers and old sack lunches. I couldn't imagine them loving it.

"Um, no," I said. "Just… no."

"But it's Americana!" Tobias cried, amazed by my refusal. "The Germans will love to ride on a real American yellow school bus. They'll have never done that before!"

You see, this was part of the problem: Tobias is German. In

terms of wedding planning, his nationality complicated my life on two levels. First, he fit the stereotype of the super-organized German who loves to plan things, so he couldn't help but be all over our wedding. Second, as a German, he had a different vision of what a wedding should be. In Germany, weddings tend to be understated affairs, completely lacking in pretension. So black stretch limousines, a phalanx of bridesmaids in identical dresses, tuxedoed groomsmen, and even fat, glittery engagement rings were as horrible for him as having our guests ride in yellow school buses was to me.

But there was another problem, too. My husband loves parties. All the parties in our relationship are masterminded by him, from the foods we eat to the candles we use. And if the party didn't rage until the wee hours, he frets about its success (which may explain why we once had a Sunday brunch that lasted from noon until after midnight). Somehow it didn't occur to me when we got engaged that, for him, our wedding would be the Mother of All Parties.

No detail of our wedding was too small for Tobias. Together, we spent hours hammering out the wording, color, shape, and size of our wedding invitations. We bickered over the appropriate flowers for the church. (He wanted wildflowers; I wanted cherry blossoms and peonies.) When visiting caterers, Tobias grilled them about their credentials as if lives were at stake, and tasted their dishes, brow furrowed, scribbling notes, as if he were a food critic for *The New York Times*. My poor mother, the traditional role of bridal advisor usurped by her future son-in-law, would tentatively offer a suggestion to me, and I'd moan, "Mom, I'm sorry... I can't handle another opinion. It's all I can do to get my own in there!"

But there was one area where I drew the line: shopping for my wedding dress. Tobias wanted desperately to go with me. "Well, at least tell me what you have in mind," he'd begged. "Nothing too formal, I hope. You know... nothing that looks like a wedding dress. And what about a veil? In Germany, brides don't wear veils."

"Forget it, Tobias!" I snapped, wondering if it were true about the veils. "You're not going to know anything about it until you see me coming down the aisle!"

"Coming down the aisle…" he'd repeated, thoughtfully. "Seems so old-fashioned. And I don't think we do that in Germany. How about we walk in together?"

Maddening.

Somehow, we did make it to our wedding day. The truth is, by the end, I really appreciated Tobias's contributions. Sure, it was annoying that we had to leave our wedding china off our bridal registry because we couldn't agree on a pattern (he wanted plain white; I wanted some design, any design), but on the other hand, Tobias had no problem handling the dirtier aspects of wedding planning. He negotiated prices with vendors with the charming ease of a used-car salesman. When the classical quartet we hired to play at the church proved themselves to be unreliable a week before the wedding, he rallied quickly to find an alternate solution, while I was frozen with horror. He gathered the paperwork for our wedding license, and planned our entire (utterly fabulous) honeymoon in the Greek Islands.

Today, eight years and two days after I walked down the aisle in my off-white gown and flowing veil, and my Groomzilla took my hand and whispered, "You look absolutely beautiful," I look at our wedding pictures and see a wedding that truly represented us. Martha Stewart might frown at our lack of color theme, the uneven number of wedding attendants, or that one groomsman (who wasn't even Scottish) was wearing a kilt, but I smile. This was our wedding: a jumble of compromises, a blend of cultures, visibly imperfect, but wonderfully, quirkily ours. Had Tobias been less involved, as I'd so often daydreamed, God knows whose wedding it would have been. Maybe Martha Stewart's?

Good thing some dreams don't come true.

~Barbara D. Diggs

Chapter 5

Here Comes the Bride

Meet the Parents

Don't handicap your children by making their lives easy.

~Robert A. Heinlein

40

Here Comes the MOG

Women are in league with each other, a secret conspiracy of
hearts and pheromones.
~Camille Paglia

Mothers of the Groom (MOGs) have been handed a bad rap. According to bridal salons across the country, they are treated as second-class citizens. Jill, an MOG friend of mine, pointed this out after a recent visit to find a dress.

"It's ridiculous," Jill told the salesgirl. "Without me, there wouldn't even be a wedding since I'm responsible for having produced the one commodity necessary for such an occasion: the groom."

The salesgirl shrugged her shoulders. "What can I tell you?" she said. "Mothers of the Groom are just not that important."

Jill invited me to join her on her next shopping expedition.

"What about that little orange and white number you bought last week?" I asked.

"The color was wrong. I tried it on, and Bill said I looked like a Creamsicle. I need your help."

The following week, we went to find something that was more MOG material. A blond beauty named Ms. Mindy greeted us as we stepped off the elevator.

"I know. Don't tell me. One of you is the MOB (Mother of the Bride)."

"I'm the Mother of the Groom," Jill said.

"Oh," Ms. Mindy sneered slightly. "Well, we have dresses for you, too. But, remember, your job is to look as understated as possible. A MOG is supposed to blend into the woodwork."

We were escorted past rows of lovely lace gowns dripping with rosettes and sequins in beautiful colors that would enhance Jill's complexion. Farther along, we stopped in front of an array of dresses that, if they had signs under them, would have read: "Drab." Ms. Mindy plucked one from the rack. "Now, here's a little something that could work," she said.

"Beige isn't my color," Jill said.

"It's not beige," Mindy corrected. "It's ecru. Ecru is a perfect MOG color."

"Ecru will make me look like an eggshell," Jill said.

"Perfect," said Mindy. "The bride's family will love it."

It suddenly became clear: The idea was to have Jill look as invisible as possible. While she tried on a variety of ecru washouts, I peered through racks of dresses reserved for more important members of the wedding: mothers of the bride. Among the collection, I suddenly spied a raspberry chiffon gown that got misplaced. I took it into the dressing room for Jill to try on.

"Now, this has definite possibilities," I said.

"Wrong," Ms. Mindy announced. "It is a smashing little number, but not for you. If you wore raspberry, the bride would never forgive you. You would look too flamboyant. But I can order it in battleship gray."

"I refuse to look like a ballistic missile," Jill said.

"Let me tell you a story." Ms. Mindy got serious. "About a year ago, I assisted an MOG who decided to wear hot pink to her son's wedding. When the bride saw her, she fainted. The MOB never spoke to the MOG again. I found out through the matrimonial grapevine that the couple divorced a year later. It's bad luck for the MOG to look too perky."

After an hour with no success, Jill and I headed to another store, this one a small bridal shop that carried a wide selection of MOG dresses. We combed the racks where Jill found a lovely dress in mauve silk.

"Are you an MOB or an MOG?" the salesgirl asked. "Because mauve on an MOG is like white on an MOB. It's simply not done. Try something in the beige family instead."

"Doesn't she know it's called ecru?" Jill whispered.

Unsuccessful in our attempt, we gave up and moved on to another store where this time a cheery woman named Angelica welcomed us with open arms.

"Forget conventionality," she said. "I tell all my MOGs to go for another kind of look that is always appropriate: the little black dress."

"Can I really wear black to my son's wedding?" Jill asked. "Won't it seem a tad depressing?"

"Black is the new gray," Angelica assured her. "Dare to be different. Dare to be an MOG who exudes class—not boredom."

Convinced, Jill found a stunning black gown with a single red silk geranium on the shoulder.

"A touch of red will add just the right hint of frivolity you need," Angelica said. "Not ostentatious, but appropriately reeking of *je ne sais quoi*."

"I love it," Jill said.

"It's so to-die-for," said Angelica, adjusting the geranium.

I kept quiet, anticipating the worst.

The day of the wedding, Jill appeared in the black gown that she had kept as a surprise to all, including Bill. All eyes were upon her as she floated down the aisle looking very *je ne sais quoi*, as Angelica had predicted. Jill's eighty-year-old mother nearly fainted.

"I can't believe you dared to wear black to my only grandson's wedding," she said.

"Relax, Mother," Jill said. "I have an MOG aura."

"Really? Maybe you need to see a doctor," her mother suggested.

Jill cornered me, champagne in hand. "Nine people asked me if I was in mourning. The rest think I look original and sultry."

Then the MOB appeared, wearing the same raspberry dress that Jill had passed up. She looked like a bowl of Jell-O. To make matters worse, during the reception, she ate so many Swedish meatballs that she popped two buttons, which flew into the salmon mousse and splattered across her face. She flew from the Grand Ballroom en route to the restroom, tripping on a pat of butter and spraining her ankle. The FOB (Father of the Bride) called 911 and slammed a Valium down her throat as the 250 guests looked on.

"I should have worn that beige dress," she moaned, as the paramedics carried her out on a stretcher.

"Ecru!" Jill and I shouted in unison.

~Judith Marks-White

41

My Daughter's Wedding

To a father growing old nothing is dearer than a daughter.
~Euripides

L ess than forty-eight hours ago, I participated in my daughter's marriage. I gave the bride away. Now a feeling of gloom hangs in the air, morose and inexpugnable. She was my firstborn, my only daughter, my little girl. I feel pride, and happiness, too. But the tears lurk inside, fighting to get out.

I thought that maybe if I wrote down what I was feeling, the purging logic of the words would ease my pain. Yet as I typed the words, tears began their trek down my cheeks, ending their journey on the keyboard below. Someone once told me that it was a bad thing to spill liquids on a computer keyboard. A bad thing? A bad thing was losing my little girl.

I alluded to the hurt I felt giving away my daughter during a toast made to the bride and groom at the reception. I spoke about all the fathers before me who had done the same thing. Yet, I told the gathering, it still pained me. I told them that my wife and I were proud to add her young husband to the family, and voiced all of the right things. But something I wanted to say, had planned to say, refused utterance.

All through the rehearsal, all through the wedding, and then at the reception, I compartmentalized this nagging, unexplainable grief. I knew that if I spoke those words, the thin membrane of this grief-compartment would explode like a water balloon. So a part of the toast to the bride and groom remained unsaid.

I had nothing against the groom. It seemed almost as if my daughter had chosen this young man to please her father. The groom, bright, caring and witty, even shared my knowledge and love of baseball, and anyone could recognize how much he loved my daughter. She is tender and tough, brilliant, and in many ways headstrong. This young husband would make a good match for her. I believed their union would be a good one, and that these two strong young people might weather any storm. I already considered the young husband a friend and believed our friendship would grow. Why then, I wondered, was I crying?

The tears first welled earlier on the wedding day when my daughter, stunning in her wedding dress, was having solitary pictures taken in the small campus chapel. The photographer placed her with her back to me, looking up at a stained-glass window as sunlight streamed through, creating brightly colored splotches of light that danced around her. The beauty of that single moment became more than I could bear. I walked out of the campus chapel with red, watery eyes. As I paced outside, the students walking to their classes seen through my eyes' tear-blurred lenses resembled those bright splotches dancing inside the chapel. But I quickly regained my composure and returned before anyone noticed that I was gone.

Then I redoubled my efforts to force the tears back down, knowing that three times within the next few hours would prove difficult to bear: when I walked her down the aisle, made the toast to the bride and groom, and during the father-bride dance. But I survived all of them in good fashion, without tears. I began to feel that maybe all of this silliness was over. Yet on the long drive home, as I gazed at my sixteen-year-old son asleep beside me—the boy who had performed the duties of brother-of-the-bride and usher so well—my feeling of pride in my son turned to tears. Crying silently, careful not to wake him, I wondered what was so wrong in my life.

Once we arrived home, just ahead of my wife and mother-in-law who traveled separately, I retreated to the privacy of the master bath and reflected on this pain, not so different from what I struggled with at the death of my mother four years earlier. Why? For another twenty-four hours, grief continued to pop to the surface. Finally, desperate to break the cycle, I determined to put these thoughts on paper.

As I prepared to write the final paragraph, the realization dawned that these tears had very little to do with my daughter's wedding, but everything to do with the simple fact that my children have grown up, a finality that I had refused to consider. I will never play horsey with them on my knees again, or carry them on my shoulders, or play All-Star wrestling on the carpet. I will never again read to them at bedtime or see their small-child wonder at Christmas. I recalled the words from the Joni Mitchell song that my daughter and I danced to on her wedding night, alone together for a brief moment:

"We're all captive on a carousel of time.
"We can't return.
"We can only look behind from where we came."

I have done my job. My wife and I have provided our children with a firm foundation to be healthy, loving, caring adults. I feel better. And now I can say that part of the wedding toast I couldn't muster before: "I may have given Rebecca away in marriage, but I will always keep the little girl in my heart."

~Jack Kline

42

Wedding Vows

To watch us dance is to hear our hearts speak.
~Hopi Indian saying

"Mom, Dad, we're engaged!" The words flowed from my son Jeffrey's lips. The announcement was not totally a surprise; we had known he had bought a ring for the love of his life, Katie. We were happy and pleased that Katie and Jeff were going to get married. As we prepared for the wedding and its attendant events, such as the shower, the rehearsal and the rehearsal dinner, the only thought that gnawed at me was that I wanted to walk down the aisle at church and dance with Jeff at the reception. Truthfully, though, it was more than a thought. It was a goal, a promise, and a vow that I had made to myself many years earlier.

More than twenty years following spinal-cord surgeries that had paralyzed me from the shoulders down, I was able to walk with a walker because of years of physical therapy. Six months prior to the engagement, I developed severe foot pain that doctors could not diagnose accurately or treat effectively.

What was I going to do? It was hard to reconcile my long-time goals with my current reality. I had to come to terms with the very real possibility of going down the church aisle in a wheelchair and foregoing my dream of dancing with Jeffrey at the reception.

I began to counsel myself. "It's no big deal, really. There are many more important things that I should concern myself with." In the grand scheme of things, this was barely a blip on the radar screen of "Things to Worry About." But despite my best efforts, there was no way to convince myself to give up on such a long-held vow. In some ways, trying to get to that place where I could accept less than my goal only made me that much more determined to achieve it!

I made an appointment with a foot surgeon. He advised me to try physical therapy and stretching exercises for my foot before going the surgery route. I did the stretching exercises religiously, and it felt slightly better. But with the wedding only a couple of months away, would my foot improve enough for me to walk down the aisle?

Of course, I had other things to worry about as well. There was shopping for my dress, planning, and sending invitations for the rehearsal dinner. I cry at weddings as a matter of routine; it is part of who I am. So getting on an even keel emotionally was important so that, during the ceremony, I wouldn't be doubled over, sobbing heavily into a soggy Kleenex. Ah, so many problems and so little time to worry about them!

But topping the list was walking down the aisle. I first mentioned it to my husband, Walter, who advised: "Instead of worrying, why not see how you do at the rehearsal? That's why they call it a 'rehearsal.'" I couldn't argue with that logic, but me being me, I still worried.

One week before Christmas and nine days until the wedding, the day of the rehearsal had arrived! As we turned into the church's parking lot, my nervousness gave birth to a whole new generation of the butterflies that had plagued me all day. Now was the moment I had both anticipated and dreaded at the same time. Now was the time for me to "do or die," win or lose, succeed or fail. All of my efforts to be able to walk down the aisle would be worth everything or nothing, depending on what happened in the next few minutes.

In the church, we were greeted by Katie's parents as we waited for the bridal party to arrive. Walter pushed the wheelchair to the back of the church so that it was even with the last pew. I gazed down the aisle; it looked very long, almost intimidating, that evening.

Originally, the plan was for Jeffrey to stand at the front of the church. He spoke to our priest and asked if he could walk down the aisle with Walter and me instead. Father John was happy to oblige. So it was settled; the logistics were in place. Now it was up to me.

On cue, with Walter and Jeffrey on either side, I stood up. Slowly and carefully, we made our way toward the altar. We stood briefly to practice lighting a "unity candle" and then we went to the front pew. We made it! I made it!

The next nine days flew by. It was Jeff and Katie's wedding day! We entered the church, which was resplendent in red poinsettias. A massive number of butterflies fluttered inside me. I waited in place with Jeffrey and Walter. The music started; I remember how easily I got out of the wheelchair! Before I knew it, we were at the altar, lighting the candle.

One vow kept, more to follow...

Katie looked beautiful as she walked down the aisle. She and Jeffrey stood a few feet away from us as they clasped hands and began their vows. When Jeff repeated "... for all the days of my life," I thought of all the times he had helped me through the difficult days of recovering from spinal-cord surgeries and the pep talks he gave me during my physical therapy sessions. I knew he would continue his caring ways with Katie, and I knew then that he would keep his promise to her and she to him. That gave me great comfort, and I managed to stay relatively composed — another vow kept!

But, still, I wasn't done.

At the reception, after we were introduced, it was time for the dances. I cried through their wedding dance, "Can't Help Falling in Love with You." Jeffrey walked over and clutched my hands. "Do you want to dance?"

Tears sprang to my eyes. "I'd love to."

He helped me up. We swayed to the strains of "That's What Friends Are For," a song that Jeffrey, at age four, sang for me when I was still in the rehab center. It quickly became and has remained my favorite song.

I looked up at my beloved son, Jeff. I told him how much I love him and how proud I am of him. He kissed me on the top of my head and said, "Mom, I am so proud of YOU!" I couldn't stop the tears this time. The dance was over soon, too soon.

Thrilled beyond words that I was able to walk down the aisle, stay composed through the ceremony, and end the wonderful day by dancing with my son, I truly know the deep sense of satisfaction and elation that accompanied those achievements.

Whether vows are made with family and friends as witnesses and pledged to your soul mate or made in private to the innermost part of your soul, they are promises to be kept.

~Donna Lowich

43

Perfectly Imperfect

You see, when weaving a blanket, an Indian woman leaves a flaw in the weaving of that blanket to let the soul out.
~Martha Graham

Aunt B gave my husband and me a handmade lace doily as a wedding present. Its delicate white threads loop gracefully, reminding me of a dew-covered spider's web sparkling in the dawn light. It is framed and hangs in our living room.

Aunt B was proud of her work. She challenged me to find the defect in it, the mistake that proved only God could make something flawless. Her work was perfect in its imperfection, I thought, though I was too tactful to say anything. Still, all these years later, I can't see the mistake Aunt B put in to satisfy God's hubris.

I'm thinking about Aunt B now because my daughter is getting married. The invitation arrived, a linocut in white and blue with birds and lanterns. It is simple and beautiful, designed by my girl and her love. I can imagine them slicing into the linoleum to carve out their names, chiseling the date and place. I see them rolling the pale blue paint onto the image's surface, splattering color on the walls, on the table, on themselves, giggling.

Like the card, they are arranging the wedding themselves and do not need my help. Still, a mother must do something special when her only daughter gets married. I decided to make her an afghan, a special afghan.

I searched for just the right project. One was too frilly, another too austere. They were all too delicate, too bold, too silly, or just too *too*. I looked through books and in racks at the yarn store. I searched the Internet. Then I found one that was just right. It was a cable knit that showed a subtle pattern, like embossed stationery. The fabric's raised portion looked like intertwining circles intersecting in knots; it seemed perfect for a wedding present. Well, maybe a little sappy, but weddings call for sappy.

Now that I had the pattern, I needed the right yarn. It had to be machine washable and dryable. I didn't want my masterpiece shoved in a closet so it wouldn't get dirty. It had to be the right color. Not too dark, otherwise the pattern would not show up. It had to be mellow and soft. I found just the right buttery cream wool, but the store was out of it. They had to order it.

A week passed. No wool. I called the store. "Oh, it should be here any day." Another week passed. Still no wool. "We'll call the distributor. Usually it takes a few days." After three more days, I called a third time. "It's coming from Turkey. It might take a while."

That night, I considered my options. Perhaps a domestic, available yarn would do. As I was on my way to search for a substitute, my phone rang. The wool had arrived. I came home an hour later with seventeen skeins of beautiful yarn. I set to work immediately.

The pattern was complicated. There were thirty-two rows, each different. I eyed the calendar. Only eight weeks before the wedding.

I summoned my courage. I am an accomplished knitter. I should be able to do this. Sure enough, I soon discovered that I didn't have to consult the pattern on even rows. The pattern was obvious from the way the yarn lay. Still, there were four different kinds of cable stitches, and each time I had to make one I had to look up the directions for that stitch. But as I continued to work on the piece, it took on a logic of its own, a logic I began to understand. I needed to consult the instructions less and less.

Time was slipping away. I had to make more progress. I decided I knew the pattern well enough to work on it while talking with my husband. Wouldn't you know, the first time I did, my husband wanted to know whether I was listening to him.

"Of course, dear, I heard every word you said."

A few days later, as I was looking at my work, I saw the mistake. It was quite a few rows back. It would take hours to rip out the knitting to the mistake and fix it. I considered the afghan and looked at the calendar. It wasn't such a bad mistake. Hardly noticeable really. I would leave my mistake.

That's when I thought of Aunt B.

My mistake was better than Aunt B's. My mistake was genuine. Besides, it would give the afghan a dual purpose. Now, it was not only an afghan, but a parlor game: Can You Find the Mistake? It would go well with my daughter's homemade wedding.

With this in mind, I continued to knit and thought of Aunt B. I'd never asked her whether she put in her mistake on purpose. Perhaps she had. Or maybe she hadn't noticed the problem until she had gone too far. Maybe she hadn't seen it until she had completed her work and blocked it or, even worse, until the fine lace had been mounted and framed.

I'll never know for sure. Aunt B died last winter. But I feel a certain kinship with her now. I know that my gift to my daughter, like Aunt B's gift to me, will be perfect in its imperfection.

~Wendy Teller

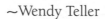

Gaining Not Losing

A son is a son till he takes him a wife; a daughter is a daughter all of her life.
~Irish saying

Honestly, my attitude was in the toilet. I had the dubious honor of playing "Mother of the Groom" for the second time in six months. The first wedding had been fraught with emotional volcanoes, causing singed feelings to rumble beneath wedding number two.

I had already empty-nested both my boys, respected their privacy and relationships, and had given advice only when asked. But it felt a lot like rejection. After all, I had invested into my sons' lives every ounce of love, patience, wisdom, and energy I possessed. I felt I was about to watch another bride and her large, close-knit family swallow the rewards of my life's work and leave my husband Bob and me abandoned by the roadside. I prepared for the June event in Rhode Island with a perpetual lump in my throat and gritted teeth.

We planned a get-acquainted party at our New Jersey beach house before the week in Rhode Island, since the two families had hardly laid eyes on each other. I was to drive from our home in south Florida on Memorial Day weekend to open the beach house and arrange catering, etc., in New Jersey. The night before I left, I had a quick conversation with Fran and Jim, the bride's parents, and quipped that I would wave at about 10:30 as I passed through Jacksonville, Florida, on my way north.

"We'll wave back!" they chuckled.

At 5:00 A.M. Sunday, I climbed into my big white cushy Lincoln Town Car, kissed Bob goodbye, and zoomed off into the sunrise. I had the huge trunk crammed with wedding gifts, clothes for cool and warm temperatures, my computer and printer, plus miscellaneous decorations for the party. Two large framed prints wrapped in a beach towel took up the back seat. As the sky brightened into a classic Florida sunshiny day, my mood became darker as I thought about what I perceived as my impending loss. I'd sacrificed a career for my kids, had been the confidant, the encourager, the tutor, the coach, and the chief cook and bottle-washer for almost thirty years... roles that would of necessity become those of the new wife. I envisioned a future of lonely Christmases and long-distance grandparenting, years of polite correspondence, and arms-length hugs.

I approached Jacksonville as the holiday crowds convened onto a stretch of road construction, where five lanes became three. Without warning, a little sports car on a right merge cut into the right lane, pushing a car halfway into the middle lane. The resulting crunch of four cars into three lanes at sixty miles per hour sent me speeding toward the median strip and directly at the metal guardrail. I swerved left to avoid the rail, which caught my rear right wheel. It hurled my car into a deadly spin, turning over twice, and landing upside down with a deafening crunch.

I hung by my seatbelt with a soothing music CD still playing, grateful the airbag hadn't deployed. I carefully wiggled fingers and toes, moved various body parts, and exclaimed "Thank you, Jesus!" several times before I realized voices were calling me outside the car.

"Are you alone?"

"Are you hurt?"

"Can you get out?"

A bevy of good Samaritans listened to my directions and forced the passenger side door open. I released my seatbelt, stopped the music, gathered my purse, glasses, shoes, and overnight bag (all scattered and covered in glass on the car ceiling), and squeezed through the half-submerged door to cheers and clapping. Although my neck hurt, I did not even have a scratch, but my beautiful car was scrunched to half its original height.

Someone asked, "Is there anyone you can call? Your husband?"

"It's 10:30!" I laughed. "He'll be in church for the next two hours. But I have the number of some folks in Jacksonville." I prayed Jim and Fran would be home.

"Hi, Jim, it's Lynne," I said as he answered the phone. "Remember how I told you I'd wave when I got to Jacksonville? Well, I'm here, but I just totaled my car on I-95!"

"We'll meet you at the hospital," he said as the paramedics strapped me to a body board and whisked me into the ambulance.

Within a few hours, Jim had retrieved all my stuff from the wrecked Lincoln, Fran had installed me in their master bedroom, and I had discovered warmth, hospitality, and friendship that dissolved my in-law fears. We really were going to become one big family when our kids married.

Miraculously, not one item packed in the car was damaged, even the framed pictures on the back seat! The accident should have snapped my neck and killed me, but a strained neck muscle was the extent of my injuries. Only a small, carved olivewood cross hanging from the rearview mirror suffered a tiny broken corner of the cross-piece. It is now suspended from the rearview mirror in my second Lincoln Town Car. That little cross from Jerusalem reminds me that the plan for my life can be revealed in upside-down circumstances and be completely unlike anything I could imagine. Fran, Jim, Bob, and I truly celebrated at our children's wedding (which could have been a funeral) and have since welcomed two adorable grandchildren together. The blended family relationships have extended our family's blessings rather than ending them.

I have amended the old saying about losing your son when he gets married. I would change it to:

Your son is your son when he finds him a wife. Their marriage can bless you the rest of your life.

~Lynne Cooper Sitton

Dad's Handout

A daughter may outgrow your lap, but she will never outgrow your heart.
~Author Unknown

I stood in the church nursery, now converted to a bride's dressing room, and stared at the two-inch by three-inch piece of paper my mom had just handed me. Her 1970s lace-covered wedding gown graced my shoulders, flowing to the ground. Despite a minor mustard-dripping incident, the day had gone as smoothly as possible thus far. But this little piece of paper that she had just handed me might be my undoing. I looked at her in confusion and asked, "What in the world... When did he...?"

"I know. It took me by surprise, too." Her deep brown eyes, mirrors of my own, looked up at me with a mischievous glint.

The night before, Mom had come down the short stairway of our tri-level home looking for my dad. When she rounded the corner into the living room, she discovered him sitting at the computer, half-laughing, half-crying, with tears streaming down his face.

"What's wrong?" she asked. "Are you okay?"

"I don't know!" he replied. He wiped his eyes, then handed her the small piece of paper that I was now holding. Adorned with a little graphic of a bride and groom at the top, the small sheet of paper read:

"I am the father of the bride. Over the last twenty years, I watched my daughter learn to walk and ride a bicycle. I bandaged scraped knees and let her cry on my shoulder when she was hurt. When she turned sixteen, we spent all morning in the car driving around the county. It was my responsibility to provide all that she needed. As I walk her down the aisle today, I will turn that job over to someone else. I am not losing my daughter today, but gaining a new member of my family. Pray with me that Amelia and Kedron will have a happy and joyous life together."

He had seen something similar at a wedding earlier that summer, and decided at the last minute to print up his own version. I held back tears, not wanting to streak mascara down my face.

While I attempted to compose myself, Mom said, "He printed off a couple hundred of these and is handing them out to everyone as they come in the door."

My eyes sprang open in surprise and adoration. "He is?"

Mom looked at me. "Everyone loves it. He's having a field day."

My heart swelled. I had a special relationship with my dad. He was a hobby magician, and from the time I was five years old, I'd been his assistant. We'd spent hundreds of hours making up silly songs and poems, nonsensical stories and skits. When we started performing as clowns, he would drive through McDonald's for a snack, just so he could ask if Ronald could come out to play.

Not long after Mom left the dressing room, Dad came in for pictures. His six-foot frame dwarfed me. When he started balding in his thirties, he decided to shave his head rather than sport a comb-over. He said that his head held so much knowledge it could no longer hold onto his hair. I often told him he looked like Mr. Clean. All he needed was a little hoop earring, which he'd threatened for years to get.

I smiled up at him and said I knew about his secret handout. He grinned, and his chest puffed out a bit.

"I just got the idea last night and decided to make it up really quick." He pulled a few out of his tux pocket to show me.

The photographer came in, and I stood on my tiptoes to give Dad a kiss on the cheek. His strong arm wrapped around my waist, making me feel small. His bright blue eyes glistened with the hint of tears even as his smile stretched ear-to-ear. I smiled through the kiss and then asked, "How did I get so lucky to have a dad like you?"

Moments later, we stood in the lobby, ready to make our grand entrance. The wedding march was coming to a close as my last bridesmaid approached the front of the church.

"Wait! Wait!" Dad said as he rushed into the other nursery, which had been converted to the men's dressing room. I thought maybe he was having second thoughts about giving me away. Instead, he rushed back out with a couple tissues. My big, strong, emotionally controlled dad—whom I'd only seen cry a couple of times—was having a hard time holding it together. And, now, I was, too.

He dabbed his eyes and asked the pastor's wife, "Does my hair look okay?" At that point, I didn't know whether to laugh or cry.

We were a happy mess walking down the aisle, trying not to giggle and completely melt down in tears all at once. It was one of the happiest moments of my life as the two men I love most in the world looked eye-to-eye in silent understanding. I was their jewel. I was their treasure. They would do anything for me.

My father stepped back and released my hand after saying, "Her mother and I." But he's never released my heart. I'll always be Daddy's girl.

~Amelia Rhodes

A Little Something for Rob

It isn't the size of the gift that matters, but the size of the heart that gives it.
~Eileen Elias Freeman, The Angels' Little Instruction Book

Just a few days before my daughter's wedding, I realized that I wanted to give her a keepsake — something from me to her to commemorate the day. We had planned to spend some time alone together the afternoon before the wedding; that outing would be the perfect occasion to present Elaine with a sentimental gift from her mom.

I found and bought an inlaid wooden music box that played "Edelweiss." The box was stained celadon green. An intricate floral design, fashioned from bits cut from different species of wood, graced its top. Elaine and Rob were both musicians; in fact, they'd met in high school band, thirteen years earlier. Elaine's favorite color was green. The box played the same song I'd sung as her lullaby, all those years ago. It was just right.

It dawned on me when I awoke the morning before the wedding that we should choose a little something for Rob. I wanted to give him a token to welcome him to the family. So my husband Rich and I decided to seek an appropriate gift. I was a bit apprehensive about choosing something he would enjoy. And only a few hours remained before my date with my daughter, the bride.

We skipped the leisurely breakfast we'd planned to create time to shop. We drove to a local museum and stormed its gift shop. After considering and rejecting several options, I found myself drawn to a basket of—rocks. The shop where we searched offered a selection of small stones engraved with inspirational words.

Browsing through the pebbles, I kept picking up a rock inscribed with the word "Joy." I would set it down to look at the other choices, but that small "Joy" stone made its way into my hand at least six or seven times.

"Rich," I said, "what do you think of this?" I held up the pebble, and my husband examined it. His raised eyebrow told me he wasn't impressed.

Considering his response, I had to agree. A rock hardly seemed to be the best gift I could dream up for my new son-in-law.

I looked around the shop for other ideas. Nothing appealed to me. I found myself returning to the basket, and once again that Joy pebble called to me. I turned to my husband again. "I think we should buy this. I don't know why, but it just seems like the right thing." Rich was accustomed to my sometimes unconventional gift choices. He nodded.

"He can carry it in his pocket tomorrow as a 'fidget stone,'" I offered.

"Isn't he wearing his dress uniform?" Rich asked.

"Yes, he is," I replied, picturing how handsome Rob would look in his U.S. Navy uniform, waiting at the altar for my daughter.

"Those trousers have really tiny pockets," Rich said.

I glanced at my watch. My daughter expected us in twenty minutes. I bought the rock.

As we raced across town to meet my daughter for our special date, Rich and I joked about the old *Peanuts* Halloween special, wherein Charlie Brown kept saying, "I got a rock." I hoped that Rob would understand why we'd given him a rock. I wasn't sure *I* understood why we were giving him a rock.

Elaine greeted us at the door, her skin glowing, wearing a serene smile. Her calm countenance reinforced my certainty that she and Rob were meant to be together.

"Mom, are you ready? I have a few last-minute errands I was hoping we could run while we're out."

"I just need a minute," I told her as I hugged her. "Is Rob here? I need to chat with him."

"I think he might be out back," Elaine said. I found Rob puttering in the garage and handed him the small gift bag holding the rock.

"This is just a silly little something," I told him. "It's kind of goofy, really…"

My voice trailed off as he pulled the tissue from the bag and unwrapped the pebble. He looked at me and blinked. Then he swallowed.

My heart sank. Had I offended him?

"I used to have one of these," he said quietly, turning the smooth stone over in his hand. "My grandmother gave it to me. Her name was Joy."

~Sheila Seiler Lagrand

Our Day

Our death is not an end if we can live on in our children
and the younger generation. For they are us;
our bodies are only wilted leaves on the tree of life.
~Albert Einstein

Wedding planning was already in full operation when I got off the plane from Paris with my newly dubbed fiancé. Matt had given Mom the greatest gift a few weeks back when he asked for my parents' blessing to propose to me during our summer trip in Europe. Mom had waited her entire life for this, to plan a wedding for her daughter, and while I was away she secretly read wedding magazines, put together sample favors, and selected cake and mother-of-the-bride gown possibilities.

Back from my trip and ready to plunge into details with her, Mom jokingly referred to the wedding as "our" wedding. As in hers and mine. "Forget Matt!" she joked. "We're the ones who have waited our whole lives for this! My April and me."

As many brides know, planning a wedding with your mother does not come without disagreements. Mom insisted that we get married inside the church. I wanted an outside affair. When the church was booked for my preferred wedding date, Mom begged me to change it. "October 2nd!" she pleaded. "What's the difference between 10/23/10 and 10/2/10?" But Mom knew that the numbers 10 and 23 were Matt's and my lucky numbers, and I wouldn't budge. October 23rd was to be our wedding day, no ifs, ands, or buts.

I did give in to some of her requests. When Mom heard me toying with the idea of having a chocolate fountain instead of a wedding cake, she nearly fainted. "Wedding cake is my favorite!" she exclaimed. "You can't have a wedding without wedding cake!"

But when Mom was diagnosed with cancer that September, everything else seemed frivolous. The date, the place, the cake... who cared about any of it if my mother wasn't going to be there to enjoy it with me? Mom seemed to be on the same page with me. "Just get me to next October," she told her doctor before adding, "preferably with my hair."

In the next year, we went through the ups and downs of battling cancer. Through the process, Mom proved to be the strong one. While we focused on her cancer, she chose to focus on getting the perfect wedding planned.

Late that following summer, Mom went in for emergency surgery. The doctor came out with some discouraging news. "It looks ugly in there. The cancer has spread. There is nothing more we can do."

Mom tried life-prolonging medications and supplements, but after a month of excruciating pain, she made a new decision. She was ready to go into hospice. "Nobody wants to see you get married more than I do, my April," she gently explained to me, "but I am in so much pain. I wanted to make it so bad, but I can't live like this anymore. I'm ready to go."

I was in shock. It wasn't fair. I told my mom we'd move up the wedding. She refused. It was too late. Everything was in place. She insisted I get married as we had planned it—as I had wanted it—on October 23, 2010.

I couldn't accept that. I couldn't get married without Mom there. A few days later, Matt and I were slated to meet with my priest. I would use that opportunity to make a very special request—a wedding, at my parents' home, with my mom as the guest of honor. This time, she was going to have to be the one to give in.

At my church, Matt and I told the priest of our circumstances. "It's really important that my mom sees me get married," I explained to him. He agreed and said that he would happily officiate the ceremony whenever and wherever we chose. "Sooner is better than later… in matters like this," he told me with his tender Irish accent. I nodded as a tear rolled down my cheek. I knew exactly what he meant.

As expected, Mom argued against the idea of pushing the wedding forward. I knew she feared that I was doing it just for her, so I firmly told her otherwise—that it was indeed for me. After promising that we would still have the October 23rd wedding as planned, Mom gave in. We set the date for four days later, September 23rd, one month away from my actual wedding.

That day when I got to my parents' home, my younger sister answered the door.

"How's Mom?" I asked.

"All done up and ready to go," she responded confidently. "She's trying to take a nap before everyone else arrives."

I headed into my mother's room. The sight was overwhelming. There, on a hospice bed, surrounded by medical equipment and pain pills, lay Mom all made up in a colorful dress and sparkling jewelry. The two sights didn't belong together. Mom was perched up, eyes open, and looking in good spirits.

"You look so pretty!" I said as I took a seat next to her on her bed.

"I'm ready to watch my daughter get married," she replied with a smile.

And so I did. In my parents' living room, members of Matt's and my family sat around with tissues in hand as we said our vows. The priest pronounced us husband and wife. Our families cheered. Everyone hugged. As I headed toward my mom, she pulled me in and whispered, "Thank you so, so much." I gave her a tight squeeze in response. I knew that I had made the right decision.

That evening, we made sure to engage in as many typical wedding activities as possible. We took pictures, made toasts, and cut the cake. You can't have a wedding without wedding cake! Although Mom was no longer taking in food, we got her to eat a small bite of what was seemingly the most delicious cake ever made. Fittingly, it would be the last thing she ever ate.

The very next night, Mom took a dramatic turn for the worse. That beautiful woman who celebrated my marriage with me just one night ago was now back in her hospice bed, surrounded by her family. In her dreamlike state, she mumbled about my shoes and transportation for the wedding. Even in this state, the wedding was her top priority. It had been the single happy thing that had kept her going this long, my family agreed.

"Everything is taken care of, Mom," we assured her. "Your job here is done."

Two days later, she was gone.

Only three weeks after my mother's funeral, I walked down the aisle with my father. It was October 23rd, my wedding day. Dad cried on the way. I knew what he was thinking, "Your mama should be here for this." As Dad handed me off to Matt and we took our seats, my mind started to wander. Is she here? Mom told me that I would always feel her love. I looked around the church at the beautiful colors and decorations, at her plans and designs. I looked at the picture of my mom set by the altar next to her mother-of-the-bride corsage and memorial candle. She was smiling at me. I felt love and happiness warm my heart.

She was there.

I smiled back. "Thank you for this beautiful wedding, Mom," I thought. "You did such a good job, and I can't believe that this day is finally here."

I laughed to myself and then added, "'Our' day is finally here."

~April Taylor Fetch

48

The Father of the Brides

A daughter is the happy memories of the past, the joyful moments of the present, and the hope and promise of the future.
~Author Unknown

Three wedding days. Three brides. One father of the brides...
Sometimes, I still get choked up thinking about my husband, that father.

I think of the way he looked on those wedding mornings as the chaos in the house swirled around him, and he stood just out of the eye of the hurricane, looking a tad lost. And he was.

But he was so much more.

And I sometimes wonder whether those brides of ours fully understood what their father was feeling on their wedding days.

Our daughters always knew that their dad came from very different roots from theirs. That he was first-generation American, with all that means.

They knew, but only sketchily, about his early years on a Central New Jersey chicken farm. Those were tough years.

A farmer's kid doesn't do after-school sports or clubs. Not when those endless chores are waiting.

Their dad didn't take anything for granted. Not luxuries, surely. Not leisure. Not college. There was no sense of entitlement back in Perrineville, New Jersey.

But there were teachers who recognized that this young man had promise. There were mentors who guided him.

And there were scholarships to college and law school or neither would ever have happened. Nor would his long run as a judge of the New Jersey Superior Court.

Maybe that's why this father of three brides was so happy and proud to give his daughters three much better childhoods than he had. Why he wanted life to be easier for them.

I'm sure he didn't remember, on each of their wedding days, that he was the first to bathe each of these tiny creatures because I was positive I'd drop them. But I remembered.

He taught our daughters how to whistle, snap their fingers, ride their two-wheelers, and march like he'd done in the Air Force. He also gave them values that endure, and a sense of worth that has sustained them.

It wasn't always easy. We all used to joke about how the poor man lived in a harem. Four women. Four sets of mood swings, neurotic worries about hair, clothes and weight. And one steady anchor through all the turbulence of three adolescences and one wife seeking her destiny.

And how the man worried. He worried about their safety, their disappointments, the student government elections lost, the teams they didn't make.

When these daughters left for college, his worrying didn't stop — it escalated. How would they fare on those distant campuses? Would some T-shirted, long-haired sophomore break their hearts before Christmas break?

They never knew how his face lit up when they remembered to call on Sundays, or on his birthday, before cell phones and e-mails, let alone texting, took hold. They never knew how he marked their final exam schedules on HIS calendar.

And then along came the men who would become the husbands of his daughters, the men he hoped would love them as he had, fully and forever.

They never knew how their father prayed, in his own way, for happy endings.

Who else would have become an instant expert on the best,

most waterproof tents for three home weddings? Who else would lose sleep worrying about the outdoor toilets for those weddings?

And who else would gamely walk each of them to their waiting husbands, bravely smiling, on three beautiful June afternoons?

Yes, it was all of this that this father of the brides, who asked nothing in return on those days, gave his daughters.

There are three photos I often turn to in our daughters' individual wedding albums.

They show a man on a dance floor holding a bride in his arms and trying hard to smile for the wedding photographer.

But each time, the look on his face is of mingled joy, pain, and bafflement.

How did it all go by so fast?

Would this new man in her life be good to her?

Would he keep her safe?

The next frame shows a father hugging his daughter, the bride, as she turns and runs to her waiting groom.

Smudged endings and beginnings are etched into those photos.

I study them sometimes, and remember how, after each wedding, we would collapse on the den sofas and just stare at the ceiling.

Neither of us needed to say it: nothing would ever be the same. Each bride was walking into her own life, and symbolically pulling the door shut.

It was just as it should be.

It was time to move on.

And I was the only eyewitness to the father of the brides as he quietly wiped away a tear.

~Sally Friedman

"That's my dad...Director of Homeland Security."

49

The Mommy-Moon

A mother's treasure is her daughter.
~Catherine Pulsifer

*I*t felt like the wedding bells were already ringing the night my only daughter made her memorable midnight call — the one that let us know her boyfriend had finally proposed. Within a matter of days, the date had been set and the event officially scheduled for a short six months away.

As plans progressed, I made several trips from Dallas to St. Louis, where the affair was to take place. We were all on a treadmill running as fast as we could to find a dress, a veil, an organist, a photographer, a florist — you know the list.

Then came a second midnight call. This time, my daughter blurted out that she and her fiancé had decided to take their honeymoon in Italy.

"Wow, that's great!" I responded. "What's more romantic than going with your honey on a honeymoon to Italy?"

The next morning, however, sipping solo on a cup of Earl Grey, I felt a little uneasy. If I was truly joyful about her visions of Venice, why did I lie in bed crying after I hung up the phone? I certainly was not jealous! Was I wishing she would not go? Or was I simply wishing that it were me going on one last trip with my daughter before she moved on to take up space in someone else's heart?

I glanced at the clock. She would have left for her early class already — and I was acting spontaneously — but I reached for the phone anyway, dialed her number, and left a message on the answering machine.

"Hey, sweetie… it's Mom. Just calling to see if maybe the two of us could find some time to go on a mommy-moon before you walk down the aisle. Maybe Chicago? Miracle Mile? Do a little shopping? Toast the future? Just one last trip together? Think about it and call me back… I'm ready if you are!"

The mommy-moon was everything I had expected—and more. Even the female relatives of the family—once they heard about it—got into the act. And at the end of a twelve-hour drive, when I arrived in St. Louis to pick up my daughter, there was a massive cardboard box waiting in her apartment. Addressed to the bride-to-be, the postmark let me know it was from all her aunts and cousins in Tennessee. The instructions on the lower left corner were specific: CONTENTS: One Bridal Party. DO NOT OPEN until you reach Chicago!

The following morning, we laughed, lifted, shoved, and grunted until we had squeezed that enormous box (plus our luggage) into the trunk of the car. Then we pulled out of the drive, took a turn toward the freeway, and headed north to the Windy City. By early evening, we were safe in our hotel room, munching down on a traditional thick-crust Chicago pizza, and watching the sun go down across the lake.

"Okay, time for the bridal shower!" said my daughter. And while she cut through the packing tape and started unloading the box full of goodies, I set up a small table and two chairs in front of the window and got out my camera.

The female relatives from Middle Tennessee had truly outdone themselves, and the two of us oohed and aahed (as brides and mothers do) as we lifted the elegantly wrapped gifts out of the packing paper and arranged them on the table.

Near the bottom of the box, we found a handful of manila envelopes, labeled in the order they were to be opened.

Envelope #1 was full of latex balloons. We split the contents and started huffing, puffing, tying, and tossing the balloons around the room.

Envelope #2 contained two silk corsages, one for the bride and one for the MOB. We pinned them on our jean jackets, baby's breath upward, and welcomed each other to our party.

Envelope #3 was marked GAMES. Inside were three bridal games, two pencils, and three prizes for the winners. (I won a potholder and a small cheese board; my daughter won a packet of recipe cards.)

Envelope #4 revealed a letter to the bride from her Tennessee aunt, who apologized that the whole gang could not join us in Chicago for the bridal shower. She assured us, however, that all their love and best wishes had been tucked in alongside the packages — along with a promise that they would all be in St. Louis to watch her walk down the aisle on her wedding day.

Over the weekend, my daughter and I did pretty much whatever we wanted, whenever we felt like it. We rose early the first day, slept in the next. Stayed on budget in one store, splurged at the next. Ate healthy one meal, pigged out the next.

We shopped the Mile, browsed the back rooms for lingerie sales, and smashed a plate (*Opa!*) at a Greek café — just for the fun of it. We taxied a little, walked a lot, strolled in silence past shop windows, and once — crossing an intersection — she put her arm around my shoulder and whispered, "I love you, Mom." We both knew that this mommy-moon was our last bit of private time — just the two of us — before she would take on her new name and new life. No surprise, then, on the last evening, drifting off the street into the back of an Irish pub, that we found ourselves in tears, listening as a local strummed a guitar and sang a familiar ballad from her childhood.

Next morning, when it came time to leave the hotel — just before heading to the elevator — we kicked aside a few of the balloons that were still on the floor and embraced in the middle of the room. I held my daughter close that day, whispering a prayer in her ear, thanking God for these few treasured days before she moved on from our family to a family of her own. I thanked Him, too, for the twenty-nine years she had blessed me as a mother, and for the joy and laughter she had brought to my world.

One month later, my daughter took her long walk from the back of the church to the altar. The honor fell to her teary-eyed father to present her to the groom, escorting her past row after row of friends and relatives (including those from Tennessee) who had traveled to witness the event.

As they reached the front of the chapel, a family friend began singing the tender words from "O Mio Babbino Caro"—and near the end, precisely on cue, dearest Daddy placed the hand of his beautiful bride into the hand of the handsome groom, and very simply and symbolically gave her away.

I sat in the second row smiling and let him have his moment. After all, in my heart, I had already given her away. And the photos of that event remain preserved in the wedding album for all to see—under the label: "The Mommy-Moon."

~Charlotte A. Lanham

50

Something Old, Something New

Something old, something new, something borrowed, something blue.
~Old English Rhyme

I woke long before the summer sun kissed the world good morning. I was unusually calm considering I was the quintessential worrier—the poster child for Murphy's Law. But on that Saturday in July, my daughter's wedding day, I was blessed with peace amid the nuptial chaos. From beginning to end, the carefully planned details were joined together in holy matrimony, which God let nothing put asunder.

And then it happened. Sunday evening, the "wedding high" came crashing down like lightning in a sudden summer thunderstorm. What in the world went wrong? She'd had the something old, something new, something borrowed, but now... I was the something blue. No warnings were posted in bridal magazines, no therapists present at bridal shows. Not even *The Best of Martha Stewart Living: Weddings* had prepared me for the hollowness I felt. My baby girl would be living across the river instead of down the hall. Just a walk down the aisle and a couple of "I dos" had left me alone in a home full of testosterone.

The sobfests I held in my daughter's honor outnumbered the days of her honeymoon. My first trip to the grocery store spawned a slight meltdown. I'd never have to buy low-acid, no-pulp orange juice again, and I could roll my cart right past the chocolate Pop-Tarts without hesitation. The laundry also had me sniffling. There was no need to mark the socks with a K; the only girl socks left were mine. I'd wander into her bedroom just to smell her. I even held her wedding gown up to me and stood in front of the mirror. I guess I was hoping to see her looking back.

After almost a month of my moping, one of the boys let me have it. "Geez, Mom, she only got married. She didn't die." His words were an alarm clock jolting me from the darkness. I realized our relationship hadn't died; it had merely changed. The ties that bound us were not broken, but stretched enough to accommodate growth. My head had to convince my heart that it was okay that she'd grown… from my child into a woman and a wife. I just needed to quit wallowing and grow up, too.

I forged ahead with my pre-wedding plans to turn her bedroom into a scrapbooking room, allowing myself one display of baby-to-bride pictures arranged on a bulletin board. Not too shrine ish, I thought. As I busied the days creating a wedding scrapbook, contentment began to seep into the emptiness. Life seemed to bloom around me again. Although I managed to climb out of my poor-me pit, her absence was still evident; there are certain things you just need another girl for. Lord knows, those boys would never know "which shoes look best with this outfit."

In time, across the river didn't seem quite so far, and grown we have… into a mother and grandmother, bearing new ties to expand and mature. And if one day her daughter is standing at the back of the church, clutching her father's arm and waiting to walk down the aisle, I pray she'll be blessed with the same peace and joy I received from heaven on that perfect summer day.

~Lela Foos

Here Comes the Bride

Chapter 6

The Wedding Party

A happy bridesmaid makes a happy bride.

~*Alfred Tennyson*, The Bridesmaid

51

Not Pretty in Pink

Rich colors are typical of a rich nature.
~Van Day Truex, Interiors, Character, and Color

Pretty in pink? Not this maid of honor. It was bad enough I had been dragged kicking and screaming to the bridal salon to pick out a dress. Now the saleswoman was trying to fob off some pink organza extravaganza on me. Ha!

At nineteen, I knew what I didn't like. And I didn't like pink. Or any other pastel color. Nor was I afraid to make my views known, quite loudly and repeatedly if I had to, which I obviously had to do with this saleswoman since she wasn't getting the message.

My sister, the blushing bride, had already picked out her dress, and so had my mother. That just left me. Having said no to ten dresses in succession, each one more hideous than the next, I could see my mother losing her patience with me. She was giving me the look that said: "If you don't pick something soon, I'll pick it for you."

I finally deigned to try on a dress that was marginally less repulsive than the other ones the saleswoman had trotted out. But when I came out of the dressing room to model it, the saleswoman made her fatal mistake.

"Oh," she said, practically wiping a tear from her eye, "this is perfect. You look so sweet."

"Sweet?" I repeated, in a sugary voice that had my mother and sister cringing in their chairs because they knew what would be coming next. "It makes me look sweet?" I repeated. The saleswoman nodded, thinking she had wrapped up a sale.

That's when I swooped in for the kill. "Then it's obviously the wrong dress for me because," I paused for a moment as I looked her in the eye, "I don't do sweet."

By this point, the saleswoman had finally figured that out. "Oh," she said in a small voice. "What kind of look are you going for?"

That was the problem. Although I knew what I didn't want, I wasn't totally sure what I did want. But it wasn't going to be pink. I said the first thing that came to mind. I said, "I want a brown dress."

The saleswoman looked at my mother, my mother looked at my sister, and my sister looked at me. "But you're so young to wear brown and…" the saleswoman began. She glanced at the expression on my face, and the rest of the sentence faded off into oblivion.

For a minute, nobody said anything. Then there was a collective sigh as they all realized the only way they were going to get me into any dress was to go along with me. If that meant a brown dress, well, it meant a brown dress.

The saleswomen retreated to the back of the store and returned carrying huge folds of material. She took off the plastic protector and unveiled this latest creation. And it was brown. But not just any brown. It was a deep rich brown taffeta with an iridescence that changed colors as the light hit it.

Victorian in style, the dress had a high collar with a small ruffle that was repeated on each cuff. The pleated bodice ended with a simple band at the waistline. From the waist down, the skirt billowed out. It was a dress you read about in a storybook.

I wanted to hate it. I tried to hate it. I really tried. But the moment I saw the dress, I fell in love with it. When I put it on and stood in front of the mirror, I felt like a princess. Even wearing my sneakers underneath the skirt couldn't take away from the sensation of stepping out of my usual jeans-and-T-shirt world into a world of elegance and grace.

I turned this way and that, peering over my shoulder in the three-way mirror, looking for a flaw. The dress moved with me, making a faint rustling sound. I found myself standing up straighter, taking smaller steps. Even smiling a little.

No one said a word. I could feel everyone holding their collective breaths. Waiting. Then I said those three little words that made it all worthwhile. I said, "I'll take it." And I did.

Oh, there were fittings that I grumbled about. New shoes to be bought and dyed. A visit to the hairdresser. But none of that could lessen the thrill I felt every time I looked at the dress or heard the slight rustling sound as I played with the material. Not that I would have ever admitted it.

The night of the wedding arrived. My sister, as befitting the bride, looked properly radiant in her beautiful white wedding gown. My mother looked lovely in her deep burgundy dress, and my father beamed in his matching cummerbund.

And me? I felt like Cinderella at the ball. I flitted around all evening, talking to people, dancing, and smiling. For one evening, I was transformed from my everyday, ordinary, nineteen-year-old self. The transformation was so complete that many of my parents' friends who had known me for years didn't recognize me.

For years after the wedding, the dress hung in a closet in my parents' home, never to be worn again. For a while, I would run my hand through the fabric, reliving the feeling I had when I put it on. Then it got pushed farther and farther into the back of the closet. A few years after I moved out, my mother asked me what I wanted to do with the dress.

"Give it away," I said, in my usual non-sentimental way. "I have no use for it."

So she did.

But every so often, I take a look at the small wedding album that I have tucked away in one of my drawers, under a pile of scarves. I peer closely at the luminous girl wearing the brown dress and remind myself that I'm still her.

~Harriet Cooper

52

Flood Damage

Filthy water cannot be washed.
~African Proverb

Six weeks before our daughter Patti's wedding to Jeff, we took the three bridesmaids' dresses to show to her future mother-in-law, Gisele.

"A friend loaned us the dresses," I said. "She was generous enough to let us borrow them this weekend to show you, and she said we could keep them until after the wedding."

"They're lovely." Gisele caressed the glimmering satin. She glanced out the window. "It's drizzling outside. Why don't you leave the dresses here where they'll stay dry? You don't want to risk getting them wet."

We agreed, for we were grateful to the friend who let us borrow the beautiful dresses. We sure didn't want to stain them.

Patti and I carried the long gowns carefully, watching to make sure the hems didn't drag on the floor. We followed Gisele into her bedroom. She was crowded for space in her mobile home and directed us to lay the dresses over the back of a chair.

"Leave them here until you come back for dinner tomorrow night," she said. "They'll be all right."

Wrong! The dresses were not all right, and we never returned for the dinner Gisele had planned.

While we slept that Saturday night, the flood of 1984 swept through Tulsa, Oklahoma. Gisele awakened to water flowing through the mobile home she shared with her son, Jeff. She waded to Jeff's bedroom to waken him. Frail and cancer-stricken, she couldn't get out on her own. Jeff carried her through the flooded trailer park to safety.

The next afternoon, authorities let us back into the trailer park with Jeff and Gisele. Jeff opened the door, and we stepped precariously around Gisele's overturned china hutch. She gasped at the sight of her beloved dishes, many of them shattered. The refrigerator lay on its side. The table of wedding invitations sat where it had been the night before, but it bore evidence of rising to the ceiling on the floodwaters. When the flood receded, the table had returned to the floor, still upright. The invitations remained in place, slightly water-damaged but not ruined.

What about those beautiful bridesmaids' dresses — our borrowed dresses? We dreaded picking our way over debris to the bedroom to see what had become of them. Gisele led the way, and she wrung her hands when she opened the bedroom door.

"Oh, dear!" she cried.

The dresses lay where we'd left them, still draped over her chair. Mud dripped from the delicate blue satin onto the floor. Heartsick, Patti fell into my arms.

"Mother, what are we going to do?"

I didn't have an answer. How could I possibly return home and tell our friend what happened? Unwilling to leave the dresses in Gisele's ruined bedroom, we dropped the sodden mess into trash bags and hauled them to Patti's apartment.

Dry cleaners weren't open, for it was Sunday of Memorial Day weekend, and people all over Tulsa were trying to deal with their flood-ravaged city. If we waited until Monday, the mud would have completely stained the satin. Patti and I had only one hope of salvaging the dresses — a slim hope, but we had to try. We dumped them into the bathtub and began rinsing off the mud. She and I took turns all afternoon on our knees, leaning over the tub, rinsing and gently scrubbing away the filth. Our backs ached, our arms hurt, and we were tired of the stench of mud in our nostrils. But the mud washed out, and the blue satin began to shine again. We hung the dresses over the bathtub, and they dried without a trace of the flood to mar their beauty.

Six weeks later, Patti and Jeff stood in the church chapel (which had also been flooded) and exchanged their wedding vows. The slightly watermarked invitations had gone out as planned. The bridesmaids were lovely in the blue satin dresses, with not so much as a stain to show what they'd been through.

Each of us has times when we're like those mud-stained dresses. We get ourselves into situations that appear hopeless. But once we wash the mud away, we uncover the underlying beauty that is still there.

~LeAnn Campbell

53

The Legacy of a Little Dress

What we once enjoyed and deeply loved we can never lose,
for all that we love deeply becomes a part of us.
~Helen Keller

I remember the day so clearly: standing in a fabric store in Florida with my future mother-in-law, Mozelle. We were shopping for fabric for the flower girl dress for my wedding. Mozelle was an accomplished seamstress and would be making the dress for her granddaughter, my future niece, Annette. My wedding would take place on September 3, 1977, during Labor Day weekend. The wedding colors were to be burnt orange and chocolate brown. The bridesmaids were going to be wearing long chiffon burnt orange dresses, and the groomsmen would be wearing tuxes of dark chocolate brown. Our three-year-old nephew, Will, would be the ring bearer and would wear a miniature beige tuxedo to match my future husband, Clay's. So, the only decision left to be made was the color and style of the flower girl dress.

"I was thinking of a simple, sleeveless, empire-waist dress with maybe some ribbon the color of the bridesmaid dresses at the waist," I said.

She replied: "I have just the perfect pattern! I have made several dresses for Annette from it, and they come out beautifully. We can make it in any fabric and use any ribbon for trim."

That day, we decided on a soft beige fabric and lining for the dress. It would be a simple, sleeveless dress with an empire waist and a burnt orange ribbon at the waist encased in beige lace. This was a special time for us as a future mother- and daughter-in-law working on the dress. When the dress was finished, she sewed a label in the dress, "Handmade by Grandma." We didn't know it at the time, but this would be one of her last sewing projects. Shortly after completing the dress, she began to develop the signs of Alzheimer's, and a few short years later, our family was robbed of the gifts of this lovely and talented woman.

The day of my wedding, my little niece was a perfect flower girl in her pretty dress with her blond hair cut in a pixie. She took her job as a flower girl very seriously and was especially attentive throughout the wedding ceremony. I remember her diligently picking up and straightening the train of my gown. Her mother, my sister-in-law, Anne, had coached her well in the proper duties of a flower girl.

Now, thirty-three years later, my daughter Natalie was planning her wedding. Her wedding would take place on October 30th. As fate would have it, she chose the same colors for her wedding as mine: burnt orange and brown. Only now, the modern term for this shade of orange is paprika.

Her choice for a flower girl was my great-niece, Bailey, the daughter of Annette, my flower girl. On the day we were driving home from shopping for her wedding dress, we began to discuss the type of flower girl dress she wanted for Bailey.

"I want it to be something simple, like what Annette wore in your wedding." Then she added, "Mom, do we still have the dress? I wonder if Bailey could wear it."

I tried to recall when I had last seen the dress. We had moved to Alabama twelve years earlier and I hoped that we still had it. It seemed like I remembered seeing it in a container with other keepsakes from my children's childhood. When I returned home, I began to search in earnest for the little dress. I located the plastic container and knelt down and opened it. At first glance, I didn't see it, but about halfway down, I saw the "Handmade by Grandma" label. So far so good, but what would the rest of it look like? Would it be in any condition to wear in another wedding? As I held it up, shook it out, and carefully inspected it, I was amazed. It looked just like it did on the day of my wedding thirty-three years ago. There was not a blemish on it.

I sat down to think about the remarkable condition of the little dress and how it came to be in my possession. It was because of my sister-in law, Anne, Annette's mother. She had saved the dress for me. I thought of Anne. She had lost her battle with a devastating illness several years before, and was no longer with us. I missed her. I remembered how we used to tease her about being a pack rat, but I am so glad that she was. She had a knack for seeing the intrinsic value of things. Most flower girl dresses are used as costumes and become torn and tattered. But this little dress was carefully preserved and passed on to me. Later, in a special family ceremony, Natalie gave Bailey a gift box containing the dress and asked: "Bailey, will you be the flower girl in my wedding like your mom was in my mom's wedding?" And Bailey said, "Yes!" She excitedly opened the box, put on the dress, and danced around the room just like her mother had thirty-three years ago. It fit perfectly and only needed to be hemmed since Annette was five when she wore the dress and Bailey would be three.

The day of the wedding arrived, and as we gathered in the bridal room before the ceremony, I looked in wonder at my beautiful, radiant daughter surrounded by this wonderful group of women. Her bridesmaids were there. Some were from childhood, high school, and college, and also her new sister-in-law, Caroline. Annette, Anne's daughter, my former flower girl, now a beautiful young mother herself, presented Natalie with a lovely monogrammed garter made from the hem of the flower girl dress after it was altered. And smiling, but choking back the tears, she said: "Natalie, I have a gift for you from my mom. She wanted you to have this sixpence to wear in your shoe on your wedding day." At that time, all of us lovingly remembered Anne, Grandma Shearer, and my grandmother Hazel who were all definitely there with us in spirit in the room.

There were other special women there in the room, too, like

my mother, Jane, who has always been a special part of Natalie's life. My sister-in-law, Evelyn, a seamstress like her mother, continued the legacy and gave Natalie a beautiful handmade lace handkerchief to carry down the aisle. It brought back memories of how her mother had made the flower girl dress for my wedding, so many years ago. Some women in the room had held my daughter as a baby, some had grown up with her, and others were just coming into her life, like her new mother-in-law, Judy, who already loved her as a daughter. These women will always be a very special part of my daughter's life.

All the women in our lives mold and shape us. And they always leave us a legacy. Like beautiful, multi-colored threads woven into the tapestry of our lives, they are forever part of us.

~Tanya Shearer

54

How Bad Skin Made Me a Better Maid of Honor

A woman seldom asks advice before she has bought her wedding clothes.
~Joseph Addison

Two months before my big sister's wedding day, I checked myself out in the bathroom mirror and spotted a giant zit. I opened a compact and covered it up. It felt poetic. I'd been covering my feelings in much the same way.

It wasn't any of the usual sibling-getting-married discontent—worrying that you'll never find your own true love; being forced to use your Beijing vacation fund for a Rhode Island wedding; wearing a bridesmaid dress that would make an Olsen twin look fat. Those kinds of complaints are just byproducts of the fact that weddings can throw a well-honed sibling dynamic out of whack like nothing else can.

Jill, who was thirty-one and marrying a great guy, never competed with me for parental attention in a significant way because, besides having parents who are diplomatic to the point of obsession (even now, we're each given the exact same number of Christmas gifts), our personalities were always opposite—appealing to parts of our parents' psyches that the other hadn't made a bid for. We differentiated, and it worked.

Jill was the tomboy, and I was the cheerleading, clothes-obsessed girly-girl. This fundamental distinction allowed us to be more amused than aggressive toward each other, even though she was just three years older than me. Plus, it was nice to have an expert to consult when I learned to whack a field hockey ball, or she got dressed for a date.

But with the wedding, she was being temporarily pushed onto my turf. Sure, I expected her to put a toe over the line—she did have to throw a big, dressy party—but I also expected her to leave much of the planning to me.

Besides not being sufficiently ladylike, she was engaged at Christmas, moved from Virginia to Colorado for her fiancé's job a few weeks later, and would be married in our childhood vacation town of Sea Isle City, New Jersey, in September. This conveniently left me with a lot of legwork back on the east coast.

I took the bus from my place in Brooklyn to Jersey, met my mom and aunts, who drove up from our home in Philly, and found a beach-front location. I asked one New York friend to hand-assemble invitations while another agreed to take photos. Frantic to prove myself indispensable, I went around calling Jill the anti-Bridezilla—a blasé bride-to-be. Thank God she had poor, organized, wedding-loving me.

But by May, Jill had settled into her new house and job, and took hold of the planning reins. She found a florist and made a creative, casual seating plan. Then she bought a dress without consulting me.

She called me at the magazine where I worked with the news. I took a deep breath and asked, "Are you at Macy's? Bloomingdale's?"

"I'm at Ross," she chirped.

I cupped my palm over the receiver in case a co-worker walked by.

"Ross?" I hissed. "Like 'I got it at Ross,' the discount store?"

"Yes!" she yelled back. She had purchased a shin-length ("tea-length," I corrected) white sundress for twenty dollars.

"As a backup?" I asked.

"No!" she laughed. "You know I hate shopping. This is it."

I made my final bid for power a few days later.

We were on the phone going over the budget. The only things left to plan were hair and make-up. Hair was too risky a job for an amateur, but make-up… Jill wouldn't recognize herself if we hired a professional, but if we left it to her she'd bring a tube of ChapStick and call it a day.

I was desperate for a new title, so I volunteered. All hail the make-up artist!

I basked in the new arrangement for a few weeks, telling everyone that I was doing my sister's make-up for her wedding, but made zero preparations. This is when my pimple rose up like a gross red oracle. After that first morning, it prospered, founding a colony of Petri dish-grade acne.

It ruined my imaginary credentials. In real life, no one would hire a make-up artist with bad skin. Worse, I'd soon be standing in front of lots of people with a face full of blemishes.

I went to see a dermatologist.

"Stress and hormones both play a part," she said. Great, I'm regressing, I thought.

"Is there a type of make-up you recommend?" I sighed. "The wedding's only a few weeks away."

After filling a prescription for antibiotics, I went straight to Sephora to find Laura Mercier's "Secret Camouflage" concealer.

I was having trouble choosing a shade for myself when I thought of Jill, who's a darker complexion than me with glossy brown hair, a contrast to my dirty blond.

What shade would I put on her? And why don't I know this already?

For the next three weeks, I took my antibiotics and studied my new tome — *Bobbi Brown Makeup Manual* — learning the difference between corrector and concealer, and that the right shade of each, blended properly, can cover all manner of sins.

By Jill's wedding day, my face was almost back to normal, and my focus was where it should be. I had a foolproof plan for her flawless, natural look.

She called my kit of brushes and pro-grade compacts crazy, then rolled her eyes but obeyed as I asked her to look this way and that while applying eye shadow. When she puckered so I could sweep bronzer below her cheekbones, her two best friends and bridesmaids, who were watching, hooted with loud laughter.

None of us had witnessed my sister making such an unselfconsciously dainty gesture in our lives. Without a word, their infectious giggles rolled over both of us until we were crying. I tried to stifle it and to scold Jill so she wouldn't smudge anything, but she grinned and stuck her tongue out at me, like she'd been doing forever.

Suddenly, I felt sure that my status with Jill was solid. All my bossiness with this wedding wasn't quite because I was jealous, or even feeling left out. I just wanted to make sure she still needed me.

And she did. Who else would she make that face at? When I looked back up at her, whether it was the make-up or my state of mind, she had transformed into the perfect bride.

I was changed as well, stepping into a sincerely supportive role and staring awe-struck while my sister welcomed everyone we know into her new life. As guest after guest told her how beautiful she looked, I completely forgot to take credit.

~Wendy Toth

The Bridesmaid Dress

A friend is one of the nicest things you can have,
and one of the best things you can be.
~Douglas Pagels

Poofy, purple, petticoat, parasol — just a few P words to describe my bridesmaid dresses. In 1998, not one of those P words would be associated with fashionable, let alone wearable. This story explains how my bridesmaids became the most grateful bridesmaids on the planet. All because of a dress choice.

"I love the dress," my maid of honor said. Not an uncommon sentiment, true or not, uttered in dress shops around the world when the bridesmaid dress is finally unveiled to the eager group of women. My bridesmaids were no different except that I knew their feelings were heartfelt.

I love purple, and I love poofy dresses. You should see my prom picture. I don't know how my dress and my date fit into the picture, let alone the car. (Maybe that's why he rented a limousine.) My initial choice of a bridesmaid dress should have been no surprise to my dear friends. What they didn't know, however, was that the dress was a practical joke.

I found a local costume shop and a friend to accompany me to the store. I searched rows of costumes to find the perfect dress. Little Bo Peep, Cinderella, Scarlett O'Hara and many others were represented. Between the petticoats I found it — a lavender southern belle dress. If you aren't familiar with the style, let me enlighten you. The skirt portion of the dress looks like a bell. The hoops and layers of petticoats help the bell keep its shape. When you walk, no chime sounds, but the forward and backward motion of the skirt makes a bit of a whooshing sound. The lavender taffeta shimmered through the white lace that covered the entire dress. The sleeves puffed over the shoulders like a mushroom top. Elastic lace gave a snug fit on the upper arm. However, my outfit was not yet complete. White lace gloves complimented the lace overlay on the dress. A gaudy purple parasol was the finishing touch. The shop clerk allowed me to take a picture when I explained the purpose of my visit. My smile for the camera widened beyond the scope of the lens.

I sent a copy of the picture to each friend through e-mail and waited.

"You've got mail," rang out from my computer. Susan was the first to reply. "It's lovely. I especially like how the lace gloves compliment the lace on the dress." Stacy sent a short reply. "So glad you found the right dress. The wedding will be great." Deanna complimented the color. Denise found a polite way to suggest the parasol might overshadow the dress. Sandy didn't say much, but didn't complain either. Each e-mail brought me great delight and barrels of laughter.

After a day or two of only positive replies about the most hideous, gaudy, purple, poofy dress anyone would have to wear, my laughter turned to tears of joy. My friends loved me enough to wear a hideous, gaudy, purple, poofy dress while holding a parasol with lace-gloved hands in public. I had to release them from their hidden torment.

We met at the bridal shop a few days after the initial e-mail. I thanked them for their kind comments and pulled the real brides-maid dress from behind a rack. It was a purplish blue (I had to have purple), flowing tank dress with optional shawl to cover their shoulders. Their wide-eyed faces turned into smiles of relief. Their misery ended. Those bridesmaids not at the store were immediately called to relieve their tension.

Although the chosen dress wasn't perfect for everyone's taste either, it didn't matter. No bride can please all her bridesmaids with the choice of the dress. Through my practical joke, I came to know that I had chosen my bridesmaids well. The day of my wedding, I was surrounded by supportive, loving, lifelong friends all wearing my favorite color—purple.

~Debbie Wong

Reprinted by permission of Off the Mark
and Mark Parisi ©2000

56

No Boundaries

It seems to me that people have vast potential. Most people can do extraordinary things if they have the confidence or take the risks.
~Philip Adams

When I was told that my three-year-old son, Paul, had autism, I felt like he had been given a death sentence. I enrolled him in a preschool where he was provided with an educational assistant. The teacher, Miss Nancy, was a lively redhead who dearly loved her class. She kept an eye out for Paul, and he found a special place in her heart. She knew instinctively that there was no limit to what Paul could do.

He quickly jumped from saying nothing to countless two- and three-word phrases. Though still shy and withdrawn, he became comfortable enough in his preschool to participate along with his classmates. At the end of the year, Nancy held a graduation ceremony for her little friends, complete with little white caps. As I watched Paul trying to fall in line with the rest of his class, copying their actions when he wasn't sure what he was supposed to do, my heart ached. Things that came so easily for the others still required major effort on his part. He did, however, graduate from preschool.

After the ceremony, I hugged Nancy tightly. "Thanks so much for everything," I whispered through tears.

She grabbed me by both arms and said firmly, "He's going to be just fine."

I stared back at her intense brown eyes as my own widened. No one had ever told me that before. For almost two years, I had felt like I was drowning in a sea of despair, fighting for every breath, fighting to find my child. Nancy had observed Paul's progress and knew how far he had come in such a short time. She had seen enough four-year-olds to know what she was talking about, and I trusted her completely. It felt like she had thrown me a life preserver that I never thought I'd see.

The following summer, Daphne, my youngest sister, asked if Paul could be the ring bearer at her wedding. I wondered if it would be too much for him, but Daphne and he were close, and I didn't want to disappoint her. So I sat down with him and wrote out his instructions.

1. Walk down the carpet toward Andrew (Daphne's fiancé)
2. Stay beside the flower girl while you walk
3. Give Andrew the ring
4. Walk back to the front row to sit with Mommy

Paul read over the words a few times. When I practiced with him, I held up four fingers, and he and I would say together his four instructions, one at a time. I showed him a wedding video and focused on the ring bearer's performance. Paul had an excellent memory, but could he put it into action?

The night of the rehearsal finally came. Paul was a little hesitant and somewhat uncomfortable standing beside Anna, who was Andrew's niece and a stranger to Paul. When they walked down the aisle, Anna walked slowly. Paul walked quickly, as if in a hurry to get it over with. As a result, he reached the front alone. I laughed nervously, surrounded by relatives and some of Daphne's friends, who weren't familiar with Paul's condition.

"That was very good, Paul, but we're not racing, honey," I said, stooping down to look him in the eye as I always did when I wanted to make sure he was listening. "Take your time, okay? Stay beside Anna next time."

Daphne's wedding day was picture-perfect. The sky was bright blue, there was a slight summer breeze, and Paul didn't protest about wearing a vest and tie. Still, I hesitated before leaving him with Daphne and Dad in the church vestibule.

"He'll be great," Daphne said, as I kissed her on the cheek, and she felt my tears.

I sat on the end of the front pew, staring back down the aisle past more than two hundred faces. I was so happy for Daphne, but so scared for Paul.

The last bridesmaid had come to the front, and Anna began her walk. Daphne gently nudged Paul to join little Anna, and I started to cry. I expected too much, I told myself. He can't do this. How could we put this pressure on him?

Paul glanced behind him at Daphne's glowing face. Then he solemnly matched Anna stride for stride, not too fast, not too slow. Perfect. The sun shone through the stained-glass windows onto his handsome face. He walked, straight and tall, up to Andrew, offered him the pillow from which Andrew removed Daphne's wedding ring, and then solemnly walked back to sit with me. By then, I could hardly see through my tears of joy for Paul's accomplishment.

Whenever Paul has a setback, I can still see Nancy's piercing eyes and hear her encouraging words. Besides knowing his multiplication tables, acing every spelling test and possessing a superior IQ, he has the purest, biggest heart I've ever had the pleasure to come in contact with. He really does have unlimited potential. He's just fine.

~Jayne Thurber-Smith

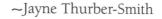

57

The Folly of Vanity

Without vanity, without coquetry, without curiosity, in a word, without the
fall, woman would not be woman. Much of her grace is in her frailty.
~Victor Hugo

*I*t seemed like a great idea at the time. We gathered at the bride's
apartment, seven ladies in long, flowing gowns that laced up the
back. We took turns pulling each other's stays (corset lacing to
those unfamiliar with historical lingo).

The tightening was subtle. "Is that snug enough?" led to, "I think
I can cinch it in a little more." And, finally, "Wow, girl, look at your
tiny waist."

After a few rounds of pulling, there we stood, a bevy of lasses
with reduced waists, exaggerated busts, hips, and, of course, little
room to breathe. But vanity had stealthily crept into our midst, and
though I couldn't bend over or even sit down, I felt like a beautiful
damsel. I'm pretty sure my voice took on a southern belle drawl.

I looked in the mirror and delighted in my pretty dress and va
va voom curves. I was Scarlett O'Hara, Marie Antoinette, and the
infamous Gibson Girl of bygone days!

About an hour into the tight lacing, I tried to eat a snack, but
my confining attire denied me any sustenance, not even a cracker.
Fortunately, I could drink, and so a margarita on ice slid down
nicely.

As the wedding hour approached, I noticed a stinging ache down
my spine along with the growing compression of my now heaving

bosom as the bottom of my lungs began to fill with fluid. My quads throbbed with lactic acid from my ill advised pre-wedding workout, and my hairpins felt like daggers stuck into my head. My feet were so swollen I could barely walk.

As I lined up to walk down the aisle, I trembled at the length of what seemed like a never-ending runner. My husband, the wedding pastor, smiled at me like a warm beacon. And guided by his big, goofy smile, I tottered toward him, semi-delirious in pain but determined to appear graceful and elegant to the large crowd assembled.

After a lovely ceremony, more pictures, and millions of seconds of searing pain, I finally sat down at the dinner table in a heap. But sitting proved even more restrictive. An old song played in the background. It was a catchy dinner-music tune, and in my state of pain-induced euphoria, I swayed to the crooner's voice. Strangely enough, it sounded like the word "salad" was being repeated over and over. Then again, it could have been my starving belly crying out for food.

"I didn't know they had such cute songs about salad," I announced to the table.

My girlfriend, Krista, also a corseted bridesmaid, but clearly retaining a few more brain cells than me, shouted, "Did you say 'salad'? It's called 'Solid as a Rock.'"

The table erupted in laughter, myself included, at the error. But then along with my laughter came a blackish sort of envelopment. The table, the guffaws… it all began to fade as I teetered on the edge of fainting.

Indeed, I was a damsel in distress.

My friend, Katherine, recognizing my flushed face and dilated pupils, quickly steered me toward the ladies' room where she tore at my laces and opened up my lungs for some much-needed air.

Returning to the table, I sheepishly sat down and inhaled my dinner. Now moderately laced, I was able to eat, dance, laugh, and enjoy a big piece of strawberry cream wedding cake without the restrictive garment of my own folly. (It wasn't too much later before Krista was begging me to let her loose, too.)

I learned an interesting lesson that day. Vanity is subtly deceptive.

I believed the corset to be glamorous, romantic, and whimsical, but in truth, I found it to be agonizing.

I should know better by now than to be duped by another promise of pretty... But then again, "The LORD knoweth the thoughts of man, that they are vanity" (Psalm 94:11 KJV).

Someone up high sure has got my number.

~Samantha Keller

58

A Wedding Gone to the Dogs

I think we are drawn to dogs because they are the uninhibited creatures we might be if we weren't certain we knew better.
~George Bird Evans, Troubles with Bird Dogs

My brother-in-law and his fiancée were getting married in a beautiful park in upstate New York. Their wedding plans were a little different from most couples, to say the least. They arranged to have their two dogs, Sadie and Clarence, attired in wedding garb. Our daughters, then six and eight, were asked to escort the dogs down a narrow walkway covered in rose petals to the waiting bride and groom, who would be standing inside a pristine gazebo.

The wedding day arrived, and things seemed to be off to a good start as Sadie, draped in a gown of flowers, sauntered down the aisle led by our younger daughter. She took a seat in the front row as Sadie, her tongue hanging out of the side of her mouth, obediently situated herself beside the radiant bride. Impressed guests nodded happily.

Next came our older daughter leading a tuxedo-clad Clarence down the aisle. As Clarence got closer and closer to his master, his eyes focused on Sadie as she sat staring in his direction. Before our daughter knew what was happening, Clarence broke free, charging toward his canine bride-to-be faster than a bull released from a bullpen. Reaching Sadie, Clarence tenderly pressed his nose against

Sadie's. The wedding guests gasped in unison. The bride and groom exchanged anxious glances while the minister attempted to take control.

"Friends, originally we were all invited here today to witness the union of two special human beings in Holy Matrimony. But as we all know, life is full of unexpected surprises. Surprise can be a good thing. Marriage should be filled with unexpected surprises, as Sadie and Clarence have shown us today. So, let's admit that this wedding has gone to the dogs... and have a doggone good time!"

The air filled with joyful laughter as my brother-in-law and his fiancée exchanged wedding vows and kisses. At their feet, Sadie and Clarence looked on.

~Mary Z. Smith

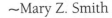

"Hey, I thought this was OUR wedding!"

Reprinted by permission of
Stephanie Piro ©2011

Decisions, Decisions

Interestingly, young people don't come to you for advice.
Especially the ones who are related to you.
~Meryl Streep

My youngest sister is getting married. That's why I'm flipping through the end of the rack where the size XL bridesmaid dresses are hanging. I'm a large-size person on a good day, and these days I'm eight months pregnant with my third child. That just makes the task of finding an appropriate dress all the more daunting. But that's what happens when you get tapped for the "honor" of being a bridesmaid—again.

Luckily, my sister is a very fashionable person. She not only reads *Vogue* magazine, she marks the pages with things she wants to buy. More importantly, she didn't throw her fashion sense out the window when it came time to choose bridesmaid dresses. There were not going to be layers of pink tulle or deep purple satin embellished with bows to draw attention to the hips. Debbie issued the most practical, flattering edict possible—our choice of any long black dress.

"Oh, you'll be able to wear it again" has been said about every bridesmaid dress since Wilma Flintstone told Betty she would get a lot of use out of that off-the-shoulder wooly mammoth sheath. But with a black dress, it might actually be true. This might be a dress that could be flattering. So along with all the other plans and preparations, the search for a dress goes on.

My mother's goal throughout the entire prenuptial process has been to get as many vital decisions settled as quickly as possible, in good taste, without unnecessary input from the "never been on a budget in her life" bride. That's why I was surprised at the list I saw on my parents' kitchen table. It was a proposed contract from a local caterer outlining possibilities for the wedding menu.

In the stapled packet of seven pages, each page spelled out more and more elaborate, elegant presentations. The first page included basic hors d'oeuvres like mini hot dogs with mustard. By page four, the choices included a personal chef creating your choice of pasta in direct competition with a Chinese food station of steamed dumplings and egg rolls. Page seven promised a parade of waiters in tall white toques, marching in with flaming hand-carved filets. Next to each item on the lists, someone had written "Yes" or "No."

"What's this list?" I asked my mother. "Is this the food you're thinking of having? Who wrote yes next to individually prepared chocolate soufflés?" I asked, as I waved the pages in front of my mother's face. I wasn't exactly jealous. I just wanted some idea of the extravaganza we were headed for.

"Oh, that's just Debbie's checklist," my mother explained, dismissing the entire scenario with a wave of her hand. "She thinks that anything less than twenty-seven choices doesn't offer guests enough variety."

On all these topics—wedding dresses, food, flowers—I have proved to be a source of unwanted, out-of-date advice. I got married twenty-five years ago—before video cameras were invented. My bridesmaids were my younger sisters who were still in high school. They wore matching pale pink gowns that I chose because I got married in August, and that's the month when my sisters are always blond and tan.

I don't know why my old fogey advice should count for anything, but I feel compelled to keep offering it. I'm the oldest child in our family, and I always saw myself as Marcia Brady. Now it's clear I'm Florence Henderson.

Every time my sister fills me in on the detail that is her obsession du jour—whether it will be mixed spring flowers in the bouquets or just roses; pastel mints or hand-dipped chocolates—I want to tell her that her wedding will be fabulous no matter what kind of candy she chooses. No one will remember the mints, least of all her. What she will remember is that her wedding day is the start of a new life together. Their wedding will be an amazing, exciting, emotional, exhausting day that signals a new beginning. It's a big decision. A grown-up commitment. But maybe it's too scary to focus on that when you're the bride-to-be. That's why she's concentrating on the mints.

In keeping with her usual sense of style, the wedding dress my sister chose was nothing short of spectacular. Debbie has spent the months since she got engaged carefully studying the pages of every bridal magazine in the world. Not content with *Modern Bride*, she read *Elle Marriage* and *Bridal Glory*. She clipped photos from *Young Bride* and *Not-So-Young Bride* and cross-filed them with clips from *Sexy You!* Then, armed with a hanging file folder, she marched into a local bridal salon to test the waters.

Maybe it was because my mother and I were trailing along in her wake, but the saleswoman quickly sized us up and pulled out the big guns—the designer gowns from the Rapture of Love collection pictured in the clippings clutched in my sister's French manicured hand. For my sister, who is a size 6, trying on the sample gowns was a flattering, fairy-tale experience. The first thing the saleswoman did was put Debbie's hair up in a loose bun and fasten a double strand of fake pearls around her neck. This immediately made her look glamorous and different. Then, she brought out various headpieces and veils, each one more beautiful and bridal than the last. The accessories made every low-cut, off-the-shoulder gown look spectacular. The worn beige carpet and dusty crystal chandelier of the bridal store faded in the background as Debbie stood on the platform in front of a three-way mirror looking like a fairy princess, more beautiful than any magazine ad she had saved.

For my mother and me, the sight of Debbie in a wedding gown conjured up a jumble of feelings. Watching my youngest sister model a cream-colored satin wedding gown was an emotional experience.

I expected my mom to cry—and she did—right after she gave the saleswoman a thumbs-up and mouthed the words, "She's out of our house!" But I didn't expect to be moved myself, just seeing my little sister swathed in satin. This is the sister who used to wear braces, who painted the names of favorite rock groups on her bedroom wall, and until very recently, devoted an entire wire cart to her nail polish and cosmetics collection.

How could she suddenly look like a princess just by trying on a dress? But she did.

I have wonderful memories of my own wedding. When I look at the photos now—after I recover from the shock of how young we all look—my memories of the day come flooding back. At the time, my wedding was elegant, special, and romantic. It was everything I dreamed of because it was mine. And that's why I'm hoping my sister plans a day that is just as special for her and her groom.

No matter what they end up choosing, it's not the hors d'oeuvres or the music we'll remember. It's the start of their married life together, and I hope she ends up with as many wonderful memories of her wedding day as I have of mine.

~Ellen Scolnic

She Should Have Been My Bridesmaid

Never forget the days I spent with you.
Continue to be my friend, as you will always find me yours.
~Ludwig Van Beethoven

I could feel my curls bouncing as I lifted the train of my dress and hurried after Stephanie into the chapel basement. She wanted to pin my hair up before the reception started because she thought the dining hall would get humid.

She led me to her makeshift salon by the fireplace and patted the chair in front of her. She put a bobby pin in her mouth as she said, "Let's get all of this hair off your neck." I sat down as she gently pulled off my veil. As she scooped up my curls and started sliding the pins against my scalp, I thought back to all of the times she used to do my hair at her family's lake cabin on Stop Island when we were in grade school. We'd come into the bathroom, our swimsuits still dripping from our latest swim, and she'd have me sit on a stool in front of the mirror while she brushed through my snarled, wet hair. I could see myself sitting there, pulling threads out of my towel with my chattering teeth as we laughed and talked to each other's reflections.

Conversation had come so naturally for us in those days. Now we had to fumble for things to say to make the time pass less awkwardly. Almost everything we talked about as she pinned up my hair felt artificial and forced, as if we really were nothing more than just a hairdresser and her client.

But I felt we were so much more than that because we had been best friends. There had been a bed at her house that nobody slept in but me, and when her little sister had learned to say her name, she learned mine right along with it. Her parents used to tell me how Olivia would toddle around, calling out for "Stephie-Loni" even when I wasn't at their house.

A slideshow of our past flashed across my memory as we made small talk about our families and plans for the future. We were riding our bikes to the gas station for candy, our sweatshirt pouches sagging with the change we had excavated from her parents' vehicles and from underneath their couch cushions. We were sitting in their paddleboat, our voices hoarse from trying to sell oatmeal cookies and sun-warmed Kool-Aid to passing boats. I saw us making comic strips in the church pews, and attempting to cover up sudden outbursts of laughter with unconvincing coughs and sneezes. I saw us locking ourselves in the bathroom at summer camp, yelling at the other girls to leave us alone as she showed me how to shave my legs for the first time. I saw her giving me her favorite rainbow-checkered boots from Scotland on a somber boat ride from Stop Island the morning after my grandpa died.

Finally, I saw us starting junior high, where Stephanie's confidence and clever sense of humor became her tickets to the popular crowd. I didn't belong in her new group of friends, and I didn't want to. But I still wanted to belong with Stephanie.

I remembered riding home with Stephanie and her dad, a Kmart bag of weekend clothes in my lap, after one of the last times I had slept over at her house. It had felt quiet and tense in the van at that time, most likely because Stephanie had just said something that had hurt my feelings. Either that or I was just being too sensitive, as I often was. More and more, it had felt like a struggle for us to come up with things to say without offending each other. I remembered how I had scratched a line in the frost-covered van window with my fingernail, and imagined it as the thread our friendship had become. As her dad drove me closer to the comfort of my own home, I wondered how much longer it would take before the thread finally snapped.

I knew it was natural for childhood friends to grow apart as time went on, but I had never thought it would happen to us. I never saw our friendship as a temporary crossing of paths. She had been my best friend, and I had assumed that had meant we would be in it for the long haul.

It saddened me that she was holding a brush instead of a bouquet on my wedding day, but it bothered me even more that she didn't seem to care. Over the years, I had made gentle attempts to pick up where we had left off in junior high, like the booklet I gave her for our high school graduation. I called it *The Adventures of Stephanie and Loni*, and it included stories of some of the zany things we had done in our childhood. In the hours I had spent working on it, I imagined her laughing out loud as she read each story, and I pictured her always keeping it safe in a box with precious old photographs and treasured letters. If anything, I had hoped it would show her how much our friendship had meant to me, but all I received in response was a card thanking me for the money and the cute book. Her parents had had more to say about the book than she did. I took it as a sign that my desire to rekindle the friendship was unrequited.

I squeezed my eyes shut as Stephanie began spraying my hair into place. After she finished straightening out my veil, I stood up, hugged her tightly, and thanked her for everything.

I could've clarified that by "everything," I had meant for the fishing derbies with her family, the matching "mushroom" haircuts, the code names we had made for the boys we liked, the friendship. But I knew it would never accomplish what I wanted it to. So instead of correcting Stephanie when she patted my back and assured me it had been a pleasure to do my hair, I simply released my embrace and told her she had done a great job. She told me not to wait for her while she packed up her bobby pins, brushes, and curling irons, so

I walked back to the reception hall alone, staring down at a bouquet that held roses as blue as forget-me-nots.

~Loni Swensen

Young at Heart

Nostalgia is a file that removes the rough edges from the good old days.
~Doug Larson

M y long-time friend Janice arrived at our girls-only luncheon grinning like the Cheshire Cat. Extending her left hand, she announced, "Look who's engaged."

In her late fifties and divorced for more than twenty years, she'd finally met a great man. We were ecstatic. She deserved to be happy. Everyone congratulated Janice as they checked out her beautiful engagement ring and quizzed her about the wedding.

"What color are our dresses?" I teased.

Another girlfriend chimed in, "I look good in black."

"Remember, we're all blondes now," one quipped.

The following weekend, I watched the movie *27 Dresses* about a woman who was always a bridesmaid, never a bride. Twenty-seven gowns, ranging from hilarious to downright ugly, hung in her closet as a constant reminder.

A few weeks later, I called some of the gals and suggested we throw Janice a shower asking guests to wear bridesmaid dresses. Enthusiasm bubbled, but there was just one big problem. Even if anyone had kept the gowns we'd worn in weddings years ago, there was only a slim chance we'd be able to wear them now, thanks to our middle-age bodies. Dresses that no longer fit were pooled for a free-for-all. Everyone eyed the formals, hoping they'd be able to squeeze into one. Some browsed garage sales, while others checked out resale shops. One found hers at Goodwill.

Who needs the Academy Awards to make a fashion statement? The day of the shower, ladies paraded in wearing long gowns and sporting beehives and bouffant hairstyles, charm bracelets jingling from their arms. Suddenly, our days as bridesmaids didn't seem all that long ago. Conversation turned to styles we'd been asked to wear in weddings that even a model couldn't have pulled off.

Guests were asked to choose the prettiest dress, the ugliest, the shortest, and the tightest. The southern belle ensemble that used more material than Scarlett O'Hara's green velvet gown won hands down for the prettiest. The girl with the ugliest formal, shoes dyed to match, had worn it in her best friend's wedding and insisted their friendship remained intact. A no-brainer, shortest went to the gal in a mini, but tightest was a close call. After much thought, we declared Large Marge the winner. Marge wasn't the only one afraid to eat that second piece of cream-cheese filled cake, iced with colorful bridesmaid dresses. Most of our vintage clothing left little wiggle room; a few were held together only by safety pins.

As Janice opened gifts, Sonny and Cher crooned "I Got You Babe" softly in the background. Instead of the number of children they'd have, we warned the guest of honor that each ribbon she broke would represent how many prescriptions the newlyweds would need. Janice cautiously unwrapped each present. We'd all participated in traditional shower games once too often, so we played ones geared toward our ages. In the unscramble-the-words game, "menopause," "Viagra" and "Depends" replaced "bride," "groom," and "wedding cake."

When it came to recognizing theme songs from popular '50s and '60s TV shows, guests triumphed. Like Mary Tyler Moore, we knew we'd make it after all. And didn't we all enjoy those *Happy Days*? The mere mention of Lucy brought gales of laughter. And like Laverne and Shirley, we'd been busy making our dreams come true.

Commercial jingles kept everyone on their toes. How many times had we wondered, "Does she or doesn't she" use Clairol? And who wasn't "Cuckoo for Cocoa Puffs"? Two days after the shower,

I still had "See the USA in Your Chevrolet" stuck in my head like Bazooka bubblegum.

As guests departed, everyone wished Janice the best. Although we may have had to squeeze into those dresses, our shower proved we were still young at heart.

~Alice Muschany

Here Comes the Bride

Marital Mishaps

*Mishaps are like knives, that either serve us or cut us,
as we grasp them by the blade or the handle.*

~James Russell Lowell,
"Cambridge Thirty Years Ago," Literary Essays

Through Storm and Flood

Two lovers in the rain have no need of an umbrella.

~Japanese Proverb

"Let's have the wedding here — in our woods!" Those were the words that my bride-to-be spoke to me the day after I proposed to her — and the words that echoed in my mind as I stood in those very same woods months later, the day after Hurricane Isabel tore through our state, leaving us with a 160-year-old oak tree lying on the ground right through the center of the area we were preparing for the wedding.

We planned to be married on the eve of midsummer 2004, in the most beautiful place we could think of: beside the brook that meanders through the forest that surrounds our Virginia home, among the beech and oak trees that have stood there for generations. Any large wedding requires months of preparation, but to hold such a thing at home requires even more! So in the summer of 2003, we began preparing the site: building a deck to be the dance floor, building over thirty terraced steps into the hillside for our elderly guests to walk down, planting flowers, and clearing brush from the place where our friends and family would sit during the ceremony.

And now facing this: the fallen trunk of a beautiful tree, nearly three feet in diameter, lying across, through, and on top of the space we were preparing.

A wedding party is made up of dear friends who are willing to help with whatever needs to be done in order for the wedding to come together. So I called my best man. "Brian, come on over. Bring a chainsaw." And he came, and the rest of our friends came, and with chainsaws and axes and brute strength, they helped us clear away the bones of the fallen giant, leaving behind a single piece: a 400-pound section of trunk to use as the altar for the ceremony, as a way of honoring the beautiful tree that we had lost.

In the months that followed, we worked harder than we'd ever worked before. After we removed the tree, we repaired the damage that the new deck had suffered when the tree fell, removed the water-logged debris from the brook, and finished the stairway down the hill. Through it all, we grew closer, knowing that all of the preparations were for a single day, but that the results of the preparations would be something we could enjoy together for years to come.

One week before the big day, we could finally breathe! Everything was done, ordered, prepared, scheduled, and ready to go. With one exception: the weather. We had no rain contingency for our eighty-five guests, and no room in our home for that many people if the rain came.

So we stood on our deck together, my bride-to-be and me, and spoke to the sky above us, requesting good weather for the day of the ceremony. "You can rain as much as you want," my lady said, "up until two days before the wedding. But we'd appreciate it if it didn't rain after that."

And the weather listened. Very closely, as it turned out. Two days before the wedding, the clouds opened up, and it rained like we had never seen. Our quiet little brook, usually only a few inches deep and three feet wide, began to rise toward the edge of its banks. There was nothing to be done but watch in awe. Those of us who were gathered at the house all went down to the deck we'd built, to stand in the rain and marvel at the power of nature. The water rose to the edge of the bank... then kept rising. And rising. Before long, the water was washing at the feet of the deck. The place where the guests were to sit, thirty feet from the bank, was inundated. The far side of the bank was even worse off — our three-foot-wide brook had turned into a 130-foot-wide torrent, so forceful that it carried whole tree trunks downstream.

"Look!" one of our friends pointed. The huge log that we had placed as the wedding altar was washing away as well.

"Come on," I said, and the groomsmen and I mounted an expedition into the rushing water to rescue the altar and haul it to higher ground.

Soon after, the rain stopped, and the waters receded, carrying with them the last remnants of the mulch we'd spread for our guests to walk on.

But the weather kept its word; there was no rain after that. We spread more mulch the next day, and set the altar back in its place. The day of the wedding dawned clear and bright.

Then, on the eve of midsummer, my beautiful bride walked down the hill on her father's arm, wearing a silver toe-ring borrowed from a bridesmaid, and bright cerulean toenail polish as her "something blue," barefoot so that she could feel the earth beneath her. She met me beside our oaken altar, and we were hand-fasted there, our hands bound together with ribbon in accordance with ancient tradition.

Through storm and flood we built the natural temple where we were to be married; through storm and flood was it cleansed; through storm and flood we found out just how close our closest friends were and still are.

Through storm and flood we learned that there is nothing that we cannot stand and face together.

~Cael Jacobs

Once Upon a Time

It is a wise father that knows his own child.
~William Shakespeare

M y father always told me bedtime stories. He never used a book, relying on his imagination, facility with words, and a wealth of personal experience. His stories involved distant landscapes, called kingdoms. Without fail, he weaved me into each adventure, referring to me as the beautiful princess. Often, what I did during the day would surface in the tales. If the beautiful princess scored well on a spelling test, she was rewarded by the king with a new quill; if she forgot to help her mother with the dishes, the princess was banished from court festivities. I held my breath waiting for my appearance in the story. I never tired of the evening ritual.

Dad changed jobs during my adolescence, keeping him away from home several days at a time. His stories were replaced with novels from the library, which I read before bedtime.

It wasn't long before adulthood and my engagement. A beautiful wedding was planned. Hotel reservations, dinner arrangements, and a host of pre-nuptial parties were scheduled.

At the same time, a serious flu epidemic hit the school where I taught, and my students were dropping out of class until attendance was almost nonexistent. I was counting my blessings and keeping my fingers crossed that I would not succumb. Things looked promising until the Friday before my Sunday wedding. Coming home from school, I felt lightheaded and tired, but chalked it up to time-consuming preparations. By evening, it was obvious fatigue had nothing to do with my condition. My entire body ached, my stomach churned, and the shivering would not stop. My mother and grand-mother hovered around me, offering chicken soup and whispering encouragement, telling me I would be fine in the morning.

I slept fitfully, and woke feeling no different from the night before. The sunshine streaming through the windows hurt my eyes; every noise was amplified until I thought my head would explode. My in-laws were scheduled to visit that afternoon. It was useless to think I could get out of bed and come downstairs to greet them. When they came up to the bedroom, my ashen face and weakened condition hardly promised a beautiful bride-to-be. My father-in-law, a feisty codger, scowled, muttering something about ruining the wedding. I was powerless to reassure him.

Things got worse. Friends and relatives called and dropped in, asking how they could help. My grandmother and mother were wringing their hands, not knowing what to do. They called our phy-sician, who said there were no medications for this strain of the flu.

In Judaism, important events are not cancelled. I overheard a phone call to our rabbi, asking if a bedside ceremony might be per-formed. My husband-to-be was the last visitor I saw that evening. Ever optimistic and cheerful, he put on a brave face, promising I would feel better the next day. Always able to lift my spirits, he made me laugh in the most dismal of circumstances, but this time, even he could not convince me. When everyone left, and I was alone for the first time all day, I thought about how many people were going to be disappointed. My wedding gown was hanging on the outside of my closet door, and I agonized over the possibility of never getting to wear it.

The day of the wedding dawned no better than the day before. My mother called the doctor once again, who repeated there were no medications, and I would just have to wait it out.

I lay in bed absolutely drained; the flu and my emotions had taken their toll. The wedding was scheduled for five in the afternoon; it was nine in the morning, and the anxiety of what was happening became overwhelming. At that moment, my father knocked on the door. Seeing me helpless and tearful, he sat on the edge of the bed. He waited a moment, looked at me, and firmly began, "I have a story to tell you. Once upon a time there was a beautiful princess who fell in love with a handsome prince. They were a loving and happy couple, making plans for a bright and wonderful future. Everyone in the royal kingdom was joyous!

"A wedding was planned. First, the royal caterers announced a wonderful feast, with the finest foods and wines, fresh succulent fruits, and a towering wedding cake that would take days to decorate. Then the royal musicians rehearsed songs composed especially for the event. Guests traveled from far and wide in golden coaches, sparing no expense for the gifts they would bring. The royal wardrobe mistresses sewed a gown fashioned from the most delicate silk, woven with pearls. Royal florists picked the most fragrant blossoms from hothouses to adorn a bouquet for the princess, with flowers that would rival her beauty. Chambermaids cleaned the palace so not a speck of dust could be found in the glistening room where the ceremony would be held.

"It was the day of the wedding. Embroidered banners flew from all the turrets. Candles, ornate silverware, goblets, and starched linens were brought from the palace storerooms and placed in the royal dining hall in readiness. And then, word reached the kingdom: An evil spell caused the bride to become ill. All activity came to a halt. A hush fell upon the kingdom.

"The prince made his way to the palace to see if the rumors were true. When he found the woman he loved bedridden and weak, he turned so she would not see a tear escape his eye. He thought it strange that she was well and healthy just a few days before. He wondered if perhaps she no longer loved him and was just pretending to be ill so she would not have to marry him. He left her chambers with a sad and heavy heart, inconsolable. The kingdom mourned, not just for the princess's strange malady, but for the broken-hearted prince, whom they had all come to love."

My father nodded his head slowly, squeezed my hand, kissed my cheek, and left my bedroom without another word.

It couldn't have been more than several seconds before the impact of his story registered. To this day, I cannot understand the sudden change that came over me. I got up from the bed, a bit unsteadily, and headed for a steamy and restorative shower. Drying my hair and styling it with my mother's assistance, I began having hope that I would not disappoint the prince. I came downstairs, and at the royal grandmother's insistence, ate a small bowl of oatmeal. She beamed as I swallowed spoonful after spoonful.

It wasn't much longer before the royal photographers came. My mother and sister helped me into my wedding gown, watched and gave advice as I applied some make-up, and accompanied me down the stairs to pose for the most important pictures of my life.

I still cannot fathom how I was able to gather the strength and will to meet the handsome prince at the wedding altar, but I did, with my father proudly standing at my side. Just loud enough for me to hear as my husband and I were joined in matrimony, my father said, "And they lived happily ever after."

~Edie Barton Scher

One Size Fits All

His clothes fit him so ill, and constrain him so much,
that he seems rather their prisoner than their proprietor.
~Philip Dormer Stanhope

*I*t was a month before the wedding. I was standing in the middle of the tailor's shop, wearing my tuxedo shirt and boxer shorts, trying to retain my composure as the tailor and his assistants wrapped their measuring tapes around my arms, my legs, and everywhere else imaginable. As the tailor took a stranglehold on my neck with his measuring tape, I tried to concentrate on Ann, my beautiful bride-to-be.

Getting to this point in our relationship had been a challenge, and not because we weren't head over heels in love with each other. We were, but getting to the altar had meant promising that we'd have the beautiful, perfect wedding ceremony she'd never had. Her last marriage had begun with a quick wedding without much family and far short of the dream of exchanging vows in a beautiful church or garden surrounded by loved ones. I'd promised her we'd have a wedding with family, flowers, and all the love she'd dreamed about since she was a young girl. And so I found myself being yanked and pulled by a gang of tailors who would have made good torturers for the Marquis de Sade.

"I have my two brothers coming to be measured for their tuxedos," I reminded the tailor. "We need to be in black, and we have to match." He nodded at me and measured the cuff of my sleeve, frowning at the fact that my arms were longer than the usual client.

"Have them here for their fittings by Monday," he said, waiting until I'd pulled up some trousers so he could measure the break in the cuffs. "Make sure they show up, or I cannot guarantee their tuxedos will be ready in time for your wedding." He made a note in his appointment book that read "Fit all Buentello tuxedos for same wedding."

Satisfied things were going smoothly, I finished up and raced off to check on the garden grotto we'd rented for the ceremony. Over the next few weeks, one detail after another fell into place. My brothers called to say they'd made their fittings. Two days before the ceremony, Larry, Carl and I walked into the tuxedo shop to pick up our suits.

The tailor gave us a proud smile as his assistants helped us into our tuxedos. I should say we tried to fumble our way into them. My brothers, who are much broader at the shoulders than I am, huffed and puffed, but there was no way they were going to fit their size 50 bodies into the size 40 jackets they were trying to put on. Me, I slipped into my tux with no problems. My suit was a perfect size 40, just like my brothers' tuxedos were. I looked at the tailor, who checked through the instructions to his tailors who had done the final fittings. All of a sudden, he slapped his head in frustration.

"Stupid idiots!" he roared, waving his clipboard around in the air. "The note said measure all the Buentello family for the same wedding, not measure all the Buentello family the same!"

My brothers started laughing. And even though for a moment I felt like was going to have a breakdown because the tuxedos weren't ready and there was no time left to fix things, I started laughing, too. I mean, nothing is as funny as watching a couple of big, burly guys laughing as their tuxedos are riding up their arms and legs.

But there was little time for us to be hysterical. After a frantic discussion with his assistants, the tailor disappeared behind a curtain. I heard a lot of grumbling and shouting, followed by the sounds of many hangers being shoved aside, boxes being torn open and thrown to the ground, and even the tearing of cloth. The tailor's voice rose and fell with alternating tones of elation and frustration. My brothers stood around in their shirts and socks while I wondered if it might not be time to go to a blue jeans motif for the wedding.

Finally, the tailor emerged from behind the curtain. In each hand he held an immaculately pressed, expertly hemmed tuxedo that seemed cut to the exact specifications of each of my brothers. Larry and Carl eased themselves into their tuxedos and stood before the collection of mirrors, marveling at the perfect fit. The tailor measured an arm and a leg and nodded approvingly. I stood up from the chair I had collapsed into and admired the beautiful suits.

"There, you see?" the tailor said, hanging his measuring tape around his neck with satisfaction.

I nodded while I watched my brothers check out their suits in the mirrors. "Pretty nice tuxedos. They match the style and cut of mine perfectly. There's only one problem."

The tailor clucked at me. "And what is that?"

I picked up the tuxedo I had put on earlier. "Mine is black. Theirs are white."

The tailor looked. He slapped his head. Yanking the tuxedos off my brothers, he turned and disappeared behind the curtain again. The shouting and banging continued.

Needless to say, we did manage to find three tuxedos that matched, at least a little. And though the fit wasn't precise, my brothers and I look great in the wedding pictures—if you look at the ones with our hands behind our backs and that have people standing in front of us to hide the fact that our pants are about two inches too short. But you know what they say about weddings: It's all about the bride anyway.

~John P. Buentello

Making Light of the Storm

The temple bell stops but I still hear the sound coming out of the flowers.
~Basho

Ah June, the perfect month for every mother's dream: a gorgeous wedding for her daughter. My Holly—a treasure, sunny-tempered, clever, the best of girls—deserved the best. Together, we had planned the wedding as she wanted it, to be held in the farmhouse garden. The night before, all prepared, we went to bed anticipating a glorious day.

I woke at 2:00 A.M. Wind roared through the trees in the pine plantation next door. Raindrops pelted the roof, and soon all other sounds were drowned out in a torrential roar. The gusts grew and shook the house until the windows rattled. Last week's tropical cyclone that blasted the Pacific had, against the meteorological predictions, turned our way.

What a catastrophe! I had nightmarish visions of the ruined wedding—the marquee, flowers and bridal avenue of potted plants and trees destroyed, torn to fragments, scattered on the wind. Holly on her father's arm, sloshing through what had been the lawn, sinking deeper with every step. The minister washed away in sheets of rain, and what guests braved the storm swallowed up in huge pools of voracious mud. Only a miracle could reduce this storm by lunchtime, so what could I do? How could I rescue my daughter's day and make it memorable despite the storm?

At first light, I got up and hurried outside. Bitter cold rain needled my face. The wind pushed so that I could barely stand. Already, the garden was a quagmire, the rain making lakes on the lawn. The marquee, half-toppled, flapped and clapped as the wind tore through it. Soon, it would collapse completely. Nothing remained of the bridal avenue, the floral displays, and the ceremonial arch. In tears, I turned back to the house, walking in the shelter of the shrubbery. Leaves ripped from the trees whirled past, flowers torn off, tumbled to the ground. In a puddle beside the path, two whole white camellia blossoms floated. I paused, caught by their beauty. The blossoms dazzled like twin stars, slowly revolving in the water.

My daughter's special day would be remembered for all the wrong reasons unless I managed to think of a solution. We couldn't have the wedding inside our tiny cottage, and the family farmhouse, badly damaged by fire four months ago, was only three-quarters restored. We'd delayed the wedding once because of the fire. We couldn't do so again, but then what choice was there?

Perhaps I could arrange the farmhouse's renovated entrance hall and two connecting living rooms. If I lit a fire in the main fireplace and made the hearth the focal point, we could hold the ceremony there. But how to soften the bleakness of new plaster and bare boards? I looked again at the floating camellias. The answer lay at my feet.

I had until lunchtime. Everyone was called upon to help. A "save-the-day spirit" prevailed. Off went family and friends to borrow pretty glass dishes and bowls, old-fashioned white linen tablecloths, and acquire hundreds of camellia flowers. While Holly's brother cooked a special wedding breakfast for the bride, groom and special guests, her father entertained them, promising me to keep them happy until the ceremony.

I phoned my florist friend Diane to help, stripped the garden bushes of any unblemished camellia flowers, and raided the neighbors' camellias. Then I made a quick trip to town where I borrowed our church's and decor shop's wrought-iron candlesticks and candelabra.

Time pressed. I drove to the farmhouse, arriving at the same time as Diane. Her car was loaded with fat beeswax candles and candle lanterns, glass bowls, bundles of ivy, and more camellia blossoms. Two enormous forty-candle candelabra filled the back seat. I hugged her gratefully.

"You're such a friend."

Diane grinned. "People are going to talk of Holly's wedding for years," she promised. "I'll make an entrance archway using tree fern branches and the candle lanterns. You do the inside."

So the transformation began.

At 1:00 P.M., I drove Holly to her wedding. The sky turned a terrible charcoal shade as the rain pelted down. The weather remained atrocious.

"Not what we planned, I'm afraid, my dear."

She hugged me, taking my breath away and threatening my ribs.

"Can't be helped," she said, trying to smile.

The storm raged overhead. It was virtually dark as I parked right up by the front door and helped Holly out.

"Oh!" she said.

The front porch was now an archway of woven fern branches hung with candle lanterns. At the top of the steps, a tall, wrought-iron stand held six globe lanterns. Flanking the steps were two huge silver bowls filled with water on which floated red- and white-streaked camellia blossoms and heart-shaped candles. Every candle flame shone like a star.

My husband opened the front door, and the guests spilled out. Some carried candle lanterns. They formed into a guard of honor, lighting the way. The other guests tossed camellia petals at the bride. Behind them, firelight and candlelight shone, making a warm mellow glow inside the house.

"Oh!" said Holly again, beginning to smile.

I handed her over to her father, who took her arm. The guests fell in behind, cheering, and Holly walked through the hallway along a pathway of red and white camellia petals strewn all the way from the front door to the fireplace in the living area. Tiny glass bowls edged the petal path, one blossom and one floating candle in each, red blossoms alternating with white ones in pairs all the way.

I slipped in the side door and joined Aidan, the groom, and the minister waiting by the fire. I couldn't wait to see Holly's face when she saw the room. I'd turned all the builders' trestles, boxes, and crates into tables for the guests to sit around, and covered them completely with the borrowed linen tablecloths. I'd arranged thick ivy ropes in swags about each table, set out bowls with camellia blossoms and floating candles, and finally placed two candelabra per table. Every windowsill, shelf, and spare surface was trimmed with ivy, candles, and camellia flowers. The church candelabra flanked the hearth, and Diane's large candelabra sat in the window embrasures on either side of the fireplace. The whole room was incandescent with a soft yellow light. Everywhere, golden stars shone—on windowpanes, in the water, in each person's eyes. The camellia blossoms, stars in their own right, added their scent to that of the beeswax candles and sweet pine logs.

Holly stopped in the doorway. Candle stars winked at her feet. The glass and the water reflected each flame over and over so that there was a Milky Way of little flame-stars. She laughed with delight, and Aidan stepped forward to take her hand. The minister beamed at them.

In the pause as the guests settled, Holly turned to me. "Mum," she breathed, "this is perfect. It's so beautiful."

That was all I needed. Who cared about power cuts and raging cyclones when this magic was happening? I watched my radiant daughter say her vows and sighed with contentment.

~P.D.R. Lindsay

66

The Runaway Who Wasn't the Bride

Dogs are not our whole life, but they make our lives whole.
~Roger Caras

Weddings have a way of driving a girl crazy. The "real-life" planning for the day she's dreamed about since she was a little girl can turn the kindest, sweetest bride-to-be into a shrill, sobbing, stressed mess if she isn't careful.

I've always been easygoing about things like that. I made it to the eve of my wedding without dissolving into tears over dress choices or seating arrangements. When my DJ canceled a week before the wedding, I took a deep breath and scrambled to find a replacement. When we had torrential downpours the night before the wedding, I told myself, "There's nothing you can do about the weather." We got a little damp going to the church for the rehearsal, but by the time we were all seated for dinner afterward, the laughter was flowing with the wine. I guess as brides go, I was pretty unflappable.

Stacey, my beloved mutt, was a different story. We were planning to leave for our honeymoon directly from the reception, and my grandparents were keeping her while we were away. I had taken her to their house that afternoon. If anything at all bothered me during the rehearsal, it was the memory of her soulful brown eyes giving me the silent guilt trip as I left. But by the time we sat down to our meal, I had pushed even that aside to enjoy the company of my loved ones.

My father got a call midway through dinner. We were all laughing and sharing bits of food from each other's plates, and I didn't even realize he'd stepped away. When he returned to our little cluster of tables, his face was grim. He whispered something to my mom, and they looked at me. I felt my heart start to pitter-patter just a little.

In addition to Stacey, my grandparents had also offered to house some of our out-of-town relatives who were coming to the wedding. A few them had not yet arrived when my grandparents left for the rehearsal. They had left a key on the back porch so our relatives could go on in and make themselves at home.

"That was your cousin," Dad told me, looking like he'd rather be getting a root canal than share what he was about to tell me. "They just arrived at Grandmom's. When they let themselves in, Stacey darted out. They tried to catch her, but... she's gone."

It took a second for my heart to start beating again. Stacey had been with me since college. She slept at the foot of my bed, and her sweet furry face and wagging tail greeted me each day when I came home. My fiancé loved her, too, and his face grew just as pale as mine. She was part of our family, and embarking on this new adventure without her just wasn't right.

Instantly, our dinner gathering transformed into a search party. Bands of aunts and uncles, cousins, bridesmaids, and groomsmen took to the streets. The rain continued to pour, and the October night was windy and chilly. But no one backed down.

The park near my grandparents' house was suddenly awash with not only rain, but women in dresses and heels and men in suits and ties who traipsed through the mud like an expert search party. My friends and family hunted tirelessly. Our high heels planted themselves firmly in the mud and wouldn't budge, so my bridesmaids and I kicked them off and stumbled barefoot over mucky ground. My elderly relatives forgot their aches and pains and climbed hills, calling endlessly for my dog. Those who weren't searching the park scoured the neighboring back yards. I still wonder what the neighbors thought, looking out their windows on that rainy night to find well-dressed but drenched men and women poking around in their shrubbery.

After a few hours, we realized we weren't going to find her. My mom and sister went home and set about making up signs. I said a tearful goodnight to my fiancé and curled up on my parents' couch. I wept long into the night, finally becoming one of those brides who loses it.

My wedding day dawned crisp and clear, finally free of rain. My head hurt, and my face was pale. I hadn't eaten my dinner, and my stomach was still too queasy for food. My eyes were raw and puffy. This was supposed to be the happiest day of my life, but my heart was heavy. I thought of Stacey out there alone, and my waterworks started anew.

The photographer arrived. Instead of finding a bride in her gown and make-up, he found a tousled, weeping lump of a girl in her flannel pajamas. My mother explained the situation, and he nodded gently and started taking shots of the bridesmaids instead. Mom nudged me into her bedroom, where she managed to get me into my dress. The make-up, however, was an entirely different story. As soon as I'd get on a bit of blush or some eye shadow, I'd drown it in tears and have to start over.

Another knock sounded at the door, and my father greeted my great-uncle. I heard him and Dad talking in whispers, and then Dad uttered a loud "Thank God!" I flew from the bedroom, a ghost of a girl in a long, not-quite-buttoned white gown that matched the color of her pale, sleepless skin.

"She's home," Uncle Don smiled. "I went back to the park at first light and found her. It seemed like she was trying to find her way home. She was wet and hungry, but she's fine, honey. Now go get married." I flew at him and threw my arms around him, laughing and crying all at once.

No bride has ever rushed so much to get ready for her big day. When I walked down the aisle, my make-up couldn't hide the blotches left by my sleepless, tearful night. There was a speck of mud on my dress from hugging the uncle who had just traipsed through a waterlogged park with my dog. But my eyes were shining, and the smile on my face had never been more genuine. Sometimes, even when things don't turn out perfectly, they are still beautiful in the end.

Years later, the memory of my sleepless anxiety has faded. What I have never forgotten is the love of the family and friends who ruined their finery and soaked themselves to the skin helping me search for my wayward pup. Of all the gifts I received for my wedding, their selflessness was by far the most precious. I am forever grateful to the uncle who searched past midnight and still rose at dawn to bring Stacey home.

A wedding is about two people pledging their love, but it is also a reminder that we should cherish the loved ones who surround us and support us through our days. I couldn't have asked for a stronger reminder of that.

~Pam Hawley

67

Buckaroos and Buckarettes

Budget: a mathematical confirmation of your suspicions.
~A.A. Latimer

My only daughter, Alyssa, was getting married in July, and planned a garden ceremony at a lovely ranch just outside town. Like a lot of modern brides, she was counting every penny while stewing over every detail, including the fact that I couldn't seem to find a suitable mother-of-the-bride outfit. But she was most upset by one of the more odious expenses she faced: providing sanitation facilities for the guests.

We found several companies in our town that specialize in portable restrooms. With company names ranging from the obvious Port-a-Potty, to the ridiculous—Honey Bucket or Royal Flush—we decided to hire Buck's, known around our area as the "go-to" place.

Until then, I thought only construction crews or outdoor concerts utilized these modern-day outhouses, but no. Lots of brides-to-be rented them for the big day. The clerk at Buck's kept a straight face as she ran through the different rental packages. For the 100 guests Alyssa planned to invite, we'd need at least two units. "We have rentals," she said, "in white instead of brown." She paused. "You know, to look more formal." A formal outhouse?

"Maybe we can hang signs on them, too?" I said.

The clerk didn't miss a beat. "Oh, yes, you have your choice of

Madames or Hommes, Guys and Gals, or our favorite, Buckaroos and Buckarettes. With color-coordinated ribbons to tie on the door handle."

"How about air fresheners shaped like wedding bells?" I grinned. Alyssa and the clerk glared.

I saw nothing wrong with a bit of bathroom humor, but by the time we left, Alyssa was upset.

Getting upset is what brides-to-be do, right? As July neared, Alyssa's nerves grew more frayed.

"Mom," she said one day, "I just heard from Uncle Fred in California. He's bringing his new wife and all ten of their kids." If the guest list grew any longer, we'd need three Bucks instead of two.

More of her plans unraveled faster than a roll of Charmin on a downhill slope. One family member refused to attend if alcohol was served, and another refused to come if alcohol wasn't served. The lilies we were growing ourselves were threatened by a late-season hailstorm. My daughter worried about everything from where on the ranch Aunt Millie might grab a quick smoke to whether the brides-maids would fit into their dresses. One minute my normally sweet daughter hated everything and everyone, the next she dissolved into tears. I began to understand why the term "Bridezilla" was coined.

I finally found a simple frock that complemented her colors of dusky pink, aqua and black, but by then Alyssa had transformed from a reasonable twenty-five-year-old to a creature who could give the Bride of Frankenstein a run for the money. And money was part of the reason why she was freaking out. There wasn't enough.

Finally, the couple sat down with calculators and agreed. Their budget was clogged with way too many guests. They might never stop arguing about whether the toilet seat should be left up or down, but they concurred about the wedding. To avoid going into debt, the guest list had to be cut in half.

To their great relief, some invitees, including Uncle Fred and company, decided they couldn't make the trip after all. By the time the number of guests had been reduced to about sixty, Alyssa and Ryan realized that another substantial savings stared them in the face.

A smaller crowd, even one plied with beer and wine, could get by with only one portable toilet.

One day before the big event, Buck's delivered one of its special white wedding "units" to the ranch. The couple nixed my "wedding bell air freshener" idea, but they hung several pine tree car fresheners inside and positioned the white facility around the corner from the main reception. To add some color, they tied aqua and pink ribbons on the door handle. Since the bride and groom were country/western fans, they hung a sign that read "Guys" across the top and "Gals" underneath.

On her wedding day, my beautiful daughter made a gorgeous bride. Since the drinkers had won out over the nondrinkers, beer and wine flowed at the reception. Everyone agreed that my daughter and new son-in-law had done a great job on a shoestring budget, and nobody complained about having to wait to use the facilities. Lucky for them, the Buck stopped here.

~Linda S. Clare

"We need to cut costs. After you marry us,
would you be able to tend bar?"

A Gift from Great-Grandma

The art of living lies less in eliminating our troubles
than in growing with them.
~Bernard M. Baruch

I have no idea how much I'm going to regret my advice when I give it. My smart, independent, twenty-five-year-old daughter has moved back home for the six months before her wedding. She seems to have everything under control until one morning when I find her curled up in her bed, fully clothed, rocking back and forth with her pink and purple quilt over her face.

All I can see of her in the shadows of her darkened bedroom is her long, straight brown hair splayed on her crumpled pillow.

"Tricia, what's wrong?"

She rocks back and forth, but doesn't answer.

"Tricia, I can't help you if you don't tell me what's wrong."

"It's just... you can't fix it!" She rocks some more and then sits straight up, hair askew. "I want my wedding to be perfect, and I just know something will go wrong."

In hopes of helping her relax, in hopes of helping her put the whole idea of "perfection" in perspective, I make a terrible mistake.

"Tricia! Of course, something will go wrong! Probably more than one something will go wrong, but it won't matter! That's what you'll talk about for the rest of your lives. That's what will give you sweet memories and something to tell your children."

She frowns doubtfully for a moment, and then her face brightens. She chuckles a little as she asks, "Like the pastor calling Dad 'Bruce'?"

"Yup! See? That's what you remember from our wedding stories, not that I had real daisies on our cake. They were perfect, just like I wanted them, but what we talk about and laugh about is the pastor calling Dad 'Bruce' instead of 'Butch'… in the vows! Twice!"

She continues to smile as she stares down at the crumpled quilt.

In the back of my mind, a little alarm goes off. I have, in effect, just promised her that nothing serious will happen, that anything that goes wrong will just be funny. I'm helping her for the moment, but am I making a huge mistake? I'm tempting fate, and fate could make me pay a horrible price.

I ignore my qualms, and Tricia and I make lists. Soon we're busy making bouquets from pink and burgundy silk flowers and talking to caterers about delivering platters of Mexican food to the reception in our yard. We joke about potential problems that could come from her future father-in-law's association with a local biker community or from her little brother's penchant for playing jokes on her.

The big day arrives. The caterers prepare tables in our yard while my husband and I drive our daughter to a stately, old brick church across from Central Park in our little town in Western Oregon. The weather is mild for a mid-summer day. I begin to wonder if there just won't be anything to joke about later if the whole day goes off without a hitch. I lose all karmic caution as I actually hope for some little mishap to prove me right and to give us a story to tell.

Before the ceremony, the photographer arranges two families, four generations on our side, along the three sweeping stairs below the altar for the official wedding pictures. The groom and groomsmen wear black cowboy boots with their tuxedos. Tricia's white cowboy boots peek out from under her full-skirted white gown.

Finally, the photographer finishes with us, and we all carefully scramble down the steps toward the aisles. I hear a scrape, a soft clatter, and chilling gasps from all around. I turn to see Tricia's ninety-year-old great-grandmother, Mary, flat on her back up against the legs of the front pew. She had tripped on the edge of the step. She is not conscious. I stop breathing.

For a moment, no one moves, and then three men surround Grandma. One of them takes her head into his lap and talks to her softly. She blinks, stunned. Her head is bleeding.

Tricia sinks onto a nearby bench with her dress deflated around her, hands clasped over her mouth. Our horror suspends time. We focus only on Grandma Mary, care only that she is all right.

Grandma opens her eyes and mumbles, "All this way... I'm not... going to miss... this wedding!" Little Grandma Mary in her blue linen suit tries to sit up just as two EMTs hurry down the aisle to get to her.

The pastor, in his full dress robes, squats on the floor next to her and gently, quietly says, "Madam, I will not start this ceremony until you have been checked out by a doctor. You might as well go. We will wait."

She looks him in the eye, ready to argue despite her position, now sitting up but leaning on one EMT while the other daubs at the wound on the back of her head. The pastor looks right back, just as determined. She says, "All right, but I won't ride in any ambulance." The EMTs carefully help her to her feet and continue to support her as my husband's father escorts her to his rental car.

Tricia and I wait together in a dressing room while guests arrive, learn the reason for the delay, and then sit to wait quietly for news of Great-Grandma.

"Mom. What if she's not okay? I actually looked forward to what silly things could go wrong. But not this..." Tricia can't continue.

I don't know what to say. I take her hand, and we wait. All thoughts of a perfect wedding vanish. We only want Great-Grandma pronounced healthy and back with us.

For over an hour, we listen to the pianist play Mozart, Beethoven, and even a little Simon and Garfunkel. Tricia and I take turns peeking out the door.

Finally, in the middle of "Bridge over Troubled Water," we hear movement and louder voices. We open the door just enough to see Grandma Mary with a huge white elastic bandage wrapped around her head like a turban. Her white curls stick out around the edges, and someone has tucked a single pink lily into the side of it.

She turns to smile at us, then waves and pats her "turban," as the pianist begins "Ode to Joy." On Grandpa's arm, Great-Grandma walks, unsteady but dignified, past the door and into the chapel. Our guests stand and applaud.

Great-Grandma's gift of her love for her family and her determination to be with us for Tricia's wedding reminds Tricia and me both that a wedding is about love and connection, not about producing the perfect event. After a long delay and with a crumpled dress and mascara smeared, Tricia really does have the perfect wedding.

~Sallie Wagner Brown

69

The Cake

In all of the wedding cake, hope is the sweetest of plums.
~Douglas Jerrold

Some women dream of the fairy-tale wedding: a future gem sparkling in silver and crystal wrapped in satin that shudders with quickened breath. I dreamed instead of a prince, and when I found him, I wanted to marry him with unseemly haste. He had a tux, I bought a dress off the rack two days before the wedding, and we ordered a small bouquet with a few corsages thrown in to assuage our conflicted families. I elected to make the cake myself.

The cake was to be the pièce de résistance, an outward channeling of the joy I felt. I pored over recipes, dog-earing candidates, and mulling combinations. I filed recipes in neat rows upon the small countertops in the even smaller Boston apartment — possibilities that were scented with vanilla and dusted with cake flour, casualties of incessant testing. I finally settled on an ethereal white cake, filled with thin layers of vibrant lemon curd and tangy raspberry, topped with rich butter cream frosting and adorned with a crown of edible purple pansies.

In the days before the wedding, I channeled my nervous anticipation in the kitchen. One day, it was stirring the gentle figure eights, cutting ribbons through seas of thickening curd. Another day, it was the earthy sourness of warming raspberry sauce that took me back to the sun-dappled tangle of my mother's patch. On the day before the wedding, I made the butter cream, drizzling hot sugar into golden eggs and pretending I didn't know about the pound of butter that followed. I filled and iced my cake, secure in my knowledge that we could feast on a little slice of heaven to celebrate our day in the clouds. I capped my confection with the lid that accompanied the cake stand and placed it in the refrigerator to await the morning.

I awoke on the day of my wedding with a mental list of things to do. The apartment buzzed with voices and sounds, and I buzzed with nervous energy. My mother, sister and I visited as we did our make-up and hair. Having made myself pretty, I went to the kitchen to do the same to my cake.

The wail brought my sister to the kitchen, and together we surveyed the disaster that had once been my joy. Overnight, the delicious butter cream had hardened to mortar and permanently sealed my masterpiece to the glass dome of the cake stand. Short of a chisel, I could not think of a single way to extricate my cake. With head bowed and tears threatening, my sister—ever the pragmatist—announced with cheery confidence, "Let's get the blow dryer. We can get it out." The cake received more primping that morning than I did. We fussed, blew, and slowly spun the cake stand until that pound of butter loosened its resolve and started to slide away.

Eschewing tradition, the groom (who was our ride to the wedding) peeked into the kitchen. I looked up from my protective hunch over the cake, dressed only in a ratty robe with a death grip on a blow dryer, and tried to smile. He tried not to. "Looks like you have everything under control," he pronounced with nodding solemnity. "I'll wait on the couch."

A hot spatula and the flowers disguised any lingering after-effects of the cake's near-death experience as it stood, coverless, on the now infamous cake stand. A few minutes in front of the mirror restored my spirits, and I emerged from my room gowned and ready for the day's festivities.

As we walked to the car, my mother snapped my favorite picture of the wedding. To the unknowing eye, it shows a happy couple holding hands with a family member trailing behind, smiling a serene smile and carrying the wedding cake. I know the difference.

The groom isn't just smiling; he's laughing. The joy on my face reads more like relief. And my sister's Mona Lisa smile? It looks like pure triumph to me.

It was delicious.

~Jill Fisher

70

Cinderella Descending

I don't like people who have never fallen or stumbled. Their virtue is lifeless and it isn't of much value. Life hasn't revealed its beauty to them.
~Boris Pasternak

On June 14th, I planned to put on the performance of a lifetime. I'd be the Cinderella in white, walking down the aisle to marry Prince Charming. It was the role I deserved, after years of being overlooked for lead parts in ballet academy recitals. Now I'd be center stage, carrying out my performance with all the poise of royalty.

And my prince? John was majoring in Acting/Directing at the University of Washington. His velvety baritone voice could melt a woman's heart. It did mine!

As two struggling artists, we were perfect for each other—he, the handsome leading man, and me, the graceful dancer. I was certain our life together would be idyllic. And our wedding, no doubt, would be flawless.

We planned a ceremony at our family's impressive church, followed by a reception in a ballroom at my mother's workplace, Seattle's elegant Olympic Hotel. As a hotel executive, Mom spent her life hosting parties for the rich and famous. I had no doubt she'd put on a flawless reception. Perfect!

I chose a full-length wedding gown with white lace over a satin sheath. It looked regal with its short train flowing behind. Gorgeous!

My brother-in-law, Tim, agreed to help with music for the ceremony by accompanying our church organist on woodwind instruments. I chose two Bach classics for our processional and recessional. Beautiful!

When the special day arrived, I entered the back of our church, arm-in-arm with the man who would give me away: my brother, Bill. Tim ceased playing introductory music as soon as we entered. I peeked through a slat to wink at John waiting at the front. Once he'd returned my wink, I felt calm and in control, confident the ceremony would be flawless.

Soon, Tim nodded toward the organist and raised a wooden recorder to his lips, then the sweet notes of "Sheep May Safely Graze" poured into the sanctuary. As the pipe organ joined Tim's flute in soft harmony, the crowd stood to watch me walk down the aisle. This was my moment... my time to shine!

Right on cue, Bill and I stepped into the open arch at the back of the church. We were about to take our first step when the sun burst from behind clouds and flooded the sanctuary. The crowd gasped as brilliant rays illuminated my path to John.

I gasped as well... but for a different reason. The unexpected rays of light served as a divine wake-up call. This was no performance! I was about to give my life away... forever!

I started trembling. Tears spilled over as I looked toward my groom. Yes, he was handsome and charming, but... I was terrified! I tightened my grip on Bill's arm, afraid to let go. However, without hesitating, he passed me to my handsome groom. John grasped my hand reassuringly as we turned toward Reverend Phillips.

While the reverend recited "Dearly beloved, we are gathered here in the sight of God..." my thoughts went wild. Omigosh, what am I doing here? This is serious stuff!

I wanted to run out of the church, but my feet wouldn't move. Instead, something else started running. While my groom flawlessly recited his vows, my nose became the focus of my attention. Why hadn't I brought a Kleenex?

Once John's resonant voice had ceased echoing off the walls, I hung my head and mumbled vows between sniffles and snorts. So much for perfection! But John saved my pride. After carefully placing a kiss on the driest part of my lips, he swept me out of the church. What an awesome leading man!

Once my nose and head had cleared, my confidence returned. Certainly, the reception would go more smoothly than the ceremony. After all, my mother and her staff were pros at that kind of thing.

The ballroom was gorgeous—suitable for my Cinderella role, with elaborate cornices, velvety wallpaper, and draperies flowing from a twelve-foot ceiling to the floor. When we arrived, Mom's associates were laying out my favorite hors d'oeuvres. They'd already placed a giant ice sculpture in the middle of the banquet table and surrounded it with bottles of champagne. Flowers were everywhere!

The man in charge, Mr. François, greeted us with a bow and showed us where we'd be forming the reception line.

"You're a bit early," he said as the staff hurried through their last-minute preparations. "But, here, sip some champagne while you wait." I'd never been a drinker, but my mouth felt so dry that I grabbed the glass eagerly.

Soon, guests began arriving. Two hundred of them wandered through slowly, chatting as they gave us hugs and congratulations. Meanwhile, Mr. François kept my champagne glass filled to the brim.

Finally, the long line came to an end. As our guests swarmed over the hors d'oeuvres, I breathed a sigh of relief and whispered to my mother, "Where's the closest restroom?"

"It's on the balcony overlooking the hotel lobby," she said, pointing toward a hallway leading to two flights of luxuriously carpeted stairs.

"John, I'll be right back," I said, and took off down the hall. My head reeled from the champagne. Nevertheless, I felt like a princess, descending the stairs overlooking a posh lobby. Every eye was on me—the bride in white lace.

Holding my head high, I didn't slow my pace when I got to the stairs. Why should I? Given my level of grace and coordination,

I always ran down staircases. Grabbing skirts in one hand, I'd just begun my elegant descent when a spike heel caught on my gown's lacy train. I tried to recover, but the champagne had reduced my knees to rubber. As I fell, the skirts tangled around my legs mummy-style. Onlookers gasped as I rolled down the stairs sideways, bouncing like a cheap loaf of bologna.

Horrified, I jumped to my feet and ran into the ladies' lounge. I hid in a stall to take inventory of the damage. Thanks to heavily padded, plush carpeting, nothing was broken or bruised… except my ego. I'd done no damage to my gown and hardly a hair was out of place. Though I was fairly certain none of our guests had seen my pratfall, I remained sequestered for a while, fearing someone might come in asking about the drunken bride. In time, I built up the courage to walk cautiously back to my wedding reception.

Now, decades later, I realize our imperfect wedding and reception were previews of coming attractions. In our early years together, John and I focused on petty imperfections and wondered why we'd married. We fought, and I'd cry, wanting to run. We took embarrassing pratfalls. But, ironically, the deeper trials that followed are the very things that drew us closer.

Six years after our wedding, John's diagnosis with multiple sclerosis finally inspired us to seek something greater than a perfect performance. Cinderella and Prince Charming needed to fall so a greater story could arise. Our "happily ever after" came only as John's struggles with MS revealed our dedication to each other.

The result? Thirty-five years of an ever-strengthening marriage and a family for which I thank God daily.

~Laura L. Bradford

71

My Perfect Wedding

When you aim for perfection, you discover it's a moving target.
~George Fisher

My future husband loaded up the truck as I added the finishing touches to my make-up. I quickly put on my pink bride baseball cap. I noticed my soon-to-be husband, Scott, accidentally left his black groom baseball cap on the bathroom counter.

Scott yelled out from downstairs, "The bags are in the truck. We are all loaded up."

I walked down the dark hallway with only the kitchen light to show me my way. As I walked out the door, the morning frost on the grass glistened in the moonlight. The steam from Scott's coffee followed him as he hopped into the already running truck.

The blue light of the clock caught my eye: 5:52. Wow, I thought. We are ahead of schedule. I handed him his groom baseball cap. Without a word, he put it on.

We hopped on the freeway. To our delight, there were no other cars on the road. It was as if the roads were open just for us. We had all the time in the world.

We continued down the highway. It was the perfect start to the perfect wedding. Wedding?

"Oh, no!" I screamed. "I forgot my wedding dress!"

"What? What? How do you forget your wedding dress?" he said.

"It's in the closet. It wasn't with the other bags."

The truck was off the freeway before I could finish my sentence. He whipped the truck around and headed back home. He flew down the empty freeway at 85 miles per hour.

"Hey, is that a cop?" he asked as he pointed to the right side of the freeway.

"No, no, that's not a cop. It's just a car," I said.

"Are you sure?" he said.

"Yes, I am sure," I said with a slightly agitated tone.

"Fine," he said, "but that looks like a cop."

"It's not a cop! Oh… but that is," I said as I pointed to the left side of the freeway.

We flew by him still going 85 miles per hour. It was too late. There wasn't time to slow down. Quickly, our brake lights lit up the freeway as the darkened police cruiser came to life. The officer pulled in behind us. We knew what was coming.

"We can't get a ticket! We don't have time for a ticket," I said.

As the sirens blared behind us, Scott said, "I can't believe you made me wear this hat!"

I let out a nervous laugh as we pulled over.

The officer slowly walked up to the driver's window and said, "Did you know you were going 85 miles per hour?"

"Yes!" we both screamed out in unison.

The officer stepped back, half-smiling, and said, "And why was that?"

"We forgot the wedding dress. We are on the way to the airport. We forgot the dress." Again, both in unison.

The officer said, "The airport is the other way."

"We are going to get the dress. It's at home. Then we have to go back to the airport." Still both speaking over each other.

The officer looked at Scott, tapped the side of his truck and said, "Slow down when you get to 70th. Officers like to hang out there."

As we pulled away from the still-smiling officer, Scott said, "It had to be the hat. He must have felt sorry for me."

We finally got home. I ran into the house to get the dress. Almost instantly, I was back out the door. Somehow, the sun had come up while I briefly ran inside. I hopped in the truck with a big smile on my face. Scott looked at me with a little less excitement.

We finally made it to the airport. Our first-class tickets allowed us to get through the lines quickly. With twenty minutes to spare, we sipped on mai tais waiting for the plane to take off.

"See, I knew we would make it," I said with a smile.

"It's too soon for me. I need another mai tai," he said with half a smile.

When the plane touched down in Hawaii, I knew we were a mere twenty-four hours away from getting married.

We quickly got to our hotel room, unpacked a few things, and then headed off to our favorite restaurant. We joked with friends and family about the little mishap with the dress. Everyone went around the table talking about what went wrong at their weddings. We all laughed as each couple shared their little wedding imperfections.

I realized that what makes a perfect wedding are the imperfections that happen along the way. It's much like a marriage. There are beautiful moments; there are stressful moments; there are moments when you just need a drink. But in a "perfect" marriage, you get through all those moments together.

~Diana DeAndrea-Kohn

72

It Won't Rain

The best thing one can do when it's raining is to let it rain.
~Henry Wadsworth Longfellow

The six-acre park next to the city hall couldn't have been a more picturesque spot for a wedding. Impeccably manicured lawns rolled gently down to a shimmering lake. Paths wound through azalea bushes, and a pavilion overlooked the entire scene.

"What do you think?" My future daughter-in-law, Lindsey, could barely contain her excitement. "Won't this be perfect for an outdoor wedding?"

"It's beautiful," I agreed.

"We'll set up the guests' chairs here." She pointed to an area under a stand of oak trees. "Reverend Spencer will stand with his back to the lake, and Jeremy and I will be married under the archway my dad is building for us."

I smiled as I pictured the charming wedding Lindsey described. Then my practical side stepped in. "Where will you dress? And what if someone has to use the bathroom?"

"The mayor's office said they would give us a key to City Hall so we could use their facilities."

"Sounds like everything is falling into place." I glanced up as a cloud passed over the sun. "What will we do if it rains? After all, it is springtime."

"It won't rain," Lindsey said with certainty.

"Okay, but..."

"It won't rain."

We worked out the rest of the details. Then Lindsey left to run errands while I stayed behind to find out about getting a key for the building. The receptionist directed me to the mayor's office where I told his secretary, Connie, what I needed. After signing the necessary papers, I turned to go and then hesitated. While I loved Lindsey's indomitable spirit, I somehow doubted she could control the weather by sheer force of will.

"Is there a room here we could use just in case it rains the day of the wedding?" I asked. "I'd hate to try to notify guests of a change in location at the last minute."

"Sure," Connie said. "You can use the boardroom. I'll show it to you."

Connie unlocked the door to a large room with high ceilings. Over a hundred chairs faced a dais ringed by a semi-circular desk that held microphones for the city council members. The rich walnut paneling and rails were beautiful but not very romantic. As Connie and I talked, I pondered how to convert the stiff, courtroom-like surroundings into a backdrop suitable for a wedding.

Then I turned around.

Twenty-foot glass walls framed two sides of the "back" of the room. "Can we open those blinds?" I asked.

"Certainly."

As we drew back the long, vertical blinds, sunlight streamed in. One window faced the parking lot, but azaleas lined the front and hid most of the asphalt from view. Water spurted merrily from a fountain in the center of the oval drive. Oaks and birches lined the parking area and side of the building.

Perfect.

Later, I told Lindsey about the boardroom. "At least now we have a contingency plan in case it rains."

"It won't rain," she said.

"But..."

"It won't rain."

The weekend before the wedding, it began to rain. And I don't mean gentle April showers. By Tuesday, it had rained nonstop. We weathered tornado warnings and heard reports of cars being swept away by floodwaters in a nearby city.

On Thursday, Lindsey called. "It's still raining!" she wailed. "Even if it stops now, everything will be too soaked to have the wedding outside."

I tried to reassure her. "I know. We can use the boardroom. It'll be all right."

On Saturday, my sister and niece helped me decorate the boardroom while Lindsey's mom prepared for the reception dinner to be held at her house. As thunder crashed outside, we ironed tablecloths and hung paper bells. My husband and some of Jeremy's friends set up a truckload of white folding chairs and dried the seats. The caterer hurried the wedding cake inside before rain could destroy the icing. Almost everything was in place.

Then the archway arrived. Lindsey's dad had carved it of 150-year-old cedar from a barn on her grandfather's farm. Double wedding rings crowned the top. We wound ivy through the latticework sides, hung white silk bouquets on the corners, and placed potted plants on either side. It looked like an archway fit for royalty.

When we pulled back the blinds, the room was transformed. Branches brushed the tall windows, giving the illusion of trees swaying overhead. Flowers bloomed throughout the grounds. We looked upon a world that was fresh and green and inviting—and dripping rain, of course. It was as close to being outdoors as we could get.

Later that day, as Lindsey and Jeremy exchanged vows before a background of gray clouds, love filled the room. Even torrential rains could do nothing to dampen the beautiful event we had come to celebrate.

I now have a daughter-in-law who still looks upon the world with a can-do spirit, and Lindsey is blessed—or cursed—with a pragmatic mother-in-law who is not a last-minute person. When Lindsey's "can-do" turns into "Oh, no! What now?" I hope I'll always be there to help her see that contingency plans can be a beautiful thing.

~Tracy Crump

Chapter 8

Here Comes the Bride

Bucking Tradition

Just because something is tradition doesn't make it right.

~*Anthony J. D'Angelo*, The College Blue Book

73

The Farm Boy and the Mongolian Circus

Oft expectation fails, and most oft there
Where most it promises.
~William Shakespeare

"Mom, I'm getting married," Shane said. "She's from Outer Mongolia."

Mongolia? We were from Kansas. How does a farm boy from Kansas find a girl from Mongolia?

Meeting Bulgan Bayaraa for the first time was an experience. She didn't speak much English, and the first thing she said to me was, "If you came to my village in Mongolia, all the people in the village would spit warm milk on you!" She smiled.

Apparently, that is an honor.

I have four grown children, and I'd been waiting for years to plan a wedding for one of them. I could picture my daughter as a bride in a white Victorian wedding gown, and my sons as grooms in tuxedos. Very traditional weddings in an old church, candles, the organ, stained-glass windows… I could almost smell the flowers and taste the tiered wedding cake.

My son and his bride-to-be wanted to plan their own wedding. I was disappointed because, of course, as the mother of the groom, I wanted to help plan it. The bride's parents were still in Mongolia and couldn't make it to the wedding.

My son was a radio personality, and Bulgan had been a performer in a Mongolian circus. The two of them had a variety of very interesting friends, and somehow they all got involved in planning the wedding.

Bulgan wanted Shane and herself to wear traditional Mongolian clothing at the wedding. The outfits had to be custom-made in Mongolia and shipped to America. I was hoping the bride would wear a white wedding gown with a veil. Bulgan wore a yellow silk dress with gold glitter on her face, neck and arms, which was a symbol of good fortune. Shane wore a leather coat made of yak skin, red pointed boots that looked like something Aladdin would wear, and a big fur hat with horns on it that looked as if he'd borrowed it from a Viking. When I had pictured my son getting married, I imagined him in a tuxedo looking like Cary Grant. With the fur hat on his head, he looked like Genghis Khan.

They decided to get married in the back yard instead of a church. There went the old church and the stained-glass windows I'd hoped for!

When the guests arrived, there were Mongolian circus performers doing various dances and a contortionist who was twisting herself into knots. The groom's friends included Hawaiian hula dancers, Samoan dancers, a country band, and a radio DJ. There were Russians who didn't speak English, Mongolians who didn't speak English, and a Chinese family that provided the buffet for the reception.

The radio DJ, who had just recently been ordained, performed the ceremony. The music was provided by a country band. There would be no organ playing "Here Comes the Bride."

The bride and groom exchanged vows and drank warm goat's milk from a silver bowl. My son had driven thirty miles to a farm early that morning to buy goat's milk for the ceremony. At last, they were pronounced husband and wife.

As soon as the vows were said, the hula dancers broke into a dance, the country band began playing a mix of country and Hawaiian music, and the contortionist was doing unbelievable things while balanced on a tiny metal pole. Samoan dancers rubbed oil all over themselves and danced a "wedding money dance" where the guests were expected to "stick" dollar bills to their exposed skin. They collected a considerable amount of money for the couple because there was hardly a guest who didn't try to "stick" money to the dancers.

No one quite knew how to react, but soon everyone, from the youngest to the oldest, was doing the hula, or at least trying to. The guests enjoyed a delicious buffet of Chinese and Mongolian food, and had a piece of bright pink wedding cake.

During the reception, it was announced that it was the birthday of one of the guests. Paper party hats were handed out by his family, and everyone sang "Happy Birthday." Many of the wedding photos showed people wearing the party hats. The Chinese family set off five hundred firecrackers for good luck.

Most of the guests couldn't carry on conversations with each other because there were seven different languages being spoken. However, there were a lot of smiles and laughter. Happiness is the same in every language.

It was a one-of-a-kind wedding for a one-of-a-kind couple. Was it the wedding I'd always dreamed about for my son? No, but it was the wedding he wanted, and he seemed happy. I didn't get the church, the ceremony, the clothing, the gown, or anything else I had hoped for.

Oh, yes, and I'd injured my right hand a week before the wedding and had to wear a cast up to my elbow. The cast would not fit through the sleeve of the dress I'd planned to wear for the wedding. The frilly, silk dress with the pink roses printed on it that I'd been looking forward to wearing and being photographed in was replaced by a dress chosen for the size of the armholes so I could get the dress on over my cast. The wedding photos look like a group of people on their way to a costume party.

I'm hoping I'll still get to plan a wedding for one of my remaining children... although a wedding without circus performers and hula dancers might seem downright boring!

~April Knight

74

You're Getting Married Where?

He spake well who said that graves are the footprints of angels.
~Henry Wadsworth Longfellow

My church is almost 200 years old. The sanctuary is enormous and features two breathtaking Tiffany stained-glass windows. One is two stories tall and depicts Christ's ascension, and the other illustrates the women at the tomb on Easter morning. Our pulpit is carved from a block of green marble, also made by Louis Tiffany. You could not ask for a more beautiful church for a wedding.

And I was married there, in a ceremony befitting the setting. While the wedding was perfect, the marriage was not. Ten years later, I was a single mother of three small children. I prayed each night for a new husband who would love my children as his own and commit to spending his life with me. And, in time, I met the man who would become my second husband.

My first wedding had been huge, a true fairy-tale extravaganza. I was a bit older, wiser now. I did not want to be married a second time in the same church; it felt wrong. This time, I wanted an intimate, family ceremony, but still a religious one with a personal connection. I can still remember with perfect clarity the day I took Eric by the hand and asked, "Would you marry me in the cemetery?"

Before you think of a sacrilegious satanic ceremony complete with black wedding gown, let me explain. I grew up across the street from my hometown's historic cemetery. Built in 1883, it is the final resting place of soldiers as far back as the American Revolution. My ancestors lie there as far back as my great-grandfather. As a little girl, my father and I took long walks there every week while he pointed out the graves of famous locals and our relatives. I learned to ride my bike there, and when my children were babies I pushed their stroller around the curving roads so familiar to me. Riverview Cemetery for me is a place of peace and happy memories.

Just past the wrought-iron entrance gates is a large marble chapel named The Grand Army of the Republic Chapel. It was built in 1897, a gift to the cemetery by Civil War veterans and their families. Carved along every side are the names of Civil War battles, and as true history buffs, the Chapel was always especially significant to my father and me. Inside, it can seat 120 people, and has a center aisle ending at a pulpit. There are stained-glass windows, candelabras, and stands for flowers. It exudes an atmosphere of serenity and beauty.

I was ecstatic to be planning my wedding, yet at the same time it was bittersweet. My parents now lived almost a thousand miles away. Neither was in the best of health, and they could not make the trip to be there. I had spent so many long childhood hours in Riverview Cemetery with my daddy; it seemed the perfect way to make it feel like he was there. Eric understood and gave me his complete support, saying the only thing that mattered to him was marrying me; whatever location I chose was fine.

With a great degree of nervous hesitation, I called the superintendent of the cemetery. It was easy to talk to her; I had gone to school with her children from elementary on through high school. We attend the same church, and she had been a Sunday school teacher to all three of my children. However, this was an unusual request.

My worries were groundless. She never thought my request was morbid and said it would be wonderful for the Memorial Chapel to be used for such a happy occasion. Not only did she agree, but she even offered me her home to get dressed for the ceremony.

The day was bright; the flowers outside the chapel were in full bloom. Since my father could not be there, my older son walked me down the aisle, and my other son and my daughter were ring bearer and flower girl. The chapel was filled with our friends and families. After we finished our vows, my older son played the trumpet recessional as Eric and I took our first walk as husband and wife.

As the years have passed, we have both begun to carve careers as dark fantasy and horror writers. It makes an interesting anecdote to include in our bios that we were married in a cemetery. But the greater truth is it was truly a beautiful and spiritual service. Even though he was not there physically, I felt my father's presence as the sunbeams streamed through the stained glass, warming the chapel with a rosy glow.

Though many people at the time thought my choice of location was gruesome, it was not. Seventeen years have passed, and I would not change a thing about that day. Our wedding may have been held in an unusual place, but for us it was unique and personal. My parents have now passed away and lie within sight of the chapel. It is quite meaningful to me that I can stand and see the memorial to the people who began my life and the spot where my current life began.

This year marks the 150th anniversary of the beginning of the Civil War, one of the darkest times for our country. I like to think of our wedding in the Civil War Memorial chapel as a commemoration of reconciliation; a way of bringing two different entities together and forming one union, stronger together than either could be apart. Symbolic of the small skirmishes and the full-blown battles we would face, joined together in union as one, we are able to withstand just as the United States has done.

~Anna M. Lowther

75

Under the Chuppah

When you sew, you have something that will last to show for your efforts.
~Elizabeth Travis Johnson

N o one is quite sure how the family tradition began. No one will stand right up and say, "I remember exactly how and when we decided to do this!"

But, somehow, when our oldest daughter Jill was to be a bride, the family Chuppah Patch Project came to life.

In Judaism, a chuppah, the wedding canopy, a cloth stretched across four poles, is fraught with symbolism, all of it lovely. It is under the chuppah that the bride and groom have their sacred space, somewhat apart from all others, sometimes with loved ones under the chuppah, too, or at least nearby. The chuppah can also be interpreted as a first home, waiting to be "furnished" with the love that binds them.

So, of course, there would be a chuppah at Jill's wedding. That symbolism was far too meaningful to ignore. But this one would not be constructed of vines or flowers or of fine silken fabric. This time, it would be constructed of individual patches with random thoughts, drawings, messages, notes or whatever struck the creative fancy of close family and friends who were invited to contribute.

The bride's two sisters spearheaded the chuppah project, dutifully sending out pre-cut patches of a simple linen fabric with brief instructions as to what was hoped for in the final product: a "canopy" composed of these patches, sewn together as a whole, and mounted.

Soon, they came pouring in. Each patch stopped me in my tracks as I discovered new aspects of our daughter and her groom. The patches were alternately wrenchingly moving, hilarious, beautifully crafted, sentimental, and always original. No two were remotely alike, as dear ones used their own lovely intuitions and memories to create this singular artifact.

Of course, there were glitches. Some didn't follow the instructions about leaving space for a hem; others used their own fabric; still others delayed and stalled and threatened to disturb the perfectly planned dimensions of the chuppah.

Certainly, there are easier ways to create this special ritual canopy. And there are surely many more handsome, perfect examples of wedding chuppahs to be found. But this wedding chuppah—this very special wedding chuppah—was crafted of memories and meaning.

There would be two more Chuppah Patch Projects in our family for the three Friedman brides. Suffice it to say that they never went smoothly or predictably, but they also meant more to these brides and grooms than any other "gift" they received.

The fact that all three weddings took place in our own garden added to both the personal feel and the emotional pull. Standing under those patchwork chuppahs was like no other experience in our lives as a family. The enormous focus on whether the bridal gown would be ivory or blush—tea-length or floor-length—faded into oblivion. The debates about menu, with intense concentration on the precise sauce for the salmon—forgotten.

On three June afternoons, there we stood, under those chuppahs. Past and present collided. All was real—and surreal. Under the chuppah, our own dreams and memories merged with this moment: a bride, a groom, a rabbi, a family. Above us, a soft breeze on all three days mercifully cooled us, and each time, somewhere off in the distance, birds chirped.

And try as I did to concentrate on the rabbi's messages at those three daughters' weddings, I was off in another place. I was remembering Jill, Amy and Nancy in sunsuits and snowsuits, not wedding gowns. I was remembering them shrieking with delight as they mastered the challenges of their two-wheelers. And a minute later—or so it seemed—they were walking down the front steps in their prom gowns. And I was, of course, remembering those last, lingering hugs that came on college campuses, ready or not.

Standing under the chuppah at those weddings, I was silently wishing for our daughters and their husbands what mattered beyond the lyricism/delirium of their new love. I was praying that they would have the sense of awe and gratitude that comes as marriage matures. The wonderful knowledge that there is someone—one constant someone—who truly cares that you're terrified of airplane take-offs, or frantic about being good enough at your job, or depressed because you think you're getting fat.

I knew, each of those afternoons under the wedding chuppah, that there may be things more mighty than that unqualified connection, but I couldn't name any. And, best of all, thanks to those patchwork chuppahs, the memories of standing together under them still come flooding back years later.

My daughters are grown women and mothers, so yes, those chuppahs are history now. But they hang prominently in each of our daughters' homes for all to see, space-stealers for sure, especially when space is tight. But then, there is probably no more important wall hanging in all the world.

~Sally Friedman

All Aboard the Wedding Train

The most important trip you may take in life is meeting people halfway.
~Henry Boye

Wedding plans involve millions of little details, and couples soon learn that each one of those details has a price tag. When my husband and I were planning our wedding, he didn't care much about the cake, the flowers, or the wine we bought. His main concern was providing transportation for our guests from the church to the reception.

He'd been to one too many weddings where he only knew the bride and groom, and the ceremony and reception were nowhere near each other. He'd had to awkwardly beg rides from other guests just to get from one part of the wedding to the other. For our wedding, he wanted to spare our out-of-town guests the same hassle.

We quickly found out just how expensive transportation can be, especially in a big city. We were getting married at a church in the heart of Chicago, with the reception at one of our regular hangouts on the North Side. On weekends in Chicago, you often see trolleys full of wedding attendants zooming around the city, so we looked into hiring one.

When the quote came back at four figures, we quickly dismissed that idea. That—and other popular transportation options, we soon discovered—were simply beyond our means.

While wondering how we would solve our dilemma, my fiancé joked, "Well, we could always take everyone on the L."

I pondered that idea. The church and reception were both located within two blocks of the CTA's Brown Line. We could buy everyone a pass, hand them out at the wedding, and ride the train together. Because the Brown Line was elevated, we'd get to see a little bit of the city, and the price was right. We could take all of our guests on the train for under $200. That was a fraction of the price for a trolley or bus.

"That's not a bad idea," I said.

"I was joking," he replied. But the more we talked about it, the better the idea sounded, and soon we were figuring out how many CTA passes we needed for the night.

Although we were pleased with our decision, it wasn't necessarily everyone's cup of tea. I made the mistake of telling a bridesmaid and a friend about our non-traditional plans at my seamstress's house while they helped me get my wedding dress fitted. Initially, it wasn't a pleasant scene.

"How are you getting to the reception?" asked one friend, as she helped me into my dress.

"We're taking the L," I replied.

"You can't do that!" they cried and immediately went into crisis mode. We couldn't possibly take the L—my dress would get ruined from the dirt on the train. They believed the bride and groom should take a limo, and my bridesmaid even offered to provide it as a wedding gift.

"First off, my dress is going to get dirty anyway," I said quietly, as to not alarm the seamstress whose work I'd end up getting filthy. "Second, no one is ever going to wear it again, so why should it matter?" Explaining why we wanted to take the L, my friends grudgingly stopped complaining, but they were still dubious.

My parents and a few other guests were a little concerned about the idea of hauling everyone on the train, but instead of upsetting us, they just decided to drive themselves from point to point.

On our wedding day, nearly fifty of our guests took us up on the option to ride the train. After the ceremony, we all trooped over to the L stop and slowly made our way through the turnstile and onto the platform. When our train arrived, we poured onto two cars and relaxed for the ride.

To our delight, my new husband and I discovered that we had inadvertently created an opportunity to spend extra time with the guests who'd traveled hundreds of miles to share our special moment. Since we were all trapped on the train, we got to see more of the people for whom we did this in the first place, and we appreciated having extra time with far-flung friends we rarely got to see.

A few stops before our destination, I jumped out of the first train car and hustled back to the second to see the rest of our guests. As I stood in the center of the crowded train, talking with a friend, I noticed the man next to me looking at my bridal getup. "Did you really just get married?" he asked skeptically.

When I gleefully replied that I had, he reached down into the bag of groceries at his feet and pulled out a bottle of red wine. "Congratulations!" he said, handing it to me.

My husband and I look forward to opening that bottle of wine on our tenth anniversary. When we pop the cork, I'll be wearing my dress with the ring of L car dirt along the bottom, and we'll toast to our celebration with family, friends, and the city of Chicago.

~Jill Jaracz

An Interesting Cast
of Characters

I am not in this world to live up to other people's expectations,
nor do I feel that the world must live up to mine.
~Fritz Perls

When my husband and I decided to get hitched on January 1, 2000, his family was all in Serbia and my parents were living in Kuwait for ten months of the year. Celebrating the millennium in the Cook Islands seemed like a stellar idea because if the world was going to end (or at least come to a halt), what better place to be than a remote tropical island?

I honestly can't remember how we decided to get married there, but it was the best decision of my life. I'd been a bridesmaid enough times to get the vicarious walking-down-the-aisle-all-eyes-on-me thrill, but also the associated stress of planning a party for more than a hundred people. Combining the honeymoon with the wedding seemed like a much more satisfying alternative, so we decided to do the wedding alone but have a party in the summer when my parents were in town.

I contacted an event planner named Anita who arranged everything for us. We booked an apartment in a small, family-run motel on the edge of the water. The day we arrived, she met us and drove us around the main island (a forty-five-minute journey) to check potential wedding spots. After finding the perfect secluded area of beach, we went to meet our minister. We wanted our ceremony to be fairly non-denominational, and Anita assured us that Danny would be the perfect officiant. After meeting him, we had nothing else to do but enjoy our vacation and see them in two weeks for our wedding.

But we did see Danny again—a couple of times, actually. The first time was for a cultural dinner show at a hotel. The dancers came out, and there was Danny, our minister, acting as emcee of the show. He spotted us right away and gave us a shout-out, which was cute, then had us come up and dance, which was less cute.

The second time we saw Danny was in our room, sitting on our dresser. He was on the cover of our *Guide to the Cook Islands*, looking like one of the natives from *Gilligan's Island*. Apparently, our Danny was a bit of a local celebrity.

On the day of our wedding, we weren't due on the beach until sunset, so I'd booked an in-room massage to relax and pass the time. Enter Divine in a muumuu. She oiled me up, ran her hands up and down my shoulders for a couple of minutes, then asked if she could have my *People* magazines. After she left, I had to have a few piña coladas to unwind.

It was time to get married. With my fiancé safely ensconced at the bar, I put on my wedding dress (fifteen dollars at the mall), and did my make-up (lip balm) and hair (four bobby pins). Anita showed up with a massive bouquet, out of which I plucked four gardenias to put in my hair in lieu of a veil.

The sky was getting very overcast, but I didn't care. My fiancé had made his way to our beach (to this day, I'm not sure how he got there) and was waiting for me to walk with him to our wedding spot. Waiting for us at our sandy altar was Danny. With another man. Wearing a blue Speedo.

Apparently, this man was a friend of Danny's and lived just behind our section of beach. He was having a barbecue and was checking water conditions before everyone hit the surf. Thankfully, Danny persuaded him to hold off on his beach party for a few minutes, and we were able to start the ceremony.

The photographer acted as best man, and Anita was maid of

honor. We said our vows, and then Danny pronounced us husband and wife. In the name of the Church of Jesus Christ and the Latter-Day Saints. There's a picture that I'm sure was taken as Danny said this because my husband and I have looks on our faces as if to say, "Umm… are we Mormon now?"

We didn't have time to ponder that question because it started to rain, a blessing from the gods but not for my dress: it became completely translucent. The true blessing was having a bouquet as big as a gladiator shield to hide my lady parts.

After the paperwork was signed in a bar across the street, we took off on our scooter and toured the island in the rain, honking and waving at everyone we passed. Back at our apartment, my new husband decided to forego the traditional carrying of the bride across the threshold and instead threw us both in the pool.

While drying off, we saw that the rain had stopped, so we ran to the beach in our towels to see the most brilliant sunset ever, then got dressed and had a romantic dinner, where I promptly fell asleep at the table.

Looking back, I can see how my wedding reflects my marriage—full of interesting surprises, overall kookiness, lots of laughs, and utter exhaustion.

~Lori Dyan

78

Bagpipes in Toronto

To have and to hold from this day forward, for better for worse, for richer for poorer, in sickness and in health, to love and to cherish, till death us do part.
~Book of Common Prayer

We were married in Toronto in October 2005. We chose Toronto because I knew the city well, having completed my fellowship in Buffalo, just over the border. Toronto is a vibrant, cosmopolitan city; it is also gay-friendly. Pam and I had met on the Internet—PerfectMatch.com—some six weeks before. It was a whirlwind romance, a flurry of emotions, joy, and travel between St. Louis and Rochester, New York. We surgeons are used to making decisions quickly and often. So the decision was not difficult. When Cupid strikes, it's hard to miss the arrow through the heart.

Pam made all the preparations. She had always wanted a ring from Tiffany, so we got Tiffany rings, seven diamonds in each one. Her dear friend Susan, a minister, agreed to officiate. The venue was the City Hall in Toronto, a gleaming semi-lunar edifice of glass and steel, set against a backdrop of older sandstone buildings. The misty rain stopped, and rays of sunlight filtered through the clouds. As we took the taxi ride down Queen Street, I remarked, "If there were bagpipes, it would be perfect." Since I'm a Scot, I love the drone of the pipes, and a piper can be found at many a Scottish wedding.

At this point, the taxi driver rolled down the window, and then we heard it: the strain of the pipes wafting through the air, playing "Scotland the Brave." I couldn't believe it—what perfection!

Our ceremony was lovely (of course, I'm biased). The Canadian judge had, by law, to officiate also, so she and Susan performed the ceremony together. We had written some vows of our own, and we used the vows from the *Book of Common Prayer*. They were strong vows; we promised to love, comfort, honor, keep, and be faithful.

Following the ceremony, before our afternoon tea at the Four Seasons, our photographer motioned us toward the Mounties lined up in a row on the green space. It was an idyllic scene—a happy couple, sunshine, Mounties, horses. So idyllic, in fact, that a busload of Japanese tourists unloaded and rushed over to snap the event for their albums. At this point, it was time to leave. We had become an event.

During our tea, a compilation of our favorite songs was played, starting with the classic by Robert Burns, "My Love Is Like a Red, Red Rose." We had two cakes—a sponge and a traditional Scottish wedding cake, which is a heavy, dense fruitcake layered with marzipan and hard icing. The tradition is that oblong pieces can be cut and mailed in specially designed boxes to loved ones who could not attend the ceremony. We sent a piece to my mother, whom Pam had met the month before. Pam had been standing with her on the curb outside her favorite Italian restaurant in Troon, Scotland, supporting her on one arm while she steadied herself with her other arm on her white stick, when my mum said to her: "It's okay for me to go now, now that Diane has found you. You are the right one."

Neither of us really felt the impact of those words till a month after the wedding, when I took the call from the nursing home that she had passed away suddenly from a heart attack, just after asking the attendant for a cup of tea. We went through her room at Westbank, the solid sandstone nursing home with a side of white pebbledash overlooking the South Bay at Troon, to pack up her belongings. The CD player had buttons and Velcro glued on the knobs, so she could recognize each one by feel. Opening the lid, we found the compilation wedding CD she had enjoyed. On the bedside table we found the box that had contained the slice of wedding cake. It was empty.

She had enjoyed the cake. She had been there in spirit to enjoy our idyllic day.

~Diane M. Radford

79

Polterabend

Men are made stronger on realization that the helping hand they need
is at the end of their own arm.
~Sidney J. Phillips

When we taxied down the runway and took off with a roar, my stomach fluttered, and John reached over, giving my hand a warm squeeze. We were heading toward Dangast, Germany, a small fishing village on the North Sea. "I don't want to die!" a child screamed in the seat behind us. After a half-hour of this, and the mother sitting stock-still beside her terrified youngster, a woman walked up the aisle from the back of the plane and did her best to comfort the child. She spoke the thick, rich German language I heard off and on while I was growing up. The little boy didn't know what she was saying, but his wide eyes focused on her, and he found something comforting in her voice.

One reason we were going to Germany was to have a German wedding. American weddings seemed so foreign to me. I was raised with a German mother and American father, and heard tales of their own wedding, so different from the serious events I was used to in the United States.

I would sit at the kitchen table with a blue-and-white-checkered cloth smoothed over it and laugh as Mom told the story of the Polterabend—the German tradition where friends and neighbors bring boxes of china to a party for the couple a night (or two) before the wedding. My parents had a Polterabend, but my beleaguered father-to-be didn't know about the tradition until there were bits of broken glass and pottery flying everywhere as he stood in the middle of it, looking at the smiling, round German faces surrounding him, his future father-in-law handing him a broom. I don't know who finally explained to him that he had to sweep up the bits to show he would be a good husband, but he finally began the task. No sooner would he have some of it neatly piled then the mischievous friends and neighbors would rush the complete pile and scatter it again while others continued to smash more Bavarian pottery.

"I want a Polterabend someday," I'd say while sipping tea from one of Mom's German china cups.

"It isn't quite how it used to be," Mom had cautioned me. "The bride-to-be has to help the groom-to-be now."

My father had rolled his eyes. "Too bad it wasn't that way before!"

I had my heart set on a German wedding. John was also eager to visit Germany again. He had been stationed in Germany when in the Army years before I met him. He loved the dark beer and tangy sauerkraut and apples next to jagerschnitzel with potatoes. He loved the old towns with cobbled streets and buildings that still bore the scars of world wars.

I was lucky to find someone willing to strike out on an adventure instead of demanding the norm. I was especially lucky on that plane beside John because he knew it wasn't just the desire for a Polterabend that drew me away from home. There was a vacancy I was trying to escape. I couldn't bear to get married with my family around me. My father, sister, and perhaps aunts, uncles and some cousins would have been there — but my mother was gone. She had died from leukemia just four years earlier. She would never see me in my wedding gown. A wedding at home would have made her absence scream out.

John knew I needed to avoid that pain on our wedding day, and he was willing to travel across an ocean and stay with my German relatives he had only met once or twice during their brief trips to the U.S.

My German aunt and uncle arranged the wedding and Polterabend before our arrival. They also left no day of our two-week stay unplanned. We stepped off the plane and immediately began a whirlwind of activity and eating. Pig knuckles, bratwurst, dark breads and beers, gravies and other good food and drink were set before us until John and I thought we would happily explode. We walked old town streets, shopped in open-air food markets, and rode bikes through Dangast to meet the "good neighbors" who would attend our Polterabend. We spent a half-hour at each home becoming introduced and having a small toast. We met "Mummy Mouse" and peeked into her small gift shop. We met "Lothar the Hunter" and his wife, Gitte, and then "Wolfgang the Woodcarver," among others. Every person was identified with a profession or hobby attached to his name — it made it easier to remember. John sat among them and laughed heartily.

The days flew by. "The wedding has not happened yet. There is still time to change your mind," Aunt Karin teased over a German breakfast of boiled eggs, liverwurst on dark breads and rolls, and coffee creamed with evaporated milk. We sat on the terrace in the garden, the sun shining warmly on my still-wet hair. I looked across the table at John, who was gamely riding the waves of each day with me. "No, I think I'll keep him," I said.

"Are you ready for your Polterabend, John?" my aunt asked.

John groaned and grinned sheepishly. "Can't we skip that part?"

My aunt's laugh burst out like a cannonball. "No, John! That is the test to see if you two will help each other through hard times!"

"THE NEIGHBORS ARE COMING!" my aunt hollered later that day. I saw a twinkle in her eyes. A sound came from a distance — at first it was faint, but then it grew. We heard an accordion and singing — raucous Dangast villagers came marching down the street with Wolfgang the Woodcarver leading the way, playing an accordion and followed by other villagers singing and carrying boxes and garlands.

A parade? An accordion? John and I laughed until our sides hurt. We looked at the warm, happy faces of the villagers and felt blanketed with love from people we had just met. They placed garlands on the doorways and a large wooden stork by the hedges. They strung a line of baby clothes over the driveway and began setting up to smash the china.

They offered us gifts as well, which neither John nor I expected. I was stunned at how personal they were. These villagers had observed us well. Soon, the first bit of pottery crashed. John and I grabbed our brooms and hurried out to the friendly laughter and taunts of the villagers. John took a deep breath and then plowed into the center of it. We would sweep, and there would be a CRASH behind us. No matter how we tried to keep on top of it, the merry villagers had more mischief to make.

"When are they going to run out of things to break?" John gasped, but there were tears of laughter in his eyes. My heart was full. I had a piece of my mother with me, and I had the Polterabend I had always wanted. I realized, though, that while it was wonderful to have, I didn't need it. I had all the proof I needed that the man I would marry would help me through hard times.

~Tanya Sousa

80

A Wedding with Tim

*The essential joy of being with horses is that it brings us in contact with the
rare elements of grace, beauty, spirit, and fire.*
~Sharon Ralls Lemon

*I*t was uncharacteristically hot and sultry on Quadra Island, British
Columbia, and I was evaporating. I have never liked the heat
except when I was a child growing up on the northeast coast of
England, and back then, like all mad dogs and Englishmen, I greeted
the sun with blind enthusiasm. But this was my daughter's wedding
day, so I thought cool, knowing I would not melt.

As I looked at Amy on her wedding day, I thought how incredibly privileged I was to have given birth to a tiny baby who became
this beautiful young woman. Amy and I had always had a good relationship. Part of the secret was that we communicated, as neither
of us liked to keep troubling thoughts and emotions inside. Any
clashes were perhaps born out of the genetic mix. Amy is of Italian/
British descent. I am obviously the Brit. The Mediterranean genes
beat out the Brits, and she inherited many things Italian: a mass of
chestnut curls, large green eyes, olive skin, spiritedness and good
teeth, although I am not sure the latter is necessarily Italian, but it is
definitely not British.

The garden was resplendent; pear and apple trees created shade
for guests, and the scarlet rhododendron bushes were in full bloom.
A multitude of flowers in large pots, strategically placed around the
grounds, added an air of celebration as they went head-to-head with

the sun. A small pond sat off to the side of the garden, and my eyes landed on the floating lily pads, wishing I could be counted among them. There was a Buddha at the water's edge sitting in deep reflection. Undoubtedly, he was sending his blessings to the pond dwellers and life beyond.

What a perfect setting. People were milling about, children engrossed in play. I was hovering around Amy, administering what I hoped were calm and encouraging words. Weddings, after all, seem to create a heap more anxiety for the bride than the groom. It was time for Amy to make her way down the garden path to stand with her husband-to-be.

"Are you doing okay, sweetheart? Anything you need?" I asked as she stood in front of the bedroom mirror with one of her best friends, Catherine.

"No, Mom, I am doing fine. Just having you here helps." I tingled with joy when I heard those last few words.

As I studied Amy, I took in the dark curls that fell naturally around her face. There was a scarlet Gerber daisy amid the tresses, comfy in its place beside her left ear. Her dress, ah, her dress—we bought it in Toronto, one-of-a-kind from an uptown store that encouraged the free-spirited girl to show through. She was a vision in white silk. A rose-coloured sash, an ally of the daisy, was tied nattily around her waistline. A pleated strapless bodice hugged her form, and gave way to solitary sheer fins of silk beginning at the waistline and flowing down the skirt, reminding me of wide blades of grass sighing in the breeze.

"Amy, would you still like your dad and I to walk you down the path?" I enquired. This had been the original plan.

"No, Mom, I think I would just like my bridesmaids to walk with me."

Feeling a momentary sense of puzzlement, I said in a cheery voice, "Okay, so we will go and sit down."

"Sure, Mom," she replied. I looked at both Catherine and Amy and felt that I was being left out of some part of this day.

Jill, the minister, came into the room at this point and said to me, "Would you mind if I spend some time with Amy alone? We have some wedding business to take care of."

I could not imagine why I was being left out of the "wedding business." However, I left the bedroom, chin up, heart in a dither, and sat with the rest of the family in the front row.

The groom, Sheldon, was a perfect match for his lovely bride. His unruly sepia-toned hair and the smile beneath could have won a thousand hearts. In an off-white linen suit, he stood waiting for Amy at the arched trellis in front of a small forest that sat at the bottom of their garden. Two solitary large trees acted as bookends to the flower-covered trellis where the young couple would exchange their vows. The breezy strains of a guitar filled the air, and everyone was seated waiting for the grand entrance. As I looked around, I was curious as to why the bridesmaids were sitting with the other guests in the front rows. Weren't they supposed to be with Amy?

It all became clear in the next moment. I was facing the house, waiting to see the bride make her entrance, when from behind the home a rather gorgeous, albeit large head appeared that belonged not to Amy, but to that of a Belgian horse. In the next frame came my daughter, sitting sidesaddle on Tim, the large and infinitely good-natured steed. There was an uproar from the guests, thrilled to see the bride astride her mount. I rose from my seat to greet her. Like all the guests, I was totally awed by the vision of Amy sitting amid the folds of her white dress, looking radiant. I was, to say the least, impressed not only by the perfect image of the bride on a horse, but by the carefully guarded secret. Sheldon smiled and walked up to Amy, offering his arms to assist in the dismount. I stood up and walked over to give her a quick kiss before they continued the ceremony.

Being a horse lover, I embraced both horse and Amy, whereupon she whispered in my ear, "Mom, Jill offered Tim for the ceremony, so I decided at the last minute to ride to the altar as a symbol of my love for you and our love for horses. I did this for you."

I was speechless. Sometimes, there are moments in one's life where there are no words to describe the feelings deep within. This was one of them.

Often, it is said that when we think of fearful or sad things, we should replace the thought with an image filled with happiness and love; mine is now Amy upon the horse and the words, "Mom, I did this for you."

~Rosalind Forster

81

Highland Fling for Two

If we could ever make red tape nutritional, we could feed the world.
~Robert Schaeberle

*K*enny was born and raised in New Jersey, but spent every summer on his grandma's farm in Topeka, Kansas. I was born and raised in suburban New York, and spent many teenage vacations on my sister's farm in Missouri. So we grew up close to each other and vacationed close to each other too.

Fast-forward about thirty-five years and the latest craze, Speed Dating, finally brought us together. We had only seven minutes of conversation. Kenny says it was love at first sight. He says that when he sat down at my table, he saw me smile and thought, "Oh, boy! I finally got a pretty one!"

I was impressed with Kenny's easy laugh and his love of art. But I had also selected three other bachelors for a second date. Kenny agreed to wait while I went through my list of worthy contenders. And, of course, no one thrilled me like Kenny. So, after fifteen months of weekend dates between two states, Kenny asked me to marry him while we went on a two-week photo-journey vacation to Scotland!

In the summer of 2005, London was besieged with terrorist bombs, and Great Britain instituted stronger guidelines for visas and marriages. The British national security response required a special marriage visa. This meant we had to submit an additional passport photograph as well as a separate application to be married in the British Isles.

I had to make many long-distance phone calls and website visits to get all the requirements outlined. It seemed that everyone wanted some kind of validation of our intent to marry before issuing the coveted marriage visa stamp in our passports.

"Send us the receipt for your wedding dress," they said.

"I'm not wearing a wedding dress. This is not my first marriage," I answered, politely.

"Well, then at least send us the names of the rest of the wedding party—the bridesmaids and your family members."

"Um, we are actually kinda eloping," I whispered.

The Scottish authorities just sighed.

At last, just ten days before our departure, I got some straight answers from the British Consulate in Chicago. I packaged up our expired passports, current passports, birth certificates, and Social Security numbers, as well as letters to "prove" we had no intention of seeking political asylum to live in Great Britain. I can tell you that sealing the tape on that thick FedEx package containing our entire identities was probably scarier than saying "Yes" to Kenny's marriage proposal!

While waiting for our marriage visas, I was busy arranging for everything from our rental car to ferry boats between the Outer Hebrides isles. Then there were the details of our wedding ceremony with the local registrar and witnesses to our vows! Through the wonders of the World Wide Web, I became good friends with the owners of one particular bed and breakfast, The Ballygrant Inn on the Isle of Islay. David and Ruby Graham agreed to stand with us as our wedding witnesses and planned all the last-minute details.

In fact, on our wedding day, we drove our little blue compact off the boat ramp of the luxury ferry in the early morning of a clear, sunny Saturday. Ruby had asked the village florist to dye fresh white roses the exact color of my cobalt blue suit for my bouquet. I hadn't even thought of flowers! The florist added a corsage for Ruby and two boutonnières for the men with a single blue rose bud, sprig of heather, and a plaid ribbon.

As we dashed into the floral shop, the owner looked up and

smiled, saying, "So, you're the Americans what've come to get married, eh?"

It was just like that wonderful old movie with John Wayne and Maureen O'Hara, *The Quiet Man*. So many people in this wee seaside town were waiting to help us celebrate our wedding!

I had read about the Bowmore Distillery on the Isle of Islay as being one of the few operations that still malted their own barley on site. That was worth seeing! Unfortunately, the Bowmore Distillery was now closed on Saturdays, as the tourist season ended on September 1st. But when I sent a return message to the website manager about our wedding day on Islay, she quickly offered to meet us at the distillery for a private tour as soon as we got off the boat!

We pulled the heavy stainless-steel paddle through about six inches of barley on the cellar floor of the distillery. After turning the barley, we were treated to several "wee drams" of every bottling on site. And so, as the day edged toward our sunset wedding by the sea, we were thoroughly warmed with the best of the "water of life."

David and Ruby were excited as they accounted for every known tradition. They had their teenage son, Ewan, release their black cat just outside the door as I dashed out to the car. A black cat is good luck in Scotland!

We had planned to be married in the garden by the sea as the sun set, but the wind was too strong for an outdoor wedding. The registrar offered to perform the civil ceremony in a charming stone cottage just beside the garden. As Sharon, the Islay registrar, was reviewing the particulars of the event with us, Kenny stepped away from his video camera on the tripod. And then it was happening! Sharon was actually asking the "I do" part! Kenny was bright red, and his collar was plastered to his neck. At last, we had exchanged all the words, and David and Ruby were signing their names to the official document. I was a little giddy when the registrar asked how we had met and come all the way to Scotland to be married. And so, while I was telling her about our fairy-tale romance, I saw Kenny step over to the camera tripod, and something made a click.

Our wedding video begins with me smacking my new husband's

arm with the back of my hand as he sheepishly admitted that he didn't have a chance to turn on the camera before that moment. Our love begins with a good hearty laugh for all! May it always be that way.

~Valorie Wells Fenton

82

"Accidental" Wedding

Winter either bites with its teeth or lashes with its tail.
~Proverb

I was the second woman letter carrier hired in Kent, Washington, back in the fall of 1968. I'd only worked there a few days when I noticed a tall, handsome man who liked to tease and joke with his co-workers. My postal case of cubbyholes, where I sorted the letters and magazines for delivery on my route, was very close to Mr. Joker's. I broke the ice when I asked if I could borrow his chair. During the next few days, I found reasons to speak to him. He spoke politely, but seemed quite shy toward me when he wasn't around others. As the days passed, I noticed him stealing glances at me when he thought I wasn't looking.

A couple of weeks later, my roommate and I decided to throw a party for a fellow letter carrier who was leaving for Army boot camp and heading overseas to Vietnam. We invited Mr. Joker, and I got to know him that night.

We liked each other and started dating. We found that we were like-minded about our personal values, many things that we both believed in and held dear, and how we wanted to live our lives. We were perfectly matched in so many ways. It was the beginning of an exciting romance that led to wonderful dreams of sharing our lives together. I fell in love with Mr. Joker, and he became Mr. Right.

Three months later, we decided to get married and bought matching engraved gold bands. We rented a miniscule cabin for $70 a month and spent all our free time gathering furniture and dishes from friends and family to feather our nest.

We wanted a very small wedding at a church that was on my postal route. The pastor agreed to perform the ceremony and counseled us on the sanctity of marriage. The pastor's wife offered to play organ music for us and be our witness, along with one of our mutual friends.

I woke up the day before my wedding to gray clouds and a big snowstorm. All the freeways were clogged with spinouts and stalled cars, and the schools were closed for the day. It meant that snow plows would be out clearing roads and pushing the snow into big heaps in front of the mailboxes on my driving route, so I'd have to be very careful with my mail truck.

As I delivered the mail on that snowy day before our wedding, my mind flooded with thoughts of the ceremony that would take place the next morning, wondering what it would feel like to be married and anticipating the weekend honeymoon we had planned.

Because of the storm, it turned out to be a long, stressful day, but my heart was happy and filled with love for Mr. Right. At my last mail stop at a big apartment building, I picked up three trays of mail and got out of my mail truck. I didn't realize the snow was so slick. When I stepped around the front of the truck, heading for the sidewalk, my right foot slipped out from under me and I fell, hitting my head on the bumper. I heard bones breaking in my right ankle and leg and felt searing pain. I knew I shouldn't try to stand.

I lay in the snow for several minutes, worrying about how my injuries would affect our wedding, until a groundskeeper came out of the apartments. He hurried over to me, saw what had happened, and went for help. When he came back, he and a fellow worker linked arms, making a chair for me. They carried me into the apartment building and set me on a couch in the office. The office manager called the post office to let them know what had happened, and then called for an ambulance. They said there were so many serious accidents on the snowy freeways that they didn't know how soon they would be able to get to me. The office manager found a warm blanket to cover me, pillows to elevate my leg, and a cup of hot tea to comfort me.

Mr. Right heard about my mishap and came to sit with me during the long wait. Two hours later, a mortuary's "ambulance" came to get me. That's right, it was the day before my wedding, and I was taken to a local doctor's office in a mortuary's transportation van. I know—icky, right?

The doctor took one look at my leg and sent me to Doctor's Hospital in Seattle. They called in an orthopedic specialist, took X-rays, and then set the multiple fractures in my foot, ankle and leg in a toe-to-hip cast. But the worst news of all was that I needed to stay in the hospital for five days.

There went the wedding!

I was so heartbroken I cried. But I wiped away the tears and decided to see if we could get married in the hospital. I asked the nurse, who checked with the doctor, who said I had to speak to the hospital administrator. He said there had never been a wedding at Doctor's Hospital, but gave us his blessing. We called the pastor to see if he would make the trek into Seattle the next morning if the roads were safe, and he agreed.

So we were back "on."

The next morning, my mother brought a frilly white blouse for me to wear in place of my wedding gown. My brother brought a Polaroid camera so he could take wedding pictures. My new mother-in-law brought a cute little wedding cake. My new sister and brother welcomed me into their family. A patient in another room sent me her bouquet of red roses, and other patients brought in their flowers to make our wedding festive.

I didn't know until later that my dad thought we were rushing into marriage too soon and tried to talk the pastor out of marrying us. My new father-in-law assured them both that we were very much in love and gave the pastor a second offering for his church.

Mr. Right and I exchanged our vows at our "small" wedding in my five-bed ward in front of a multitude of doctors, nurses, caregivers, patients (walking, on crutches or in wheelchairs), and their friends and families.

Despite all the unforeseen changes, it was the most wonderful and memorable wedding any new bride could hope for. And I have five faded Polaroid pictures, plus a yellowed, local newspaper article, to prove that dreams do come true.

~Carol Hurn

"Congratulations! Even your X-rays are radiant!"

My Husband Married a Woman Named Donna

You can fall in love at first sight with a place as with a person.
~Alec Waugh

Sunlight danced across the turquoise water, and a warm breeze filled our sails, propelling us and our dreams into an uncharted future. Captain Alex stood barefoot on the stern of his sailboat with its tiller held between his knees and the mainsail's sheet in hand. With a rich, melodious accent, he joined our lives together. "Do you, Duke, take this loving woman, Donna, to be your wife?"

Donna? But my name is Dawn!

Well, let me start at the beginning. Duke and I are the type of people who enjoy an uncomplicated life, so when we planned our wedding, simplicity was key. Duke had traveled extensively, so when he offered to take me to Roatan, the most beautiful island in the western Caribbean for our wedding and six-week honeymoon, I immediately agreed. He'd been coming here for the past five years and had fallen in love with the island and its people.

Because we planned to spend a lot of time exploring the coral reef that hugged the island, we spent more time choosing masks, snorkels, and fins than a wedding dress. The simple outfit I chose had tiny beads sewn on the bodice of the sleeveless top and on the hemline of the flowing ankle-length skirt. True to his uncomplicated nature, Duke decided to buy his wedding clothes when we got there.

Visitors would be foolish to wear expensive jewelry in a country where people earn eight dollars a day, so we purchased two inexpensive bands for the ceremony. We followed suit with our clothing, bringing items that were faded or old and only taking shorts, T-shirts, sundresses, and swimsuits, which we rolled up to save space in our canvas suitcase.

I had minimal travel experience, so when we boarded a plane in New Orleans, I felt as if we were traveling to another world. And we were, I realized, at first sight of land. Tall mountains with steep slopes covered in dense green jungle poked through the clouds as we descended to the coastal town of La Ceiba, Honduras. We landed on an airstrip cut from the jungle and then took a puddle jumper to the island of Roatan thirty miles off the coast.

We chose to stay in a cabin on Mermaid Beach, and after settling in we set out to explore West End village. The sun set with an explosion of rose and orange that spread over the water as we walked the white sand beneath the palm trees on the beach. Soon, a trillion stars lit our way. We followed a sand road and the sound of distant music, and came upon a home and yard crowded with people. A young man shared a drink with a corpse that lay in a wooden coffin balanced on two chairs in the yard.

These island people didn't mourn the man's death. They celebrated his life. A band played, and people danced. Friends and family shared a meal. It was a simple ceremony that said it all. I knew we'd come to the right place to be married.

In the following weeks, we snorkeled and scuba dived, rented a Jeep and explored the island, hung out with the native islanders, and generally became part of the community. We attended both churches in West End village, but neither of them seemed to be the right choice for our wedding.

We took a trip to the clinic in Coxen Hole to take the required blood test before marriage and received cards stating we were disease-free. With another stop at the town hall we finalized our paperwork.

A two-hour ferry ride brought us back to the mainland, and La Ceiba bustled with activity. The street market held wares of every variety and gave us a chance to see how the Hondurans lived their daily lives. Guards armed with AK-47s were posted at the haberdasheries' doors, and shopkeepers with guns in their belts followed us as we shopped for Duke's wedding shirt.

With just two weeks left, we decided to get in some sailing. We planned a day trip with our Belizean friend, Captain Alex. I secretly believed he was a pirate. He'd salvaged the twenty-five-foot sailboat after a storm and now made his living by taking tourists on day trips to snorkel and fish.

On our way to an outer reef, he drummed on the side of the boat to attract dolphins. They came! Hearts racing, we donned our snorkel gear and eased into the clear blue water. A pod of hundreds swam by us close enough to touch. We felt one with all God's creatures. Suddenly, we knew where to have our wedding ceremony and asked Alex to do the honors.

Duke, handsome as ever in his Honduran shirt and contented smile, held me close as we waited for Captain Alex and his wife, Mariana. We barely noticed they were late. Our hair blew in the wind as we listened to his poetic words that bound us together. I didn't even really mind being called Donna. I tossed my bouquet of island flowers into the water, and we kissed as Captain Alex blew into a conch shell to finalize the event.

We held our reception on the beach in front of our cabin. Our island friends came and enjoyed the cake our friend Dora had made. Alex slurred his words as he congratulated us, and we realized he'd been drunk all along. Mariana confided that it was Alex's birthday, and he'd been celebrating at the bar before she'd found him and reminded him he was to marry us that day.

Finally alone, we watched the sunset end the day.

"I love you Donna," said my new husband, pulling me close.

~Dawn Baird

Chapter 9

Here Comes the Bride

Never Too Late for Love

*Happiness often sneaks in through a door
you didn't know you left open.*

~John Barrymore

84

Un Bel Di
(One Fine Day)

For I'm not so old, and not so plain,
And I'm quite prepared to marry again.
~W.S. Gilbert, Iolanthe

"For heaven's sake, Annalee, you're just going on a date. You don't have to marry the guy!"

My sister's words rang in my ears as I hung up the phone. As we talked, my voice had displayed the anxiety of a schoolgirl. She assured me that my first date with Joel would go well and that I shouldn't worry. Easy for her to say. I had been abandoned after twenty years of marriage and had lived alone for the past twelve years. The idea of dating at fifty-three years old made me uneasy. Would I know how to act? How would I respond if he tried to kiss me? I'd called my younger sister for some reassurance.

Actually, Joel and I had been getting to know each other for quite some time. We first met when I came to his church as a guest speaker. After the service, we chatted over a cup of coffee. Six months later, I'd taken a job with the church as an assistant pastor and moved into a townhouse, which as it turned out was only a half-mile from Joel's home.

Joel was a gifted musician, and when I needed a guitarist to help on the worship team, he agreed to play. Every Wednesday evening, the musicians gathered in the basement of my townhouse to practice for the Sunday service. Often, after the others left, Joel and I lingered. We'd pray together. He had gone through a divorce seven years before, and we had a lot in common. I liked his honesty and sincerity, and his sense of humor. He spoke with clarity and had a wonderful vocabulary that added to his appeal. I learned later that he had a degree in English.

I looked for opportunities for us to be together.

One summer evening, I planned to attend a singles' dinner sponsored by our church. I carefully chose the outfit I would wear, hoping Joel would notice. Everyone was asked to bring a contribution to the meal. Joel brought cheesecake with blueberry sauce that he'd made himself. A man who cooks. I was impressed!

After our meal, we played croquet, and everyone else finished the game but me. Embarrassed, I kept hitting the ball in an attempt to finish, but Joel didn't seem concerned. He stood by yelling, "It's Annalee's turn!" With each stroke, he'd repeat, "It's Annalee's turn!" I roared with laughter. I knew then that I was falling in love. I also knew I was fighting my feelings. Trusting someone enough to be in a serious relationship again seemed too much of a risk.

It had been eighteen months since I first met Joel, and I was becoming more and more attracted to him. Besides all his talents and character traits, I thought he was really cute! I didn't learn until later that he was attracted to me and was having similar feelings. He was fighting his feelings just as hard! After his divorce, he had resigned himself to bachelorhood.

Then, one autumn day, I expressed to Joel my disappointment over a cancelled trip to New York City. Some friends had invited me to go to Manhattan with them, but their plans had changed. I love the Big Apple, and it was fall—my favorite season. I yearned to go.

"I'm thinking of going into the City anyway," I mused. "Maybe I'll go see *Madame Butterfly*."

"By yourself?" Joel asked.

"Yeah. Why? Do you want to go?"

I paused for a moment. Did those words just come out of MY mouth?

"Sure, I'll go with you," Joel quickly responded.

"Do you like Puccini?" I asked.

"I don't know. I've never seen an opera."

"Well, that settles it! You must see an opera. I'll go online for tickets and see what's available for Saturday."

With a crispness in the air and the leaves in their splendid array of colors, Joel picked me up for our trip to the City. When I answered the door, he blurted, "Look at you! You look terrific!"

Yes! I thought, trying not to act excited that he'd noticed. I was wearing a dressy black and white pantsuit that seemed to fit the occasion.

In the car, we shared our excitement over seeing the opera, and I inadvertently made a remark about being on a date. "Is this a date?" Joel inquired, almost gasping. He hadn't been on a date for thirty-three years and, at fifty-four years old, he was just as nervous as I was to be having an official romantic encounter.

When we arrived in New York, we enjoyed a delicious meal al fresco at a restaurant across the street from Lincoln Center where we would be viewing *Madame Butterfly*. With an hour to spare before curtain time, we walked up Broadway to a record store. There we searched for a specific version of Handel's *Messiah* that Joel had been looking for. In the display case was the CD he wanted. He looked at me in amazement and said, "I've been looking for this for years!" Our eyes met, and we knew we both found something we had searched for—but only dreamed of experiencing.

The New York City Opera offered a magnificent production of my favorite opera, and we savored every note. As *Butterfly*'s aria "Un Bel Di" floated up to our fourth-tier seats, we glanced at each other in wonder at the beauty of the music—and the moment. When it was time to leave, we took advantage of the balmy, autumn evening and walked up Broadway once again. This time, Joel offered me his arm. We joyfully walked arm in arm, lingering in the magical feel of the night.

When we arrived in our hometown, it was well past midnight. We'd talked all the way home and then, suddenly, there was a lull in our conversation. I took the opportunity to tell Joel how much I enjoyed getting to know him and that I valued our friendship. His response was simply, "Really?"

"Yes," I continued. "It has stirred some feelings that I didn't think could be stirred again."

"Really? What kind of feelings?"

"Deep feelings. I've been waking in the middle of the night for about three weeks thinking of you."

"REALLY?" was all Joel could get out in his shock at my confession. Then he added, "I've been doing the same thing, Annalee. I've been waking up thinking about you."

By now, we were in front of my townhouse. Joel stopped the car and turned toward me.

"I'm in love with you, Annalee."

"I'm in love with you, too, Joel."

He leaned toward me.

"May I kiss you?"

"Yes!"

After we shared a tender kiss, Joel asked, "Will you marry me?"

That night, we pledged our love to each other.

By Monday afternoon, I had picked out my wedding gown of ivory satin and lace, sprinkled with pearls and sequins. The next six months were filled with planning, shopping, and making sure all the details were arranged for our wedding. We celebrated with a large wedding attended by friends and family. My younger sister was my matron of honor. Joel wrote a love song and sang it to me during the ceremony. We rejoiced in the love we'd found in each other.

At our reception, we danced the afternoon away. Yes, we had an afternoon wedding because we had reservations to see an opera at 8:00 on our wedding night. After seeing *Butterfly*, we purchased season tickets to the opera, and the last scheduled performance of the season was on the night of our marriage ceremony.

Following our reception, we drove into the City—where it all began. We checked into a hotel across the street from Lincoln Center and made our way to our seats to see *La Bohème*. I was wearing that same black and white pantsuit that I'd worn on our first date. Only this time, I had baby's breath and silk flowers from our wedding in my hair.

We held hands as we listened to another love story by Puccini. We had begun our new life together as husband and wife, remembering "one fine day"—when good friends began their journey as lovers for a lifetime.

~Annalee Davis

85

Pink Hibiscus

Grow old with me! The best is yet to be.
~Robert Browning

My fortieth birthday fell on a sunny April spring day. The rose and lilac scents began to drive away the memories of the snowy winter. I looked forward with hope, but one dream began to slowly fade. I was single and felt my prime fading away. Dreams of husband and children filling the quietness of my home became more and more out of grasp. Sadness crept over me; loneliness surrounded me. Over the next year, a pain began to take over my body, then fatigue and a feeling something wasn't right. I visited several doctors. Eventually, one had the answer.

"We found a tumor. It is most likely cancer," the doctor said.

"Is it life-threatening?" I asked as tears welled in my eyes.

"It is quite possible. We won't know until the surgery," he replied.

I placed my dreams on hold, not knowing if there would be another birthday, let alone a husband in my future. After surgery to remove the tumor, I was declared cancer-free. Life moved on with a new normal.

Flowers gave me hope during that time — the hibiscus being my favorite. It brought me visions of beaches, warm sand, and happiness. Four years later, a picture I had of a pink hibiscus flower caught a man's eyes. We met, spent time together, and fell in love.

"I knew if you loved the hibiscus that you would understand me," he said. He was from Jamaica.

He told me he wanted to be with me forever. At forty-five, my dreams were finally coming true. We talked about our future. I was so happy. One day, the doctors thought they had found another tumor in my body. I had more tests, and I was fine. As I was coming out of the doctor's office, there was a message from my dad on my phone.

"Remember the lump on my neck?" my dad asked. "The test came back. It is cancer: Hodgkin's lymphoma," he said through his tears. I began to shake. I cried, knowing what he would have to go through—the pain, the needles. His treatment would be chemotherapy. He began to fight the fight. My new boyfriend was by our side. He was the first person I called, and he held me when I cried.

Four months later, my boyfriend told me he wanted me to meet his mom and grandma, whom he called Mamma. We booked the tickets for the Caribbean paradise and planned a few days on our own at the beach town of Negril. He had a doctor's appointment a few days before our flight to follow up on some tests. He called me at work.

"I didn't want to worry you. The tests confirmed what the doctor thought. It is prostate cancer," he said. The wind was knocked out of me. The ugly word was invading my life again. The disease invaded the two most important men in my life at the same time. We went on the trip. We didn't tell his family. We were in denial as we sat on the beach watching the clear blue waves lap against the shore. The breeze softly stroked my skin. I turned my face into the breeze, and a pink hibiscus flower caught my eye. It slowly waved back and forth, calming me.

On an April night two months later, he got down on his knee, looked at me with his beautiful brown eyes, and held up a vintage platinum ring. The hand-engraved band with the simple, elegant diamond turned my dream into reality.

"I love you, and I want to spend the rest of my life with you. Will you marry me?" he asked.

"Yes," I replied, with tears in my eyes.

My dad finished his last treatment that month and went into remission. My fiancé had surgery four months later in July. The needles and pain were back in my life. I held him as he felt the pain. The prognosis was encouraging. The cancer was removed. The healing began, and the reality of another new normal entered my life.

The wedding planning began. Colors were blue and purple, his favorite and mine. Engagement photos were taken on the beach with a pink hibiscus flower tucked behind my ear. Six months later, in a garden full of trees with fall leaves blazing reds and yellows, my dad walked me down the aisle toward my new husband. His silver hair had grown back, and he was tan from the Indian summer sun. My husband-to-be smiled at us as we walked toward him. The three survivors embraced each other, surrounded by loved ones, and stepped into our dreams and joy of the future.

~Shelly Bleggi Linton

86

Better than Prince Charming

Love one another and you will be happy. It's as simple and as difficult as that.
~Michael Leunig

*I*n April 2007, my mother got a second chance at her happy ending when she met Jody. They are now planning their June 2011 wedding.

My mother hasn't always had the best of luck with men. She and my biological father broke up soon after she announced her pregnancy with me. When I was four, she split up with my younger brother's father, and he left the province soon after my eighth birthday.

She dated a few men over the years, but they didn't last very long. I dreaded the day when she told us that she had a new boyfriend. I hated them because none of them were good enough for the one person who had dedicated her life to being a wonderful mother, who sacrificed everything for the happiness of her children. My mom had always been there for me, and all I wanted was someone who would always be there for her. She deserved her Prince Charming more than anyone I knew.

Then along came Jody. He was perfect for her. He wasn't like the others. From the moment I met him, I felt comfortable around him.

One spring night, I sat down with my mother and asked her what made her fall in love with Jody. "I love him because he's considerate, thoughtful, and down-to-earth," my mother had told me. "And I can just be myself around him."

They fell in love almost instantly, and the relationship moved quickly. By October 2007, they had moved in together.

Two years later, in October 2009, he proposed.

Earlier in the year, Jody had asked our permission to propose to our mother, and my brother and I eagerly agreed. He was better than Prince Charming. He treated us like a proper father should, and we were thrilled that he wanted to spend the rest of his life with our mother.

The day before we were going to the Rockton Fair, where he was planning on proposing, my brother and I made up excuses to leave the house for a few hours because Jody was picking us up down the street. He had asked for our help and his daughter's help in orchestrating the proposal.

"I'm going to my friend's house, Mom," I said, praying I wouldn't smile and give it all away.

"And I'm going to the mall with some friends," Ethan said more casually.

"Do you want a ride? It's raining outside," Mom replied.

"No!" I had to restrain myself from saying it too loudly. "We need the exercise, but thanks for the offer."

Ethan and I quickly left the house before she suspected something was amiss. We walked through the rain toward the silver van that was waiting for us down the street.

We drove to my aunt's house where we spent hours setting up the message, "DENISE, WILL U MARRY ME?" which spanned the entire length of her enormous green lawn. I left, satisfied that the next day would be one that we would not soon forget.

The next day, after having a fun-filled day at the fair, we headed over to the helicopter area. Two of my aunts and their husbands were there after already having their helicopter ride.

As my mom and Jody were lifted into the air, I became excited. It suddenly became more real. The next time we saw them, they would be an engaged couple! Words cannot describe how happy I was at that moment. I was bursting at the seams with joy.

"We're going to be stepsisters!" Jordan and I laughed and hugged each other happily.

When we saw the helicopter appear in the sky, coming back toward us, we started jumping up and down.

My mom jumped out of the helicopter first. She held up her hand, showing the sparkler Jody had placed on her finger only moments before. She ran across the field. I hugged her and told her how thrilled I was for her. Then I told her where we really went the night before.

"I was actually planning on driving to New Hamburg to see you yesterday," my mom admitted to her new fiancé.

It was a good thing she never did because the entire proposal might have been ruined had she decided to make the drive to New Hamburg that night. I like to believe it's because it was meant to be.

My mother had found her soul mate at forty-one years old. She had found the man who knew all of her flaws and loved her even more because of them. She had found the man who wanted to stand up in front of everyone they knew and swear to love her forever. And she had found the man who wanted to take on the responsibility of being a father to me and my brother.

My mom's very own love story shows that true love is out there for every person. It goes to show that no matter how old you are or what your past holds, there is someone out there who will love you with every fiber of their being for everything that you are. Love is going to find you when you least expect it, and it's going to sweep you off your feet, no matter if you're twenty-five or sixty-nine. You can find love at any age.

~Stephanie McKellar, age 17

My Valentine

Now join hands, and with your hands your hearts.
~William Shakespeare

"Should we marry on Valentine's Day?" he said. Having lived in America for some time, I knew this was meant to be romantic, but for me, a Russian immigrant, February was still associated with the holiday my former country celebrated on February 23 — Red Army Day. That wasn't a romantic holiday, but it brought color to the vast whiteness of the Russian winter, as red flags flew everywhere, and Russian citizens felt secure, as the radio blasted endless military marches, including the reassuring "The Russian army is stronger than any!" Also, since we had no Father's Day, it was an occasion to show our appreciation for the males in our lives. Wives gave presents to their husbands, and schoolgirls handed little souvenirs to their male classmates. All of this quickly went through my head, but aloud I said, "It's a great idea!"

Then we discussed the place. My American fiancé and I, both middle-aged, had different religious backgrounds, so we decided to get married in a courthouse.

"Shall we make a reservation today?" I asked.

"There's no rush," he said. "Americans rarely marry in courthouses."

The next day, we applied for a marriage license, and I started hunting for a dress. A month before Valentine's Day, I called our local courthouse.

"We have no space available on Valentine's Day. Do you want to schedule on the next day?"

"Absolutely not!" I slammed down the receiver and collapsed into a chair. I had already sent invitations, and a perfect dark-red velvet dress hung in my closet.

Why in the world did I listen to him? Well, making a scene even before we got married wasn't a good idea, so I picked up the phone and called every courthouse within a sixty-mile radius. They were all full except one.

"If we marry on Valentine's Day, we'll have to do it in Fulton," I told my fiancé.

"Perfect!"

Was he referring to the small Missouri town forty minutes away?

"Don't you see how symbolic it is?" he continued. "That's where Churchill gave his Iron Curtain speech at the beginning of the Cold War, and Gorbachev spoke after it was over. If the Cold War hadn't ended, you and I would never have met!"

He had a point. Therefore, on a typically gray Missouri Valentine's Day, we and our witnesses hurried up the stone staircase of the old Fulton courthouse. Everybody was nicely dressed, and I even had a borrowed mink coat thrown over my shoulders.

As we got to the porch, the doors of the courthouse opened, and two policemen escorting a man in handcuffs and leg irons emerged from the building, walking directly toward us. My heart sank. This was surely a bad sign.

"That's kind of symbolic," I heard my bridegroom say. "Getting married and losing your freedom, so to speak."

"That's not funny!" I wanted to say, but everybody chuckled, and I burst into nervous laughter.

In a minute, we entered a courtroom and joined another couple to be married that day. They were young, dressed in worn-out jeans and Budweiser sweatshirts, chewing gum.

Neither the coldly formal courtroom nor the look of this couple (nor the chained man at the entrance) was what I had envisioned for my wedding day. As I was about to share this thought with my groom, an elderly judge in a long robe with a black patch over one eye entered the room.

"Symbolic?" I asked my almost-husband. "Half-blind justice?"

He winked at me.

The young couple was called first. They got up and, still talking and chewing, approached the judge. His good eye stared at them piercingly until they spat out their gum and quieted down.

"We are gathered here today," the judge began, and a tingling sensation started traveling up my spine, making me straighten up in my chair and clutch my hands together.

"Marriage is a relationship of love," the judge's voice filled the courtroom. "There will be times of stress, sacrifice, and sorrow."

I was barely breathing.

"For better or worse, for richer or poorer, in sickness and in health…"

Suddenly, it struck me. At our ages, forty-five and fifty-three, we could be close to "sickness" already. There was no telling how many healthy years we'd have, or how many years together. We wouldn't celebrate our sixty-fifth anniversary, as my groom's parents had done, nor even the forty-eighth, like my parents.

"I pronounce you husband and wife. You may kiss and embrace."

Now, it was our turn.

"We are gathered," the judge started again. Having just heard the same words, I felt detached, and my mind wandered.

I remembered myself at the Moscow airport hours before leaving Russia—surrounded by my family, my mother crying, not knowing if she'd ever see me again. Then I saw myself in America—a scared immigrant with no English, trying to make it in this new world. Later still, I saw a middle-aged woman warily gazing into a mirror—resigning herself to a life with no love and romance.

Old memories swirled around me. Was I doing the right thing? What did I have in common with this man, born on the other side of the world? Wasn't it too late to start all over again? I became lightheaded. To steady myself, I put one arm around my groom's waist and leaned on him; he squeezed my hand with his elbow. This subtle gesture broke the spell. The room stopped spinning, images from the past melted away, and it felt right to stand next to this man in the presence of these witnesses, on this Valentine's Day—and for the rest of our lives.

Now, the courtroom was quiet. Everybody was watching me. I straightened up, smiled, and still holding on to the man next to me, said, "I do."

~Svetlana Grobman

The Wrinkled One

A happy marriage is a new beginning of life,
a new starting point for happiness...
~Dean Stanley

*T*hirty years after my last date, I re-entered the dating scene. I nervously joined a matchmaker service, but expected to meet few, if any, wonderful men. I was wrong.

"Hi, are you Patt?" The question was posed by a man waiting near the reservation podium wearing the striped tan polo shirt and glasses I was told to expect. His easy smile relieved the usual awkwardness of a first date.

Our conversation was lively and nonstop. When I ordered ostrich, he did not freak out at my weirdness. After dinner in the parking lot, we sealed our deal with the still unforgettable kiss he planted on me. I discovered my soul mate and so did he.

Over the next several months, I renewed my acquaintance with internal butterflies and that special tingle. Life was again a glorious mystery worth exploring. We jointly proposed and planned a party to celebrate our mid-life love — at the dog museum.

Although I had "been there," I had not "done THIS." Mid-life love was new! Even shopping for a traditional wedding dress with my daughters was different and proved hilarious. Automatically, well-intended sales clerks steered me in the direction of "mother's dresses" and riddled my daughters with bride-type questions.

"Hello and welcome... When is your big day...? Wow, that's

great… How many bridesmaids…? Where is your wedding…? What type of gown do you have in mind?"

We conspired and tag teamed in a comedy routine.

"Talk to the wrinkled bride," my daughters would reply sternly with an open hand and palm forward.

I continued the merriment by grinning broadly with raised arm and pointing a finger downward to the top of my head. Not intending rudeness or embarrassment, we invited them to laugh with us—and they did.

I was fifty-one. Numerous excursions and try-ons yielded zero possibilities until finally my daughters heartily endorsed a sequined halter-top number and a long, slick white satin skirt with a train. The dress was perfect. The ensemble subtracted years and pounds while highlighting my "assets."

Each of our combined five children agreed to be in our wedding party—tuxes, fancy dresses, and flowers—the works. Time zoomed forward to our big day and the typical tizzy of mini-disasters. That day brought the unexpected repair of an overnight flat tire, which was soon upstaged by a wardrobe malfunction.

My younger daughter's last-minute snacking splattered stains on the top of her shimmery two-piece chartreuse gown. Unrattled, we spot cleaned it. She hung the semi-wet garment by hand out the van window. Fortunately, she did not lose her grip as it flapped dry in the wind while we sped to the dog museum.

When we made our late entrance, the nearly 100 guests were milling about the museum, fascinated by dog memorabilia. Our canine enthusiast guests commended us for our "dogtastic" location.

Although the minister performed a lackluster service, I delighted in the warm support family and friends showered on our celebration of love. Soon the glorious scent of cheese-filled mushrooms, beef tenderloin, hot rolls, and assorted goodies swirled in waves around us.

After dinner, the karaoke DJ was a resounding hit, highlighted by our newlywed dance. Joined by an eight-year-old nephew wearing a plastic monkey mask, my husband and I donned dog masks—Dalmatians because our ages totaled a bit over 101. Of course, the theme song was, "Who Let the Dogs Out." Guests cheered and barked to the music.

Although we requested "the gift of your presence only," my husband's poker-hunting-fishing crowd (whom he has known for decades) cooked up delightfully bizarre surprise gifts. After our honeymoon, we gathered family and a few friends for the opening.

As we unwrapped the first gift from the group, my husband and I exchanged quizzical looks because it was a… toaster? Mmmmm, yes—not just something else packed in a toaster box. As I grabbed the second package from the men and their wives, my husband and I locked eyes and telepathed a shared observation, "These packages are exactly the same size."

In fact, not only were they the same size packages—they were seven identical toasters with UPC codes conscientiously cut away! So much for cashing in on returns. Amidst uncontrollable laughter, we posed for the friendly paparazzi with seven toasters stacked vertically between us.

Remarkably, we found greeting cards featuring toasters and sent them as notes of thanks. One month later, the same pranksters bestowed seven individually gift-wrapped loaves of bread on my husband as birthday gifts. (I was slow to catch the extended joke.) Our tale of seven toasters and loaves lasted for years as we discovered a series of creative ways to re-gift the toasters—even some back to the group itself.

We plan to grow older together and will not let things grow old between us—with our wedding as the benchmark for surprises, laughter, and spice. Our mid-life marriage extends beyond a simple approach to the sunset years or a boring rerun of past mistakes or pleasures. As Dean Stanley wrote, "A happy marriage is a new beginning of life, a new starting point for happiness…"—at any age.

~Patt Hollinger Pickett, Ph.D.

My Piano Man

Where there is great love, there are always miracles.
~Willa Cather

As I moved into my mid-thirties, still single, I couldn't deny that I still hoped to get married. A decade earlier, a man I loved had ended our relationship because he didn't feel ready for a marriage commitment.

Brokenhearted, I had moved away and undertaken new challenges that included mission service and graduate school. Always, somewhere, I also had the opportunity to play piano for church. Then my parents died within months of each other, and my life screeched to a stop. My only sibling, my sister, was swamped with a young family and a small business that was a four-hour drive from our parents' home. So I dropped out of graduate school and moved home to settle affairs and empty the very full three-bedroom house.

Some days, I felt nearly overwhelmed by the memories as I doggedly cleaned out closets and drawers. When I needed a break, I'd go to the family piano, a dinosaur upright that for decades had been a fixture in my parents' dining room. Sliding onto its wobbly bench, I'd open a hymnbook and sing old favorites.

Now, like everything else, the piano needed to go. Because I'd been working my way through graduate school across the country, I had minimized my belongings. I couldn't keep it. My sister and I agreed that she should inherit it so that her young children could learn piano.

The day my sister and husband moved the piano out, I felt like I'd lost an old friend. The dining room wall looked so stark with the piano gone. As I vacuumed up decades of dust, I thought about that man I had loved. I hadn't heard from him since we broke up. I presumed he had found someone else to marry.

But life had to go on. Months later, the house emptied, I returned to graduate school 2,000 miles away from my family "roots"—and from "him." Though at times I longed for a piano of my own, I always had access to one—a college practice room, the church I attended, even upstairs from a basement bedroom I rented for a few months.

Still, I struggled with being single in my mid-thirties. I hadn't dated in years. But now, launching into a career, I had new goals to pursue. I wasn't prepared for the phone call that came one brisk March afternoon. I'd been getting a lot of wrong numbers lately, thanks to a popular girl at a nearby university having my number mistakenly listed as hers in the school directory.

But this time the man calling wanted to talk to me.

"This is Rich Zornes," he said. "Do you remember me?"

Remember him? It had been eight years! I had never expected to hear from him again. My knees buckled, and I slid to the floor. Through mutual friends, he had gotten my phone number. Now nearly thirty-six, he hoped I would consider renewing our friendship. Our calls, correspondence, and a visit moved toward a marriage proposal. His parents were thrilled and had a special wedding gift in mind.

The living room in my soon-to-be husband's meagerly furnished home had an empty wall. They had something that had sat unused since their last daughter married and left home. And so, in the flurry of wedding week preparations, came their gift offer: their piano.

~Jeanne Zornes

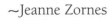

90

Remember the Watermelons

Faith is reason grown courageous.
~Sherwood Eddy

I am scared out of my mind. A big, fat-knuckled hand grabs my throat, and I feel like I'm choking. I'm off balance, dizzy, and lightheaded with fear, shaky and unfocused. You might wonder what has predicated this terror. Did I just learn I'm facing a fatal disease? Am I the victim of a violent crime and having flashbacks of a masked man lurking in the shadows?

No. I'm simply getting married in mid-life. Okay, late mid-life. I thought this was what I'd wanted for so long, but it's five days before my wedding and I can taste dread in my soul. I know I should be happy, excited even, but for now, my fears are front and center. I've been through this before. Although it was a brief marriage, a lifetime ago, I know the pain of separating, extricating oneself from another and divorcing. Remnants of that pain still resonate deep in my psyche.

So what am I really afraid of? I ask myself that question in calmer moments. My first response: It will go badly. We'll be perpetually angry with each other; our home will reek of tension and silence. We'll become strangers, disconnected from one another. Or worse, screaming and yelling will become our mode of talk. That image is familiar as I know I lived it growing up. Don't get me wrong; there were some carefree, happy times when my parents seemed relaxed. I can even recall moments of affectionate teasing between them, and I would giggle at their playfulness. But there are too many memories of walking on eggshells, feeling sad and nervous, wondering why they couldn't just get along.

Now my logic tells me I don't have to repeat prior experiences. As a psychotherapist, I even stress this to my patients. "You don't have to carry on the tradition," I tell them when they express their fears they will not be adequate parents, or lovers or partners. "You can do things differently," I encourage. I try to focus on my own advice, wanting desperately to believe I have the power to create something better. I realize it's not all up to me, but I do have a significant contribution to the state of the marriage. I also know that when all is said and done, it's a leap of faith we all take when we make a life commitment.

Faith. My mind drifts to a recent experience with my fourteen-year-old daughter. Several months ago, she planted watermelon seeds by the side of our small, red brick home. Picture this: little sun, thin, dry soil, crumbly to the touch and weeds sprouting everywhere. I tried my best to dissuade her. "Why don't you plant flowers in the front yard? Or what about tomatoes again? They were so sweet and tasty last year."

She would have nothing of it. She sang as she worked, digging the grainy dirt to bury the shiny black watermelon seeds. I knew she was in for disappointment, and I wanted desperately to shield her from it.

"Laura," I said gently, "try not to get your hopes up. It just might not work here. We just don't have the right kind of soil."

"Mom," she said, sighing, "I know the watermelons will grow. It will just take a month or two. You'll see."

For weeks, she came home directly from school and rushed to the side of our house, green hose in hand to water the barren ground. Each day when she finished, I gave my little speech. "Don't get your hopes up, sweetie. This will not be your fault. The ground is just too barren."

And each day she would sigh as though she were talking to a headstrong child. "Mom, just wait; I know what I'm doing. Have a little faith."

Two months passed, and my doorbell chimed early one evening. My elderly neighbor was standing there, disbelief shining on her face. She urged me to come outside quickly. I ran to the side of my house and saw three small balls, cradled in dark green vines. Green and white flecks of color streaked across them. I yelled for my daughter, and we both stared at the budding fruit in silence. Then she jumped up and down, a grin bursting on her face. "I told you, I told you. You just need to have a little faith, Mom."

Faith. I savor the word on my tongue. My hands are shaking as the reality of the next five days hits me. I take several, long, deep breaths, exhaling slowly, allowing bits of calm to seep through my body. Okay, then, I make up my mind resolutely. I will leap off the cliff.

~Bari Benjamin

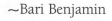

91

A Senior Bride and Her Wedding

Everyone is the age of their heart.
~Guatemalan proverb

I was forty when I finally divorced, and I swore that I'd never love or marry again. I decided I'd gracefully grow old alone.

Shortly after my divorce, I relocated from New Jersey to Georgia for my job. I worked hard on recovering, recuperating, rearranging, and reorganizing my life in my new home state. I also chose to ignore the handsome man who was trying to pursue me. Every chance he got, he was at my workstation, and every time he asked me out, I politely turned him down. I was perfectly content.

Three years passed, and he remained the same, but by this time, I was the one who was beginning to change. I was now in my mid-forties, my broken heart had healed, and I was ready to start dating.

I began to wait and hope that Wilson would ask me out again; this time, I was going to say yes. One day he asked me if I would like to go fishing with him. I thought to myself, "Wow, just when I make up my mind to say yes, he asks me to go fishing! I would've preferred him asking me out to dinner rather than catching it." However, I smiled and said, "Yes, I'd like that."

I prepared a nice picnic lunch, and we went to a picturesque park, where among nature's most beautiful settings, he patiently taught me how to fish. At the end of the day and with our last worm, I caught my very first fish. On the way home, we stopped by a taxidermist to have my tiny brim stuffed and mounted. It was a date filled with fun, laughter, and good conversation. It also turned out to be the most romantic first date I had ever had—and we didn't even kiss!

We dated for almost ten years, and neither one of us ever talked about the taboo subject of marriage. One Christmas, we were out doing some shopping. As always, I'd be in and out of jewelry shops or have my face pressed against the window of one while he stood back and patiently waited. But this day, much to my surprise, he came in with me and told me to pick out any ring I wanted. We both laughed nervously. I was laughing because I didn't know what kind of ring he meant, and I was afraid to ask. He was probably laughing because he knew my taste, had an idea of the price, or quickly realized he had put his foot in his mouth and was laughing to keep from crying. However, I was going to put the confirmed bachelor to the test.

I picked out the biggest diamond that looked the best on my dainty little finger and said, "This is it! This is what I want!"

He laughed and said, "Okay, but I didn't say I was going to buy it. I just told you to pick out what you want!"

We had a good laugh, and I didn't think anymore about it since we really weren't in the marrying frame of mind.

On New Year's Eve, we came in from church, and he poured us some champagne and got down on one knee. I really thought he was looking for something, so I told him to get up before he couldn't. (Remember, we're at the ages where we don't do any unnecessary bending and kneeling!) But he took out a black velvet box, took out the ring I had picked out, and asked me to be his wife. Before I could say "Yes" he got up and sat on the couch next to me, saying, "I wanted to be romantic, but I have to do this sitting down!" We hugged, kissed, and toasted.

A year passed without us making any kind of wedding plans. On February 1, 2009, he was lying on the couch watching TV, and I was doing dishes. He said, "Hey, Valentine's Day is on Saturday this year. Let's get married!"

I said, "What's the hurry?"

He said, "Do you remember when you had your first chemother-apy treatment?" I had been diagnosed with breast cancer in January 2003.

"Yeah," I said, "it was on Valentine's Day."

He said, "Ever since then, Valentine's Day has never been the same for you. I want it to be a day you can love and cherish, instead of always reminding you of chemo, cancer, and sickness. I promised you back then that I'd give you a Valentine's Day you'll never forget, one that'll make you happy, but as much as I tried I could never figure out that extra-special something to do. But now I have: I want us to get married on that day."

How could I say no?

Since we decided it was going to be a small, intimate house wedding with immediate family and friends, I ran around for the next twelve days looking for the perfect dress, shoes, cake, and decora-tions, and planning a menu. I spent most of that time looking for something to wear. Two days before the wedding, I was simply worn out and still hadn't found anything. I sat with my head between my hands crying and on the verge of calling it off. It was just too much in such a short time.

Finally, my fifteen-year-old granddaughter said, "Come on, G-Ma. Let's go to the mall. I'll find you something." I could just imagine what she'd pick out! But somehow she found the perfect off-white dress for me, and I even came across the perfect shoes. Then we picked up her girlfriend, and they fixed and boxed the wedding favors while I wrote out our vows. At the last minute, everything started falling perfectly in line.

My husband and everybody else cried as he read his vows. My bouquet was off-white roses with a red one in the center, which I placed in front of my mother's picture in memory of her since she had recently passed, along with giving a rose to each person who had a special meaning to me. Since everyone was old, already married or too young to think about it, there was no need to toss the bouquet. There were well wishes as we toasted, ate and danced our first dance as husband and wife amidst iridescent bubbles, before partying the night away.

Tired and ready to leave for our honeymoon suite, we stepped outside and, to our surprise, a white 1947 Chevy with a chauffer stood beside the open door. As we tearfully waved goodnight to our loved ones, we heard sniffles and whispers about what a beautiful wedding it had turned out to be.

We couldn't stop talking and thinking about the day as my husband and I slowly drifted off to sleep in each other's arms. My husband was right: Valentine's Day will always be a day I will remember—not for the illness, the chemo and the pain, but for the love, the happiness, and the wonderful memories of our wedding day.

~Francine L. Baldwin-Billingslea

92

The Second Time Around

Come, let's be a comfortable couple and take care of each other!
How glad we shall be, that we have somebody we are fond of always,
to talk to and sit with.
~Charles Dickens

I've been to a wonderful wedding. It was not one of those June extravaganzas in a hotel ballroom with a bride done up in lace, a cast of thousands, and a six-course feast.

This wedding was carried off in a dauntingly small living room. The bride wore a navy dress that was not even close to the coveted size six or eight. The groom had a receding hairline, a visible paunch, and crinkly lines around his blue eyes that spoke of a thousand smiles.

Most of us had come to this midweek wedding straight from work, notified not by an engraved invitation on ivory stock, but by a breathless, last-minute phone call. "We're doing it!" was the message, a study in brevity if not wit.

I had known this woman in an entirely different life, back when she had shared her name with a fine and funny man who died at forty-one on a street corner—a sudden, unmerciful death from a massive stroke.

I had watched her move through the terrible, agonizing shock of loss, then pick herself up and turn to the business at hand: raising three children without the man with whom she'd expected to share old age.

Her groom had a similar tale of love and loss. Cancer. A blur of treatments and hospitals. And then the not-so-sudden death of his wife and soul mate.

In adjoining suburbs, unknown to one another for years, these two had struggled. Neither was the sort for mixers or singles cruises.

Then, last year, someone had said, "Why not?" and arranged for a middle-aged widow and a widower on the far side of fifty to meet at a party.

No trumpets blared. No cymbals clashed.

But one night, my friend told me that this new man in her life had a fine sense of humor, and that when they'd talked about movies, they'd discovered that they both loved the same ones.

By fall, they'd arranged the intricate process of meeting one another's adult children, and, in his case, grandchildren. It wasn't quite like in the storybooks. Her middle son found her beau tedious; his oldest daughter wondered whether they'd talked about a pre-nup, and had reviewed one another's economic interests and limits.

But this widow and widower heeded something their presumably wise kids didn't factor in: the rekindling of hope. Maybe there truly could be a Chapter Two. Perhaps two lonely people could blend their lives and grab a second chance at happiness.

There was inevitably a certain caution, born of pain on both sides.

There was a certain reserve about making that ultimate commitment. Loving, they both knew, could cost a lot.

But it still came to pass that on an ordinary Wednesday night, two people who would never make the pages of romantic bridal magazines stood ready and willing to take that vast leap of faith that is marriage. The mood was definitely mellower than passionate and wildly romantic.

I cried so many tears at that wonderful wedding that my eyes were puffy and swollen. Even the rabbi wept.

The wedding toasts had a certain intensity about them that you don't see at the weddings of breathless twenty-somethings.

The one I'll remember best came from the middle-aged groom to the bride in her sensible navy dress: "I'll warm your feet when they're cold, my darling," he said with a gallant smile.

And at least some of us understood just how much that promise means.

~Sally Friedman

Here Comes the Bride

Chapter 10

The Honeymoon

Your honeymoon tells the world—and maybe you—
who you are.

~Ginger Strand

The Getaway

Things do not pass for what they are, but for what they seem.
Most things are judged by their jackets.
~Baltasar Gracian

With three cops aiming two pistols and a shotgun at my bride, her hands shaking uncontrollably, I came to the realization that my groomsmen were right: Marriage would be tough.

Brittney and I had barely begun our lives together, and we were already targeted as Bonnie and Clyde.

Welcome to the Friday night of our honeymoon.

It all started at 5:00 P.M. on January 18, 2008, when I pulled into the GaPac Community Federal Credit Union parking lot on Alabama and James streets to deposit our wedding checks. I'd been a member there ever since I saved $20 to open an account. I knew most of the tellers, and my aunt was the manager. Every visit was cozy.

Except for this one.

After a smiling teller congratulated me for tying the knot, I strolled out of the bank and plopped into my 2003 yellow Ford Mustang decorated by a buddy of mine in white letters on both doors with "Caleb & Britt."

Then I picked up my bride of six days at Bellis Fair Mall and headed toward northbound Interstate 5. That's when I saw red and blue lights flicker in my rearview mirror.

I went through the mental checklist:

Speedometer? Fine.

Lights? On.

Windshield? No cracks.

Full and bright, the lights now filled my rearview mirror. I pulled over. My journalist instincts kicked in as I began thinking what I'd need: license, registration...

"Put your hands where I can see them!" the officer shouted.

My checklist vaporized as the officer barked: "Roll down the window. Turn off the car. Put the keys on the roof. Open the door—slowly."

I did. All of this has to be a mistake, I told myself.

"Drop to your knees. Hands on head. Crawl backwards."

"Can I ask what this is about?" I said, turning my head toward him.

"Look forward!" the officer snapped.

He then told me, in a Bruce Willis *Die Hard* sort of way, that we'd talk later.

Cuffs clicked into place, and the officer searched me: Pens. Reporter's tape recorder. Gum. Wallet. Cell phone.

Oh, no, not the inside pocket of my jacket, I thought.

Yes, the inside pocket. The officer pulled out a two-by-two-inch booklet: *Sex for Dummies*.

"Bachelor party," I said.

The officer chuckled, and I shared a nervous laugh with him.

So, we're cool, right? I thought.

Ha. No.

I noticed a second officer to my left and two more to my right. And, to my horror, three drawn guns pointed at my eighteen-year-old bride, who had been homeschooled until college, had never lived away from her parents, and still covers her eyes when the flying monkeys appear in *The Wizard of Oz*.

I needed air. Quickly. To yell. To jump high or grow green skin and break the cuffs.

But, instead, I exhaled, and as the air squeezed through my trachea, I said, "This is our honeymoon."

I would like to say it came out clearly with some bite. Truth is, though, I sounded more like Rex in *Toy Story*. I don't like confrontation.

One of the officers escorted me to the hard backseat of a squad car. Over the radio, I heard myself referred to as "suspect" three times. An officer then took my handcuffed Brittney to one of the six other squad cars that had responded.

After some time, an officer opened the door. He told me a bank had been robbed and that the suspect got away in a yellow Mustang… one decorated with white letters on both doors.

I asked him which bank had been robbed, and then told him I had just been to GaPac. The officer reached for his radio and relayed that the "suspect" had just confirmed that he had been at the GaPac Community Federal Credit Union.

"My aunt is the bank manager there," I said.

Hope! I thought. They can't honestly believe I'd rip off my aunt's bank and make a get away in a YELLOW Mustang, right?

The officer slammed the door shut. My face drooped.

Through the squad car's front window, I watched as a handful of lawmen eased up to my Mustang's trunk with their weapons locked and loaded. They flipped the trunk open and crept back.

Surprise, I thought.

The trunk revealed one duffle, two toiletry bags, and some clothes I had bought from the Aeropostale clearance rack.

The officer opened the door to talk to me again. Before he could say anything, I asked him if he knew an officer friend of mine, whose daughters happened to be the flower girls at my wedding just days ago.

The officer's eyes said he did know him. Then he looked down at a piece of paper in his hand and read me my rights. Shut the door again.

I felt like punching myself in the face.

Finally, after several minutes, I was asked to step out of the squad car. A witness had come from the bank. I walked with an officer past several red and blue lights until he asked me to look toward a particular vehicle with tinted windows.

I stood for about a minute, observing the congested traffic around me. Oh, and the people in the cars. I thought some might nose plant in a ditch, what with their faces plastered to their windows.

Caleb Breakey was one bad dude, I thought.

For a brief time, anyway.

Apparently, "Tinted Windows" was satisfied. An officer unlocked my cuffs, reunited me with my bride, and jotted down our names and dates of birth. He then asked if we had any questions.

I couldn't resist. "Can I take some pictures for our honeymoon?" The officer said to knock myself out, so I grabbed the digital camera out of my car and had a lawman snap three quick photos.

So for all of you folks out there planning an extravagant getaway after your wedding, think twice. Just go deposit your wedding checks at your local bank and walk out.

Who knows? Your bank receipt might show—as mine did with a transaction time of 16:48:43—that you were within thirty feet of a bank robbery that remains unresolved to this day.

Just make sure you take *Sex for Dummies* out of your inside pocket.

~Caleb Jennings Breakey

Reprinted by permission of Off the Mark
and Mark Parisi ©2011

94

Our Honeymoon Adventure on Pancake Bay

By failing to prepare, you are preparing to fail.
~Benjamin Franklin

erhaps I should have been suspicious of the whole outdoor-adventure honeymoon idea when a mosquito flew up under my bridal veil. It buzzed around my ears and nose as I was trying to hold still and concentrate on saying "I do"—an ominous sign I ignored. And what does "rustic" really mean? That was the question I should have asked.

After our reception, we climbed into our little green Vega and drove across the International Bridge to Sault Ste. Marie, Ontario, to begin our wedded bliss. Our first night, only one strange thing happened. When we stepped into our hotel room, we saw two men who looked like bums sleeping on our bed. No problem. We were still in civilization. We got another room.

Late the next morning, we set out for Pancake Bay. On the way, we stopped for lunch at McDonald's. While we sat at our picnic table, a brazen seagull dive-bombed us and stole our French fries. Another warning sign I naively ignored.

Yes, I thought as we walked up the path to the resort office, Pancake Bay is truly a scenic wonderland. I envisioned romantic strolls along the clean, sandy beach and secluded, intimate hikes along trails winding through the forest, just me and my beloved. Perhaps we would spot some peregrine falcons, moose, or black bears (in the far distance, of course). Actually, we did experience wildlife, but none of that sort.

Once we got our key, we happily explored our rustic cabin. It had a front porch overlooking the bay, beautiful knotty pine floors, and a kerosene stove in case the weather turned chilly. What it didn't have was electricity or running water—unless having a toilet that flushed with some kind of chemical solution counts. But there was no place to shower, no place to cook. A week of cold food wasn't what I had had in mind. That afternoon, we did discover a shower house down the trail, but our excitement died when we learned the resort provided no towels. We hadn't counted on that, either. But we were young and in love—as unprepared as we were, we would manage cheerfully.

Our first night, a dramatic storm hit, with thunder, lightning, and pelting rain. We snuggled in the dark, feeling as though we truly were having a grand adventure. I realized that if it rained all week, however, we would be stuck with nothing to do. We hadn't considered that we might not be able to spend our free time outside. Canoeing in the rain wouldn't really be all that romantic.

But the next day dawned fresh-washed and glorious. After a cold lunch of bread and peanut butter, we decided to hike along the beach with no particular agenda other than to commune with each other and with nature. It was there that my husband was attacked. Bears? No, not mere bears. The creatures were far more ferocious and voracious. They ate my husband alive. Soon, he was covered with itchy red bumps. "Aye-yuh," said an old geezer passing by. "No-see-ums." When we mentioned our problem to the lady at the resort counter, she just shrugged and said, "Burn a coil." Yeah, right. Like we had thought to bring coils with us. But at least the weather was warm and sunny, so warm in fact that my husband turned off our kerosene heater before we went to bed that night.

By the middle of the night, we were being suffocated by the

terrible smell of kerosene. My husband manfully got up and tried to take a look at our heater, but without a flashlight in total darkness, there was obviously nothing he could do. We had to open our windows. And while fresh air could then get in through the screens, so could the no-see-ums. As we pulled the sheet over our heads, I said to my husband, "I hope the fumes give them all a headache." We started giggling like a couple of kids at a slumber party.

In the morning, after another round of bread and peanut butter, we discovered with the resort proprietor that whereas my husband had turned off the flame of our heater, he hadn't turned off the kerosene, which had leaked out and pooled under our cabin. We were embarrassed, but there was nothing for it but to apologize for our mistake and hope the fumes would dissipate eventually. We couldn't hope the same about the clouds of biting bugs, however. We were beginning to wonder if perhaps we should have thought through our honeymoon plans a little more carefully.

That night, we were awakened by a cracking sound and a jolt, and the strange tilting of the bed on my side. What in the world could have happened? Without a flashlight, we already knew it would be pointless to try to investigate. We waited uneasily to see if anything else would happen, but when all was quiet, we eventually drifted back to sleep.

In the daylight, we were dumbfounded to see that one leg of the headboard had actually fallen through the floor. What, oh what, would the resort proprietor think when we confessed that we, the honeymooning couple, had caused our bed to break right through the floor? I was mortified. The kerosene incident had been bad enough. Was there enough kerosene still left in the ground that we could just burn the cabin down so we wouldn't have to confess to him? Only a fleeting thought.

"He might see the humor..." said my husband, taking my hand to comfort me, looking at me hopefully.

In spite of my chagrin, I giggled. "Maybe he could use our experience in his promotional literature."

"Red hot vacation spot for lovers..."

"So hot your bed will fall right through the floor."

We had a good laugh and then a long hug.

Once my husband inspected our bed more closely, he discovered that a knothole in the pine floor under one leg had given way.

"You know," he said tentatively, "it wouldn't be a crime to change our plans."

"Actually, they'd probably be relieved to get rid of us," I said.

"They might even pay us to go."

We spent the last half of our honeymoon in Sault Ste. Marie, Ontario, and had a delightful time. Hot food and hot showers never felt so good.

As I look back now on this experience after thirty-eight years of marriage, I can see that in many ways, our adventure on Pancake Bay was a perfect introduction to our married life. We were venturing into foreign territory and having new experiences that we weren't entirely prepared for. There have been plenty of tough times along the way, plenty of times when we've had to make adjustments and change plans. But we've found that no matter what, it always helps to focus on our love and to see the funny side of life. So far, married life has been a great adventure, just not always the adventure we thought we were signing up for.

~Ann McArthur

Locked Out!

My heart to you is given:
Oh, do give yours to me;
We'll lock them up together,
And throw away the key.
~Frederick Saunders

My husband and I were married along the rugged, magical shores of Lake Superior in northern Minnesota. We said our vows on a pebble beach at a resort in the tiny town of Lutsen. Our wedding day was perfect: there wasn't a cloud in the sky, and the sounds of lapping waves and loon calls permeated the air.

All our guests had traveled up to the resort to be with us on our special day, and to make the weekend a sort of mini-vacation. Per our request, everyone was staying in the main lodge. No one knew that my husband, Mark, and I planned to stay in the resort's nearby condos before heading out on our Canadian honeymoon the next morning. We had kept it a secret because we didn't want any of our groomsmen playing tricks on us.

So, after we said our vows, greeted all our guests, and had dinner, Mark and I got into our car (which had been covered in the words "Just Married"), opened the sunroof, and waved to all our guests as we drove into the sunset. Really, we just pulled out of the parking lot onto the main road and took the next turn into the condo parking area, but no one knew that—they thought they had just sent us on our way to Canada!

We parked our car, lugged all our baggage up the condo stairs to our unit, pulled out our magnetic key card, swiped it, and... nothing! We tried, unsuccessfully, to swipe a few more times before we realized we had a problem on our hands. If our keycard didn't work, what would we do? We couldn't go back to the main lodge because our guests had just sent us off, and we had already made our memorable exit. The only other alternative was to call the front desk and have someone bring us a new card. So, we decided to knock on the door of the neighboring condo and see if they would let us use their phone.

As we knocked, we heard a woman's voice behind the door say, "Wouldn't it be funny if it was the bride and groom?" When the door opened, there were two women standing there, a mother/daughter pair, and they began screaming, "It IS the bride and groom! Oh, my goodness! We just saw you get married through our window! Come in, come in!" We must have been quite the sight, standing there dressed in our wedding finery with a bunch of suitcases around us.

They told us that they had watched our wedding that afternoon through their picture window, and they were very eager to help us. Once we told them what our problem was, they even offered to run to the main lodge to pick us up a key. We thanked them, but said we could just call down and someone from the front desk could probably drive up a key just as easily.

Mark made the call, and as he did, the women were telling us that the mother, Margaret, who was in her seventies, had just gotten re-married, and that her daughter, who was in her mid-forties, had come along with them on their trip to help them get around. As they were telling me all this, Margaret began waving to a man I hadn't noticed at first. He was sitting in a chair facing the opposite direction, looking out the big picture window while shaving with an electric razor.

"Hank! Get over here! Come and meet the bride and groom!"

He glanced up and saw her waving, turned off his razor, stood up slowly and walked over to us. He didn't say a word as his wife began telling him why we were there—that we were the bride and groom from the wedding they had seen earlier.

By this time, Mark had finished calling the front desk, and he turned to join the conversation. Silently, Hank reached into his pocket and pulled out his wallet. He shuffled through the bills, pulled out $100, and tried to hand it to Mark.

"Oh, no, that's nice of you, but it's too much," Mark said.

Hank kept trying to hand it to him, and Mark kept trying to defer the gift. Finally Margaret grabbed the bill out of Hank's hand and said, "If the groom won't take it then the bride will!" as she shoved it out to me. So... I took it! We thanked them over and over for their very generous gift, and then maintenance arrived with our new key. It worked, and we were finally able to begin our honeymoon.

So, what did we do with the $100? Well, we were so blown away by how generous the couple had been that we decided to use it on something that would always remind us of our honeymoon and that special time. When we got to Canada, we bought a beautiful print of the Canadian landscape that hangs in our home to this day. It was a honeymoon experience we'll never forget!

~Laura Smetak

96

Honeymoon Havoc

*The trouble with weather forecasting is that it's right too often for us
to ignore it and wrong too often for us to rely on it.*
~Patrick Young

*I*n 1966, I married a man who had custody of his three daughters, ages seven, five and three. The two older girls were our flower girls, all dressed in bright yellow and so excited to be in a wedding! The youngest was guarded closely by my husband's parents so that she would not run out into the aisle and try to be a part of the festivities!

When it was explained to the girls that Daddy and their new stepmother would be off on a honeymoon just after the wedding reception, Donna, the oldest of the girls, cried. Daddy tried to comfort her and make her understand that we'd only be gone for three days, driving from Claymont, Delaware to Atlantic City, New Jersey and back. All three girls could not fathom why they couldn't go with us! It made it hard to leave them, but we promised as soon as we returned that we'd be fixing up their bedrooms at the house we'd purchased and getting ready to move into it as a family. We said our goodbyes at the reception, witnessed some tears all over again, and tried to dry our own tears inconspicuously as we sauntered to our getaway car.

The only thing I really remember about the drive to Atlantic City in our car decorated with "Just Married" signs was a moment on the freeway that we passed a car packed full of nuns. All of them smiled and gave us the thumbs-up sign!

I remember being a shy, nineteen-year-old new bride, about to take on a marriage with three built-in children. I admittedly was a little frightened about it, but I already loved the girls and their father to the point where there was no turning back. My enthusiasm and faith that we could make a wonderful life together were giving me the hope to jump into this wholeheartedly.

Since it was the middle of June, I had a suitcase packed with summer things. I figured a nice dress to wear to an upscale restaurant, a bathing suit, and an assortment of tank tops and shorts were all I needed. The forecast called for a little rain the next day, but we figured it would be short-lived, and we'd have lots of wonderful time on the beach.

Boy, were we wrong! A hurricane off the coast of Florida took a different turn from what they had projected, and no sooner were we checked into our motel when the rain and wind started! With the television in our motel room tuned into the weather forecast, we discovered we were in for hurricane winds and heavy rain the whole stretch of our honeymoon. I'll never forget the size of the waves, larger than I'd ever seen before! I used our movie camera to film wave after crashing wave from the motel windows. I wanted to always remember this!

When it got close to dinnertime, we'd decided on a nice restaurant on the boardwalk where we could eat seafood for dinner. I put on my dress and fancy shoes and realized it was sleeveless, and the temperature had dropped at least ten degrees out there! Poking my head out the door onto the balcony, the cold air and rain washed over me and I shivered. There was no jacket or umbrella available because I had not even thought I'd need those things in the middle of June at the beach!

My husband ran down the boardwalk to the nearest store in search of an umbrella or rain cover-ups that he could buy. No luck. He returned looking like a drowned cat.

All I could do was improvise. I grabbed the only "cover" I

had—a large, gaudily striped beach towel—and wrapped it around myself. My husband grabbed a newspaper and spread it out over our heads as we dashed for our car in the parking lot.

I guess we turned a few heads that evening in the restaurant, but we had some great laughs about the whole situation! We went from dinner to a movie—the only movie playing on the boardwalk that night—*The Ten Commandments*. (A little irony there with the roaring waves in the background and the parting of the Red Sea!)

It wasn't long after we were back in our motel room that we realized how much we missed his girls. Neither of us had to say it out loud, but we knew we were thinking the same thing. Why stay here another night in a hurricane when we could be back with them, getting ready to start our new life together as a family? As we snuggled close, I looked up at him and said, "Would you mind if we went home tomorrow instead of staying another night?" I could tell by the look in his eyes that I was a woman after his own heart and always would be!

And so we drove home to the delight of three little girls and began our life together. Forty-five years and six children later, I can say it was well worth a short honeymoon to begin our great adventure as the Walker family. We often unveiled the old movie camera over the years and watched the footage of wave after roaring wave coming into the beach at Atlantic City—not to forget the short clip of me running to the car in a fancy dress draped with an ugly striped beach towel!

~Beverly F. Walker

97

The Stranger's Offer

We often take for granted the very things that most deserve our gratitude.
~Cynthia Ozick

The day after my husband John and I were married on Saturday, August 2, 1980, we were in the emergency room of a Chicago hospital. We had been involved in a head-on collision on the Dan Ryan Expressway.

When the accident occurred, John had been driving us to our hotel at O'Hare Airport where we hoped to catch a flight the next morning to the Bahamas for our honeymoon. On a late Sunday afternoon, the multi-lane roadway was packed, presumably from people returning to the city after a weekend away.

One car tried unsuccessfully to merge onto the roadway. Unfortunately, there was not enough room, and it hit a car. This action caused a domino effect involving four cars. Our small two-door, closest to the median, felt the final impact, as a big black car was spun around into our lane.

When the crash happened, I wasn't wearing a seatbelt and hit my head on the windshield. (It was not a law then for passengers to wear a seatbelt.) Thankfully, John had worn his seatbelt and was unharmed.

An ambulance transported John and me, wearing a thick neck brace, to a hospital. Three hours later, after undergoing a series of tests to determine possible damage to my body, the doctors released me. I was thankful to not even have a headache.

However grateful John and I were for having our lives spared, the fact was that we were stranded. Our car had been towed to a repair shop. We were three hours from home and family. And we knew no one in the Windy City. John and I slumped in the stiff waiting-room chairs, exhausted from the wedding and the accident, and desperately trying to decide what we should do.

It was near midnight, and our plane left at 6:00 A.M. If we could get to the airport tonight, we could spend the night there and catch our flight the next morning. A nurse told us the bus lines were closed. "A taxi will charge $45," she added. We gulped. That was more than a young farm couple could afford.

A man sitting across from us in the waiting room stood. "I'll give you a ride to the airport," he said. He looked to be in his sixties and wore a respectable-looking raincoat while leaning on a cane. He explained he was in the ER because his mother had had an episode with her blood pressure and needed to stay overnight. He was ready to leave.

Tired and shook up, John and I looked at each other. It seemed risky to get in a car with a stranger, but no other plan presented itself. We accepted the offer.

"I was in a car accident myself several months ago," the stranger said, limping as he led us to the hospital parking lot. The limp, he said, was due to the accident. "I'll always walk with a cane," he added. He unlocked the doors to a modern, clean sedan, and we climbed in. The leather seats felt good, and I curled into the back seat, nearly oblivious to what was being said by the two men in the front seat.

The stranger continued talking to John as he drove us deftly through the night. He described his narrow escape from death and how he had had to be cut out of the wreckage. In the backseat, I had nearly nodded off when the stranger's next words seeped into my consciousness. "I'm thankful to be alive," he said.

Thirty minutes later, we arrived at the airport terminal. The stranger helped us retrieve our luggage from the trunk. Then he handed John a $10 bill. "Buy your new wife a good breakfast," he said. Numbly, we thanked the stranger. Then he got back in his car and drove off into the night.

To this day, we have no clue as to his identity. But we know this man performed a miracle that night. What could have been a blight on our first days together after our wedding has become one of the best memories John and I share. The stranger helped us see that instead of feeling sorry for ourselves after the car accident and having to spend the second night of our marriage in the hospital and airport, we should be thrilled to still be together and able to go on our honeymoon.

We regret not learning the stranger's name to send him a thank-you note, but John and I have tried to give back by spreading his generosity and kindness to strangers we meet. We think he would be happy about that.

~Kayleen Reusser

98

Happily Ever After...
After the Honeymoon

No vacation goes unpunished.
~Karl Hakkarainen

My husband Mickey and I were married on a cold, blustery November night in my hometown of Omaha, Nebraska. A honeymoon in Jamaica sounded ideal: warm days on the beach, Duke and the boys playing steel drums around the pool, plenty of time to just focus on us—a welcome respite from Chicago where we both lived and worked.

We left right after the ceremony, stayed at a motel near the Omaha airport, and left the next morning for our paradise island.

All went well until we arrived in Montego Bay and discovered our luggage did not. Having only the winter clothes on our backs, we were decidedly overdressed. Undaunted, we bought bathing suits in the hotel gift shop and headed to the beach. We spent the day drinking piña coladas, napping on our lounge chairs, reading, and talking. Ahhh. Luggage? Who cared?

I should have. As a redhead with fair skin and freckles, I had no business spending that much time in the sun. By the end of the day, I was the color of a chili pepper and radiated just as much heat. My skin felt two sizes too small, and I was chilled and felt nauseous. Not a pretty picture.

Back in the room, now with our luggage, we applied what little we knew of first aid for sunburn. We (carefully) slathered my body with aloe lotion and covered my scorched skin with Mickey's pajamas. Then I proceeded to retch my way through the next twenty-four hours. I remember lying on the bathroom floor, my hot face against the cool tiles, feeling totally dejected. I looked up at my new husband and said sorrowfully, "Happy married life." Luckily, he laughed.

When I finally felt good enough to go back in the sun, it had disappeared, replaced by torrential downpours. There went our plan to hike the waterfall. The next time the sun did appear, we were 125 feet underground on a cave exploration we had previously scheduled and paid for.

Sunburn and drenching rains weren't our only honeymoon disasters. One of the first nights at the hotel, Mick dropped his new wedding band down the drain. A gasp, a gurgle, and it was gone. I knew he was totally unaccustomed to wearing jewelry of any kind, but I had a little trouble understanding why he couldn't wash his hands wearing the ring. At midnight, the hotel maintenance man begrudgingly took the sink apart and found Mick's ring in the elbow joint of the pipe. Luckily, I laughed… sort of.

Despite everything, we did have a wonderful time together. It was a honeymoon, after all. For us, it turned out to be a good test of the vows "in sickness and in health," although I don't think Mick planned on being tested quite so soon.

This year, we're celebrating our forty-fifth wedding anniversary! That's a lot of years of ups and down, triumphs and disappointments, surprises and compromises. Sometimes it seems we're more head-to-head than eye-to-eye. But we've built a foundation of love and trust that has carried us through the rough spots. Two children and seven grandchildren later, we're still talking things over and working things out. And, luckily, we're still laughing.

~Myra Lipp Sanderman

99

Honeymooning in a Clown Car

It is only in adventure that some people succeed in knowing themselves—
in finding themselves.
~André Gide

*H*ere comes the bride… and the groom, and the matron of honor, and a groomsman, and a baby, and a dog, and… a radiator?

Our wedding was nowhere near a fairy tale. Well, on the other hand, maybe it was, seeing how most fairy tales have rather eccentric plots. My husband and I met while we were both seniors in college. We dated for about four months, got engaged, planned a wedding for seven months, and were married almost one year to the day we met.

And because we both participated in the Cooperative Education Program, alternating between school and work each semester, we still had another two years of college to go. So we had neither the money nor the time to go on a honeymoon. Instead we headed straight to our little cheapo apartment in Tuscaloosa, Alabama, and waited for classes to start at THE University of Alabama (as my husband likes to call it).

Oh, did I mention that my younger sister had gotten married the year before, and that she, too, was a college student—married to a college student? I guess falling in love in college and getting married without giving it too much thought runs in my family. But my sister and her husband, on the other hand, had already started a family—one baby girl and a dog. And like us, they, too, were continuing their college studies, but at Mississippi State University (MSU) in Starkville, Mississippi, which is located between Tuscaloosa and my hometown of Rosedale, Mississippi.

Prior to these whirlwind romances and weddings, my sister and I had been roommates and best buds at MSU. So, naturally, my sister was my matron of honor as I had been her maid of honor the year before. Her husband was also one of our groomsmen.

Well, something very interesting happened during the preparations for the wedding. My brother-in-law's car broke down and needed a new radiator. (I'll just refer to his family from here on out as "the stranded family.") I don't recall how the stranded family, baby girl, and dog made it across the state of Mississippi for the wedding, but they did. Yet there was still a problem. How would they get back to MSU after the wedding?

Since we were the only car heading back that way, it was only proper that we should give them a ride. Right? But did I mention we drove a Volkswagen Beetle? And I don't mean the newer model of the Beetle. We had the original Beetle—the one with the trunk in the front and the engine in the back—the one with the teeny-tiny seats.

And, even though our trunk was loaded down with our luggage and wedding gifts, we still managed to find room for the stranded family's luggage as well as their new radiator.

When we went to pick up the stranded family at the home of my brother-in-law's parents, my brother-in-law's great-grandmother took one look at our super compact car, then narrowed her eyes and said, "The next time you come, you might want to drive a bigger car."

I couldn't have agreed with her more. Yet, somehow we managed to squeeze our matron of honor, a groomsman, a baby, and a dog into the tiny backseat of our lime-green Volkswagen Beetle and ride for three whole hours across the entire state of Mississippi. Whew! Can anybody say, "Honeymooning in a clown car?"

~Linda Jackson

A Life of Surprises

A first-rate marriage is like a first-rate hotel: expensive, but worth it.
~Mignon McLaughlin, The Second Neurotic's Notebook

I met my husband my first day at work. He was training to be a Branch Manager, and I was called in to substitute for Karen, who was going on maternity leave. Peter came up to our desk and asked Karen if she had any Benadryl.

"Jayne, this is Peter," Karen introduced as she dug out the medication.

"Hi, Jayne," Peter replied, and with a straight face added, "Karen and I do drugs together."

I was surprised at first, but then laughed at the joke — and he's kept me laughing ever since.

We started dating a few weeks later, and when he proposed after two years, I had no doubt I was the luckiest woman in the world.

We agreed that I would plan the wedding, and Peter said he would plan the honeymoon on the condition that it would be a complete surprise for me. I was hesitant, but I knew I couldn't take care of everything in the six-month time frame we had, so I agreed.

The wedding was beautiful, and we were exhausted after the last dance at midnight. Peter's brother, Jamie, our chauffeur, helped me into the back of his car as Peter got in on the other side. We were on a strict budget, so no limo for us! I didn't mind; Jamie's car was nice enough, and so was he. I knew we were having a send-off party the following day at his parents' house to open wedding gifts and thank everyone, so we weren't going far.

"Where are we driving to?" I asked sleepily.

"You'll see," my brand-new husband smiled, as I snuggled contentedly into him.

We drove downtown to one of the fanciest hotels in the city. As Jamie opened the door for me, I frowned at Peter and said, "We can't afford this!"

"I have a friend in charge of housekeeping," he winked. "We got a great rate, so don't worry."

We gave Jamie a goodbye hug as he announced he would pick us up at 1:00 P.M. the next day. Minutes later, Peter carried me across the threshold of a beautiful suite overlooking the harbor. There were chocolates on the pillows and a beautiful fruit basket holding a note from Peter's friend John that read: "Enjoy your night. This is my wedding gift to both of you."

We enjoyed the beautiful surroundings of our solitary confinement for twelve uninterrupted hours. We ordered room service for breakfast, fully intending to pay for it, as well as the room on which John had already been promised a huge discount. But when we checked out and Peter held out his credit card, the front desk clerk tore up our bill, saying, "Your money's no good here!"

After a warm and wonderful send-off party with family and friends, we drove together out of the city. I wasn't surprised when Peter took the airport exit. Peter loves the Caribbean and had been there a few times before. But this turned out to be a decoy. Instead of parking, Peter pulled up to the ATM. I flashed a puzzled look at him, and he said innocently: "Just need to get some extra cash. You didn't think we were flying somewhere, did you? I remembered you telling me about staring at all those ads of the Pocono Mountain resorts in the back of the bridal magazines with your friends. How could we go anywhere else? With the money we saved from airfare, we can afford it."

I was totally and pleasantly surprised and thrilled. It was a twenty-four-hour drive, but we both enjoy road trips and took turns driving. Peter broke up the drive halfway, having booked a cozy suite in the heart of the White Mountains in New Hampshire.

We spent a week in an all-inclusive honeymoon resort situated on a beautiful lake that had all the amenities that a young energetic couple could want. We had breakfast delivered to our door every morning, then spent the day either on the driving range, roller skating, swimming, rowing, playing pool, tennis, squash… We never ran out of things to do! We ended each day around the dinner table with other happy newlyweds.

Twenty-four years later, Peter says I did a great job planning the wedding. I say my honey planned the best honeymoon a girl could ever want, and he's been pleasantly surprising me ever since.

~Jayne Thurber-Smith

Honeymoon in the Outhouse

A human being is an ingenious assembly of portable plumbing.
~Christopher Morley

Neither my fiancé nor I were big on lavish weddings. We'd both just graduated from college in southern Illinois, moved to Denver, Colorado, and were hard at work at our first real, better-than-minimum-wage jobs. Neither of us had vacation time coming. Neither of us had any relatives in the state of Colorado. And we certainly didn't have the money to spend on a big wedding.

So, one day we simply said, "Let's do it." And we did. There were thirteen of us in the tiny chapel, and later we all went out to our favorite hangout and drank margaritas and ate popcorn to celebrate our nuptials. When I look back on it, I think the wedding and the reception thereafter may have had something to do with the state of the honeymoon.

Ah, yes, the honeymoon. We both managed to get Monday off, and since the wedding was on Friday night that gave us three days. The groom, being a geologist who loved rocks and strange, natural formations and earthly occurrences, announced Saturday morning that we were going to drive to Yellowstone National Park, more than 400 miles away. That man loved to drive, but I wasn't too sure about spending the bulk of my three-day honeymoon cooped up in a car.

But this was back in the sixties when men still got their way about almost everything.

So we drove. And drove. We'd jump out of the car, eat a fast meal, and get right back in the car. I oohed and aahed at the incredible scenery that whizzed by at seventy-five miles per hour. When we reached snowdrifts that were eight feet tall in northern Wyoming, he paused for five minutes to take my picture next to them. I stood there in my sleeveless blouse and summer-weight slacks in early June and made a snowball to throw at my groom.

Back in the car, we drove for hours, winding our way through mountainous roads toward Yellowstone. We arrived at dark and spent the night in a primitive, cold cabin. By noon Sunday, after a huge brunch loaded with "mountain man" eggs, sausage and pancakes the size of plates, I began to feel awful. I thought back to the week before the wedding and realized I'd been constipated for an entire week. The excitement of the wedding, worrying about taking a day off work from my new job, irregular meals and spending eleven hours in the car the day before had not been good for me.

As I sat on a long wooden bench with a couple dozen other Old Faithful watchers waiting for the spectacle, I felt as if I was carrying the weight of the world in my gut. Misery was my middle name as I watched my new husband pacing back and forth, waiting anxiously for his geological wonder to blow.

This was my honeymoon, for heaven's sake! I couldn't let this go on.

Holding my stomach in pain, I swallowed my shyness and gathered my courage. "Honey, I need some prune juice. Would you mind going to the camp store to see if they have any?"

My groom, who wasn't too crazy about the possibility of missing the start of Old Faithful's show, dashed into the store and returned in record time, handing me a quart of room-temperature prune juice.

As we sat there waiting for the explosion of one of the world's greatest natural wonders, I drank my juice. We waited, and I drank. Suddenly, the geyser put on her show, spewing hot steam hundreds of feet into the air. I watched and drank my prune juice.

After the show, we climbed back into the car for a driving tour of the huge national park. When a bear cub ambled across the road and climbed up to the window of the car in front of us, I snapped a quick photo, finished off my quart of prune juice, and wished I were back home in a nice tub of hot water, easing my intestinal pain.

As we neared the park exit later that afternoon after a long drive through Yellowstone's immensity, Mother Nature and the prune juice grabbed hold of my stopped-up digestive system and started the rumblings of a geyser in my gut that felt as if it would rival that of Old Faithful.

"Bob! You have to find a bathroom! I have to go! Now! Please, get to a bathroom! Hurry!"

My groom sped up for half a mile and then slammed on the brakes. "It's up there." He pointed to a dense forested area.

"Up where?" I started to panic. I didn't see anything but a huge hill and thousands of trees.

"Right there, off to the right. See that building? It's an outhouse."

I shot my husband a look that would have caused flowers to wilt and slammed the car door as I bolted out. I stumbled up the steep hill and dashed toward the outhouse, noting that it was much darker up there in the forest.

"There better be lights in this place," I mumbled to myself.

It was a two-seater outhouse. No lights. No toilet paper (except for napkins from our lunch). Nothing except spider webs all over the place. I hoped that my new husband had the car windows rolled up and couldn't hear what I was up to there in the woodland privy. I sat there in that smelly pit, terrified that a bear or a snake would amble in.

That night, in our hotel room, the prune juice continued to do its work. My husband plopped down on the bed after adjusting the TV set that was hooked to the wall up near the ceiling. "Honey, I know you don't feel too good, but how would it be if I adjust this TV so you can see it from in here? If you leave the door open, you can watch from in the bathroom, and I can watch it from the bed. At least you won't be so lonely."

I sat there on the Motel 6 toilet, watching TV, as my husband spent the night alone in the bed on the other side of the bathroom wall. Welcome to the real world of marriage, I thought to myself as I gently fondled the huge, soft roll of toilet paper before me. I actually said prayers of thanksgiving to the Almighty for that little bit of paradise... that nice, shiny white bathroom where I spent the third and final night of my honeymoon.

~Patricia Lorenz

Meet Our Contributors

Monica A. Andermann lives on Long Island with her husband, Bill, and their cat, Charley. In addition to several credits in the *Chicken Soup for the Soul* collection, her writing has appeared in such publications as *Skirt!*, *Sasee*, *The Secret Place*, and *Woman's World*.

Dawn Baird is pursuing a Bachelor of Specialized Studies degree (BSS) in journalism, literature, and creative writing at Ohio University. She is a freelance writer of nonfiction and fiction works, published both in print and online. E-mail her at dbaird.wordsmith@gmail.com.

Francine L. Baldwin-Billingslea is a mother, grandmother, breast cancer survivor, and a newlywed for the second time around, who has recently found a passion for writing. She has written her memoir, *Through It All*, and has been published in over eighteen anthologies, magazines, and online in the past five years.

Kathleen Basi is a stay-at-home mom, freelance writer, flute and voice teacher, liturgical composer, choir director, natural family planning teacher, scrapbooker, sometime-chef, and budding disability rights activist. She puts her juggling skills on display at www.kathleenbasi.com.

Bari Benjamin, LCSW, BCD, is a former English teacher turned psychotherapist, and she practices in Pittsburgh, PA. Marrying in late mid-life, she has begun writing seriously, and has had several essays published in adoption and step-parenting magazines. She is currently working on a memoir.

Laura L. Bradford enjoys sharing the misadventures that caused her to turn away from her vanity and become a woman of faith. This Cinderella didn't see the greatness in her handsome prince until she humbled herself and helped him fight a thirty-year, losing battle with multiple sclerosis.

LaTonya Branham graduated from Antioch University McGregor and Wilberforce University in Ohio. She is a college administrator and adjunct professor. LaTonya is the author of *CultureSeek* and *Spirit Seek*. She was also a contributing writer in *Chicken Soup for the Soul: Devotional Stories for Women*. Learn more at www.LaTonyaBranham.com.

Caleb Jennings Breakey is self-conscious about writing in the third person. He thinks it's a little weird. But he should still tell you that he's a writer, youth mentor, and crazy lover of Jesus. He and his sweetheart, Brittney, passionately teach writing and character at high schools, colleges, and conferences. E-mail him at calebbreakey@gmail.com.

Sage de Beixedon Breslin, Ph.D., is a licensed psychologist and intuitive consultant and an accomplished author. Her latest publications have been written to inspire and touch those who have struggled with life's challenges. Her books, stories, and chapters are available on her website at www.HealingHeartCenter.org. E-mail her at Sage@HealingHeartCenter.org.

Sallie Brown is a teacher, traveler, gardener, dog lover, and writer. She lives on Hood Canal in Northwest Washington State where her surroundings make it difficult to concentrate and, at the same time, inspire her writing. E-mail Sallie at salliebrown@proaxis.com.

Lori Bryant is an author, speaker, and inspirational storyteller. She has spent the past twenty-five years serving and loving people. Her passion is to help others find freedom and live life to the fullest! She recently co-authored *Zoe Life Inspired, a Daily Devotional* and *Conversations of Courage II.*

Marty Bucella is a full-time freelance cartoonist and humorous illustrator with over thirty-five years of experience. His work has appeared in most major magazines, as well as on greeting cards, calendars, on the Web, advertisements, textbooks, syndication, etc. To see more of Marty's work, visit his website at www.martybucella.com.

John P. Buentello is an author who publishes essays, fiction, and poetry. Currently, he is at work on an anthology of his published short stories and completing a new novel. E-mail John at jakkhakk@yahoo.com.

Julie Burns lives in Tennessee. She has published numerous works of fiction and nonfiction, including stories in *Guideposts* magazine and several in the *Chicken Soup for the Soul* series.

LeAnn Campbell is a retired special education teacher. She has over 1,500 published works, including a mystery series of books for middle-grade readers available at www.oaktara.com. Visit LeAnn's website at leanncampbell.vpweb.com.

Linda S. Clare is the author of three nonfiction books and a novel, *The Fence My Father Built* (Abingdon Press, 2009). She teaches writing at Lane Community College and is an expert writing consultant for George Fox Evangelical Seminary. She lives with her family in Eugene, OR. Contact her through her blog at godsonggrace.blogspot.com.

Harriet Cooper is a freelance writer and has published personal essays, humour, and creative nonfiction in newspapers, newsletters, anthologies, and magazines. She is a frequent contributor to the *Chicken Soup for the Soul* series. She writes about family, relationships, health, food, cats, writing, and daily life. E-mail her at shewrites@ live.ca.

Tracy Crump publishes *The Write Life* e-newsletter, moderates an online critique group, and enjoys teaching other writers at conferences and through her Write Life Workshops. Now she not only has a daughter, but a sweet little granddaughter, Nellie. Visit Tracy at TracyCrump.com and WriteLifeWorkshops.com.

Annalee Davis is an ordained minister who graduated summa cum laude from New Brunswick Theological Seminary in 1999. She is a speaker, writer, musician, and adjunct professor. She enjoys traveling, reading, sewing, quilting, and spending time with her grandchildren. E-mail her at reverendannalee@comcast.net.

Diana DeAndrea-Kohn is a freelance writer and a small business owner in Washington State. She is married to her husband, Scott, and she has three boys: Kenny, Alex, and Brodie. Diana enjoys reading, writing, and running.

Barbara Diggs is a freelance writer and copywriter living in Paris, France, with her husband and two sons. In addition to writing for magazines and business clients, she blogs about raising multicultural children and things to do in Paris with kids. Learn more at www. barbaradiggs.com.

Lori Dyan worked in the communications industry for eighteen years before pursuing her dream of writing fiction. She now writes women's fiction and children's books from her home in Ontario, Canada, where she lives with her husband and two children. Learn more at www.loridyan.com and www.restlesswriters.ca.

Shawnelle Eliasen and her husband, Lonny, raise their five sons in Illinois. Shawnelle home teaches her youngest boys. Her writing has been published in *Guideposts*, *MomSense* magazine, *Marriage*

Partnership, *A Cup of Comfort* books, numerous *Chicken Soup for the Soul* books, and other anthologies. Follow her adventures at Shawnellewrites.blogspot.com.

Kate Fellowes' working life has revolved around being a words editor for a student newspaper, reporter for the local press, and cataloger in her hometown library. She's the author of four novels, and numerous short stories and essays. She and her husband share their home with a variety of companion animals.

Valorie Wells Fenton and her husband live in a bungalow on the state line between Kansas and Missouri. Valorie is a mother of three talented daughters, grandmother of six amazing children, and even a great-grandmother. She enjoys gardening and feeding the birds. Valorie is a certified hypnotherapist in her home office.

April Taylor Fetch lives in Northern California where she works as an elementary school teacher. April enjoys traveling with her husband, and spending time with her friends and family. She also enjoys writing children's stories and hopes to one day get them published. E-mail her at aprilfetch@yahoo.com.

Jill Fisher is a stay-at-home mom of two little boys and a former elementary teacher. Jill's cake stand has survived four moves and 1,200 miles without a scratch, and it resides in a place of honor on the highest, dustiest shelf in the basement. E-mail her at yellowsmoke1010@hotmail.com.

Kristi Cocchiarella FitzGerald has degrees in English and theater. She is a freelance writer of poetry, historical fantasy and science fiction, and articles on costumes. She resides in Western Montana where she lives with her husband, Geoff, her two Shih Tzus, Panda and Koala, and her cat, Moose. E-mail her at kristi.d.fitzgerald@gmail.com.

Barbara Flores received an MFA degree in writing from Bennington

College at age sixty-two. She has published three books and recently completed a memoir, *Separated, Acting Badly*. Barbara lives in Florida with her Westie, Lola, and new husband, George—they're still celebrating. E-mail her at bfbarbaraflores@gmail.com or www. barbaraflores.net.

After raising three children, **Lela Foos** received an associate's degree in English in 2002. She is an elementary school paraprofessional and works with children in Special Education. Lela enjoys reading, gardening, and spending time with her family. She has also written several children's books.

Rosalind Forster received her Master of Social Work degree from McGill University, Montreal. She teaches Critical Thinking and Sociology. She loves to read, hike, and spend time with loved ones. Rosalind plans to write inspirational books using words that travel to the heart of the reader. E-mail her at ros.forster@sympatico.ca.

A longtime essayist, **Sally Friedman** writes about what interests her most: relationships, family, and life cycle events. She is a graduate of the University of Pennsylvania and has been a contributor to local, regional, and national newspapers and magazines for over four decades. E-mail her at pinegander@aol.com.

Victoria Grantham is a freelance writer whose work has appeared in *The New York Times*, *New York Post*, *New York Daily News*, YourTango, *American Lawyer*, and *Downtown Express*. She lives in NYC with her husband, son, and two pound puppies.

Svetlana Grobman is a former Russian engineer and editor, as well as an American librarian. She came to the United States in 1990. Here she found a new life, a new job, a new husband, and a new passion—writing. Currently, she is working on her memoir.

Johanna Hardy is a student at Northern Michigan University working toward a degree in writing. She enjoys riding horses, reading, working with children, playing softball and Ultimate Frisbee, and creating and playing music. After graduation, she plans to continue writing and hopefully work in publishing. E-mail her at indigorose@rocketmail.com.

Pam Hawley also writes short fiction and is working on her first novel. Her work has appeared in *eFiction* magazine and *The Spirit of Poe* anthology. She lives in Baltimore, works in higher education, and enjoys reading, hiking, ferrets, and cheering for the Pittsburgh Steelers. E-mail her at sixweasels@comcast.net.

Jennifer Heeg enjoys spending time with her husband, Aaron, and two children, Alex and Ava. She firmly believes everything happens for a reason and God only gives you what you can handle. With no prior publication experience, Jenni feels truly honored to share her story in the *Chicken Soup for the Soul* series.

Carolyn Hiler is an artist living in the mountains outside Los Angeles. When not drawing, painting, or hiking with her two adorable mutts, she works in private practice as a psychotherapist in Claremont, CA. Carolyn posts cartoons almost every day at www.azilliondollarscomics.com, and she sells funny things on Etsy at www.etsy.com/shop/AZillionDollars.

Former teacher **Gina Farella Howley** currently lives out her dream Mom career. Her three boys, all under seven years old, consume much of her time. When they are not awake, she is thinking about them, writing about them, and looking to make a name for herself as an author someday.

Carol Hurn lives near Seattle, WA, with her two dogs, Bear and Budha, and zany cat, Mister. She loves getting together with her three grown daughters and two grandchildren. She enjoys playing video/computer games and is working on her fifth romance novel.

Linda Jackson received her degree in math and computer science from The University of Alabama. She left her career in information technology to raise a family and pursue writing. She is the author of two novels, and this is her second story in the *Chicken Soup for the Soul* series. Please visit her website at www.jacksonbooks.com.

Cael Jacobs and his wife, Elizabeth, are the ministers of a small church in rural Virginia. They live on the land where they were married among the oaks and beeches, along with an imprudent number of cats. Cael uses his writing as a tool for teaching. E-mail him at cael@shadowgrove.com.

Jill Jaracz is a freelance writer who writes features about credit cards, authentication technology, and how things work. Jill also enjoys traveling and being a roller derby official. Please visit her website at jilljaracz.com.

Samantha Keller is a blogger, freelance writer, and mother to three mischievous munchkins. Sam is feisty with her pen and has a knack for finding both God and humor in the smallest details. You can find more of her writing and wit at www.scrappysam.com.

Jack Kline lives with his family, dogs, and horses near Louisburg, KS. He began writing following the marriage of his daughter. The bug had bitten. He has numerous published short stories and nonfiction pieces.

April Knight is a freelance writer and artist. She spends winters in Australia with her son where they search for buried treasure with metal detectors. She hasn't discovered a treasure yet, but it is a great adventure.

Sheila Seiler Lagrand lives in the foothills of Orange County, CA, with her husband, Rich, and three dogs. By day, she works as the operations manager for a registered investment advisory firm. Otherwise, you'll find her boating, cooking, enjoying her grandchildren, and blogging at godspotting.net. E-mail her at sheila@godspotting.net.

A freelance writer, **Jennifer Lang** has been published in *Parenting*, *Yoga Journal*, and *Natural Solutions*, among others. Her essays have appeared in the *South Loop Review*, *San Francisco Chronicle*, and on ducts.org.

Charlotte A. Lanham is a frequent contributor to *Chicken Soup for the Soul* books. She is an active member of the Society of Children's Book Writers and Illustrators. E-mail Charlotte at charlotte.lanham@sbcglobal.net.

P.D.R. Lindsay is busy. She wants to write all day, but must tutor writers and teach English to non-English speakers to pay the bills. She farms trees to save the planet, and runs a writers' retreat to help writers finish novels and a home-stay to give English language students a holiday.

Although **Kris Lindsey** has a B.A. degree in social work, her chosen career was stay-at-home mom until her daughters forcibly retired her by growing up. She enjoys writing, leading Bible studies, time with her hubby, and scuba diving in Fiji. Kris also writes about God's help for hurting emotions at www.krislindsey.com.

Shelly Bleggi Linton received a Bachelor of Science degree and MBA degree from Brigham Young University. She is a writer and business owner. She lives with her husband and cat, Tiger Lily, in Oakland, CA. She enjoys exploring the world, biking, reading, and renovating their 1920s home. E-mail her at sableggi@hotmail.com.

Patricia Lorenz, author of thirteen books, including *Life's Too Short to Fold Your Underwear*, has contributed to sixty *Chicken Soup for the Soul* books. Mother of four and grandmother of eight, Patricia speaks at various venues around the country and follows her dreams while she's still awake. Learn more at www.PatriciaLorenz.com.

Donna Lowich works as an information specialist, providing information to people affected by paralysis. She enjoys writing about her family and personal experiences. Other hobbies include reading and counted cross-stitch. She lives with her husband in New Jersey. E-mail her at DonnaLowich@aol.com.

Anna Lowther is a wife, mother, and writer living in Ohio. She primarily writes dark fiction as does her husband, Eric. They recently renewed their vows in the same chapel where they wed eighteen years ago. E-mail her at anna.lowther@yahoo.com.

Margaret Luebs is a graduate of the University of California, Berkeley and the University of Michigan. She has taught technical writing and worked for several years as a technical editor in Boulder, CO. She and her family now live in California where she is working on a novel.

Rita Lussier's column, "For the Moment," has been a popular weekly feature in *The Providence Journal* for twelve years. She was awarded First Place in the 2010 Erma Bombeck International Writing Competition, an honor she also won in 2006. Her writing has been featured in *The Boston Globe* and on NPR.

Judith Marks-White is a *Westport News* (CT) columnist of "The Light Touch" where her columns have appeared for the past twenty-six years. She is the author of two novels published by Random House/ Ballantine: *Seducing Harry* and *Bachelor Degree*. Judith teaches humor writing and lectures widely.

Debra Mayhew is a pastor's wife and homeschooling mom to six (usually) sweet and adorable children. She also happens to own the world's greatest dog. She loves good books, long walks, and empty laundry baskets. Debra blogs about this and that at www. debramayhew.com. E-mail her at debra@debramayhew.com.

Ann McArthur has always loved reading and writing stories. In her teens, she entertained at slumber parties by spinning adventure tales featuring her friends as the smart, brave heroines. Now she writes mostly for adults. Look for her first literary inspirational novel, *Choking on a Camel*.

Stephanie McKellar is a current high school student, scheduled to graduate in 2012. She plans to attend university in Fall 2012. Afterward, she would like to work as an author.

Recently, **Lava Mueller's** fourteen-year-old daughter discussed alterations she plans to make on the wedding dress. Her younger brother had a better idea. "Give it to me," he said. "I'll sell it and buy video games." That's a lot of video games. E-mail Lava at lavamueller@yahoo.com.

Val Muller is a writer and teacher living in Virginia. She is the author of *Corgi Capers*, a middle-grade mystery novel. You can keep track of her at mercuryval.wordpress.com.

Alice Muschany lives in Flint Hill, MO. She plans to retire soon, leaving more time for her hobbies that include swimming, hiking, writing, and photography. Her grandchildren live nearby and not only make wonderful subjects, but they keep her young at heart.

Dani Nichols is a freelance writer and editor from Southern California. When she's not writing, she works part-time as a therapeutic horseback-riding instructor. She loves ocean kayaking, good coffee, new places, swimming, cooking, and hanging out with her husband, Adam. You can read her blog at www.wranglerdani.com.

Marc Tyler Nobleman is the author of more than seventy books, including *Boys of Steel: The Creators of Superman* and *Bill the Boy Wonder: The Secret Co-Creator of Batman*. His cartoons have appeared in more than 100 international publications. At noblemania.blogspot. com, he reveals the behind-the-scenes stories of his work.

Caitlin Q. Bailey O'Neill is a freelance writer and editor previously published in *Chicken Soup for the Soul: Food and Love*, *Chicken Soup for the Soul: Thanks Dad*, and *Chicken Soup for the Soul: Empty Nesters*. This story is for her Prince Charming—Christopher O'Neill. E-mail her at PerfectlyPunctuated@yahoo.com.

Betty Ost-Everley lives in Kansas City, MO. When she's not working as an administrative assistant, advocating for her neighborhood or directing the church choir, she is an advisory board member for the Heart of America Christian Writers' Network. Internationally published, she has pieces in several anthologies. Follow her at www. thoughts.com/BettyOE.

Mark Parisi's "off the mark" cartoon appears in newspapers worldwide. You can also find his cartoons on calendars, cards, books, T-shirts, and more. Mark resides in Massachusetts with his wife and business partner, Lynn, along with their daughter, Jen, three cats, and a dog. Visit www.offthemark.com to view 7,000 cartoons.

Patt Hollinger Pickett, Ph.D., a licensed therapist and certified life coach, writes with humor from a warm, no-nonsense perspective. Dr. Pickett draws from her personal life blended with over twenty years in practice as a relationship expert. She has a book ready for publication. Contact Patt through www.DrCoachLove.com.

Sharon Pipke has spent a lifetime working as a nurse and ranch wife, and raising three children. She is semi-retired, and loves spending time with family and friends or reading. She hopes her story will strengthen someone's faith in the power of prayer.

Stephanie Piro is a cartoonist, illustrator, and designer. She is one of King Features' team of women cartoonists, "Six Chix" (she is the Saturday chick). She also does the cartoon panel *Fair Game*. Her work appears all over, from books to greeting cards. In addition, she designs gift items for her company Strip T's and her CafePress shop. Learn more at www.stephaniepiro.com.

Jennifer Quist is a writer and researcher based in Western Canada. She's published poetry, fiction, radio essays, and nonfiction. And seventeen years later, her wedding dress still fits.

Diane M. Radford is originally from Troon on the west coast of Scotland. She currently resides in St. Louis. When not engrossed in surgery or writing, she enjoys golf and spending time with her family. She is working on a memoir. E-mail her at info@dianeradfordmd. com or visit www.dianeradfordmd.com.

Sara Rajan earned her bachelor's degree in English literature from Saint Mary's College, Notre Dame. She has kept a written journal since the age of seven, and is the founder and editor of the online literary magazine, *Literary Juice*. She currently lives in South Bend, IN, with her husband, Dinesh.

Kayleen Reusser has written nine children's books, and has published articles in books, magazines, and newspapers. She and her husband, John, have three fantastic grown children. She has written several stories for the *Chicken Soup for the Soul* series. She speaks to children and adults about writing. Contacted her at www.KayleenR.com.

Amelia Rhodes lives in Michigan with her husband and their two children. She enjoys running, gardening, knitting, and volunteering in her children's classrooms. Amelia is a regular contributor to several online magazines and is completing her first book. She blogs regularly at www.ameliarhodes.com.

Karen Robbins is a columnist for PositivelyFeminine.org. She has been published in regional, national, and online publications, including Yahoo.com. Karen coauthored *A Scrapbook of Christmas Firsts* and *A Scrapbook of Motherhood Firsts*. Her first e-novel is *Murder Among the Orchids*. Karen and her family live in Ohio.

Sallie Rodman is an award-winning author whose work has appeared in numerous *Chicken Soup for the Soul* anthologies. She lives in California with her two pets, Mollie and Inky. Mary and her husband live nearby, and they meet often for dinner. E-mail her at sa.rodman@verizon.net.

Sioux Roslawski is the wife of Michael, the mother of a wonderful daughter and son, the mother-in-law of a wonderful artist named Jason, and the grammy of Riley. In her spare time, she rescues Golden Retrievers for Love a Golden and writes (of course).

Mitali Ruths lives in Montreal, Canada, with her husband and two girls. She received her medical degree from Baylor College of Medicine in Houston and trained at Texas Children's Hospital. She enjoys traveling, taking pictures, and making sandwiches. E-mail her at mitali.ruths@gmail.com or visit her blog at www.montrealzen.com.

Myra Lipp Sanderman is continually amazed to find material for her writing in everyday life. Her newspaper features, children's stories, and personal essays have often come from a family experience, an interesting conversation, or a shared emotion. She recently won Highlights for Children's Fiction Contest. She welcomes comments at Rojo42@aol.com.

Edie Scher's essays and articles have appeared in several national magazines and newspapers, including Rodale and Hearst publications and *The New York Times*. Her children, granddaughters, family, and good friend Max are constant sources of inspiration. She currently teaches at the Academy for Allied Health Sciences, Scotch Plains, NJ.

For more than twenty years, award-winning writer **Ellen Scolnic's** work has appeared in publications, including *The Christian Science Monitor, Parents* magazine, *The Philadelphia Inquirer, Jewish Exponent,* InterfaithFamily.com, iVillage.com, and parenting newspapers nationwide. She is the co-author of the best-selling *Dictionary of Jewish Words.* Read more at TheWordMavens.com.

Tanya Shearer lives in Alabama with her husband, Clay. Their family includes a wonderful son, daughter, and son-in-law. She enjoys taking her dog, Cornbread, for walks and writing children's books, devotions, and Christmas stories. She stays busy working with several student mentoring programs and community fundraisers.

Lynne Cooper Sitton (1947-2011) was a writer and illustrator who lived in South Florida. Her poems and artwork have been published in children's textbooks and greeting cards, and her stories have been published in several books. She was president of the American Christian Writers' Broward County Chapter for five years.

Laura Smetak lives in Minnesota with her wonderful husband of six years and their twenty-month-old son. Laura received her bachelor's degree from Northwestern College in St. Paul and is currently working on her master's degree in teaching at Hamline University. E-mail her at lrsmetak@gmail.com.

Mary Z. Smith writes regularly for the *Chicken Soup for the Soul* series as well as *Guideposts* and *Angels on Earth* magazines. When she isn't penning praises to her heavenly Father, she enjoys being with family or walking outdoors. Mary has written an inspirational fiction book entitled, *Life's A Symphony*, available at Amazon.com.

As if being a CPA wasn't enough of a laugh riot, **Jean Sorensen** began entering humor contests, where she was introduced to gag writing. Eventually she began drawing her own cartoons and was hooked. Jean's cartoons have been published in numerous national magazines, including *Good Housekeeping*, *The Saturday Evening Post*, and *Funny Times*.

Tanya Sousa is a guidance counselor and author from Northeastern Vermont. She has written children's books and magazine articles, and specializes in stories that inspire and encourage kindness to all living things.

Kate Sugg holds a Bachelor of Science degree in psychology from Endicott College and a Master of Science degree in mental health counseling from Pace University. She enjoys spending time with her family and friends, and loves reading and writing short stories with her amazing one-year-old daughter who inspires her to be her very best.

Loni Swensen received her Bachelor of Fine Arts degree in creative and professional writing from Bemidji State University in 2006. She dreams of writing books, singing for others, and working alongside her husband to help kids regain hope as well as other things thought lost. E-mail her at loni.swensen@gmail.com.

Ronda Ross Taylor lives in the Seattle area with her husband, Eldon, and a couple of parrots. She has two grown sons, two charming daughters-in-law, and a granddaughter who calls her "Gaga." When she's not writing, editing, or volunteering in school libraries, she can be found swimming at the Y.

Wendy Teller writes historical fiction, nonfiction, and humor. She's the 2010 recipient of the Richard Eastman Founder's Prize for Prose. Wendy's current projects involve Eastern Europe in the early twentieth century. She works as a software consultant. Wendy and her husband live in Bloomington, IN. E-mail her at wendy@wendyteller.com.

Jayne Thurber-Smith is an award-winning writer for various publications, including *Faith & Friends*, *Floral Business* magazine, and

The Buffalo News, and is a sports contributor for cbn.com. She and her husband's favorite activity is being included in whatever their four kids have going on. E-mail her at thurbersmith@cox.net.

Wendy Toth's work has appeared in *The New York Times*, *The Philadelphia Inquirer*, *Weight Watchers*, *Parents*, *Spa*, iVillage.com, Petside.com, *New York Press*, *Newsday*, and more. She lives in Brooklyn with her boyfriend and two rescue cats, Boris and Zoe, who've taught her that pets make everything better. She can be found at wendytoth. com.

Julie Turner is a writer and Web editor living in Boston with her husband.

Beverly F. Walker lives in Tennessee and cares for her husband who is battling cancer. She enjoys writing and scrapbooking pictures she takes of her grandchildren. She has many stories in the *Chicken Soup for the Soul* series.

Debbie Wong is a wife to Robert, mom of Grace, Olivia, and Joseph, speaker, singer, and author. She recorded "Heart's Desire," co-authored *Weddings 101*, and contributed to *Hugs Bible Reflections for Women* and *An Expressive Heart*. Her passion is to encourage women to dream again and discover their full potential in Christ. Learn more at www. debbiewong.net.

Dallas Woodburn is the author of two collections of short stories and editor of *Dancing With The Pen: a collection of today's best youth writing*. Learn more about her nonprofit youth literacy organization Write On! at www.writeonbooks.org and follow her blog at dallaswoodburn. blogspot.com.

Jeanne Zornes has written hundreds of articles and seven Christian-living books, including *When I Prayed for Patience...* (Kregel). She holds a master's degree from Wheaton. She and her husband, a retired teacher, live in Washington State, and have a young adult son and daughter. She blogs at jeannezornes.blogspot.com.

Heather Zuber-Harshman is a writer, speaker, and legal writing professor. She is currently working on a mystery novel and short stories while posting stories about faith, cooking, traveling, and humorous experiences on her blog at www.HeatherHarshman. wordpress.com. In between writing projects, she enjoys bicycling, traveling, snowboarding, and camping with her husband, Dale.

Meet Our Authors

Jack Canfield is the co-creator of the *Chicken Soup for the Soul* series, which *Time* magazine has called "the publishing phenomenon of the decade." Jack is also the co-author of many other bestselling books.

Jack is the CEO of the Canfield Training Group in Santa Barbara, California, and founder of the Foundation for Self-Esteem in Culver City, California. He has conducted intensive personal and professional development seminars on the principles of success for more than a million people in twenty-three countries, has spoken to hundreds of thousands of people at more than 1,000 corporations, universities, professional conferences and conventions, and has been seen by millions more on national television shows.

Jack has received many awards and honors, including three honorary doctorates and a Guinness World Records Certificate for having seven books from the *Chicken Soup for the Soul* series appearing on the New York Times bestseller list on May 24, 1998.

You can reach Jack at www.jackcanfield.com.

Mark Victor Hansen is the co-founder of Chicken Soup for the Soul, along with Jack Canfield. He is a sought-after keynote speaker, bestselling author, and marketing maven. Mark's powerful messages of possibility, opportunity, and action have created powerful change in thousands of organizations and millions of individuals worldwide.

Mark is a prolific writer with many bestselling books in addition to the *Chicken Soup for the Soul* series. Mark has had a profound influence in the field of human potential through his library of audios, videos, and articles in the areas of big thinking, sales achievement, wealth building, publishing success, and personal and professional development. He is also the founder of the MEGA Seminar Series.

Mark has received numerous awards that honor his entrepreneurial spirit, philanthropic heart, and business acumen. He is a lifetime member of the Horatio Alger Association of Distinguished Americans. You can reach Mark at www.markvictorhansen.com.

Susan M. Heim is a longstanding author and editor, specializing in parenting, women's and Christian issues. After the birth of her twin boys in 2003, Susan left her desk job as a Senior Editor at a publishing company and has never looked back. Being a work-at-home mother allows her to follow her two greatest passions: parenting and writing.

Susan's published books include *Chicken Soup for the Soul: Devotional Stories for Tough Times*; *Chicken Soup for the Soul: New Moms*; *Chicken Soup for the Soul: Devotional Stories for Mothers*; *Chicken Soup for the Soul: Family Matters*; *Chicken Soup for the Soul: Devotional Stories for Women*; *Chicken Soup for the Soul: All in the Family*; *Chicken Soup for the Soul: Twins and More*; *Boosting Your Baby's Brain Power*; *It's Twins! Parent-to-Parent Advice from Infancy Through Adolescence*; *Oh, Baby! 7 Ways a Baby Will Change Your Life the First Year*; and, *Twice the Love: Stories of Inspiration for Families with Twins, Multiples and Singletons.* She is also working on a fiction book for teens and young adults.

Susan's articles and stories have appeared in many books, websites, and magazines, including *TWINS Magazine* and *Angels on Earth*. She writes a parenting blog, "Susan Heim on Parenting," at http://susanheim.blogspot.com. And she is the founder of TwinsTalk, a website with tips, advice and stories about raising twins and multiples, at www.twinstalk.com.

Susan and her husband Mike are the parents of four active sons, who are in elementary school and college! You can reach Susan at susan@susanheim.com and visit her website at www.susanheim.com. Join her on Twitter and Facebook by searching for ParentingAuthor.

Thank You

As always, we are truly thankful for all of our contributors. We know that you pour your hearts and souls into the stories that you share with us, and we appreciate your willingness to open up your lives to other Chicken Soup for the Soul readers. We can only publish a small percentage of the stories that are submitted, but we read every single one, and even the ones that do not appear in the book have an influence on us and on the final manuscript. We strongly encourage you to continue submitting to future Chicken Soup for the Soul books.

We would like to thank Amy Newmark, our Publisher, for her generous spirit, creative vision, and expert editing, which have transformed Chicken Soup for the Soul into the relevant and beautiful series it is today. We're thankful for D'ette Corona, our Assistant Publisher, who works so well with all of our contributors to secure permissions and bios, and clear up any discrepancies in the stories—all while seamlessly managing twenty to thirty projects at a time. We'd like to express our gratitude to Chicken Soup for the Soul Editor Kristiana Glavin, for reading the thousands of stories submitted for this book and narrowing them down to several hundred finalists. And we would be lost without Barbara LoMonaco, Chicken Soup for the Soul's Webmaster and Editor, who always has a kind word to share; and Madeline Clapps, for her proofreading expertise.

We owe a very special thanks to our Creative Director and book producer, Brian Taylor at Pneuma Books, for his brilliant vision for

s. And, finally, we appreciate all of our wonder-
d friends, who continue to inspire and teach
and give us the freedom to create books that
in people's lives.

Improving Your Life Every Day

Real people sharing real stories—for nineteen years. Now, Chicken Soup for the Soul has gone beyond the bookstore to become a world leader in life improvement. Through books, movies, DVDs, online resources and other partnerships, we bring hope, courage, inspiration and love to hundreds of millions of people around the world. Chicken Soup for the Soul's writers and readers belong to a one-of-a-kind global community, sharing advice, support, guidance, comfort, and knowledge.

Chicken Soup for the Soul stories have been translated into more than 40 languages and can be found in more than one hundred countries. Every day, millions of people experience a Chicken Soup for the Soul story in a book, magazine, newspaper or online. As we share our life experiences through these stories, we offer hope, comfort and inspiration to one another. The stories travel from person to person, and from country to country, helping to improve lives everywhere.

Share with Us

We all have had Chicken Soup for the Soul moments in our lives. If you would like to share your story or poem with millions of people around the world, go to chickensoup.com and click on "Submit Your Story." You may be able to help another reader, and become a published author at the same time. Some of our past contributors have launched writing and speaking careers from the publication of their stories in our books!

Our submission volume has been increasing steadily—the quality and quantity of your submissions has been fabulous. We only accept story submissions via our website. They are no longer accepted via mail or fax.

To contact us regarding other matters, please send us an e-mail through webmaster@chickensoupforthesoul.com, or fax or write us at:

Chicken Soup for the Soul
P.O. Box 700
Cos Cob, CT 06807-0700
Fax: 203-861-7194

One more note from your friends at Chicken Soup for the Soul: Occasionally, we receive an unsolicited book manuscript from one of our readers, and we would like to respectfully inform you that we do not accept unsolicited manuscripts and we must discard the ones that appear.

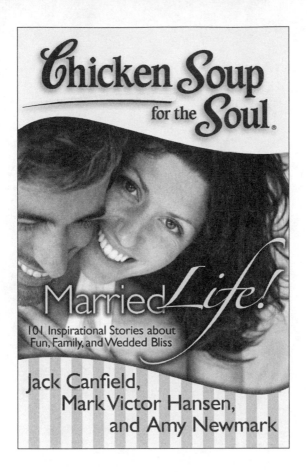

Chicken Soup for the Soul®

Married Life!

101 Inspirational Stories about Fun, Family, and Wedded Bliss

Jack Canfield,
Mark Victor Hansen,
and Amy Newmark

Marriage is a wonderful institution, and in this fresh collection of stories, husbands and wives share their personal, funny, and quirky stories from the trenches. This book will inspire and delight readers with its entertaining and heartwarming stories about fun, family, and wedded bliss. Whether newly married or married for years and years, readers will find laughter and inspiration in these 101 stories of love, romance, fun, and making it work.

978-1-935096-85-6

Classics for Lovers

Chicken Soup
for the Soul

www.chickensoup.com